ADDICTIONS AND NATIVE AMERICANS

ADDICTIONS AND NATIVE AMERICANS

LAURENCE ARMAND FRENCH

PRAEGER

Westport, Connecticut
London

Library of Congress Cataloging-in-Publication Data

French, Laurence, 1941–
    Addictions and Native Americans / Laurence Armand French.
        p. cm.
    Includes bibliographical references and index.
    ISBN 0–275–96349–7 (alk. paper)
    1. Indians of North America—Alcohol use.   2. Indians of North
America—Drug use.   3. Indians of North America—Gambling.   I. Title.
    E98.L7F74   2000
    362.29'12'08997—dc21   99–32094

British Library Cataloguing in Publication Data is available.

Library of Congress Catalog Card Number: 99–32094
ISBN: 0–275–96349–7

First published in 2000

Praeger Publishers, 88 Post Road West, Westport, CT 06881
An imprint of Greenwood Publishing Group, Inc.
www.praeger.com

Printed in the United States of America

The paper used in this book complies with the
Permanent Paper Standard issued by the National
Information Standards Organization (Z39.48–1984).

10 9 8 7 6 5 4 3 2 1

CONTENTS

INTRODUCTION

Substance abuse represents the major health problem plaguing American Indians, both historically and today. A major factor was the introduction of fortified and distilled alcohol, first by the Europeans and later the Americans, to an indigenous population whose physiology (metabolism and neural compensation) was not accustomed to this concentration of ethanol. Another factor was the introduction of alcohol outside of traditional customs and folkways. While there is evidence of substance use during aboriginal times, notably of fermented corn or cactus juices and psychoactive agents such as peyote and cocoa leaves, these substances were confined to prescribed rituals and were not abused. Moreover, in most instances the concentration of psychoactive agents consumed during aboriginal times was minimal compared to today's standards. Clearly, the departure from prescribed aboriginal customs and ritualistic use of psychoactive substances, combined with the increased potency of psychoactive agents introduced by Western groups, has contributed greatly to the substance abuse problem among American Indians and Native Alaskans.[1]

By all accounts, alcoholism is the number-one killer among American Indians. A review by the prestigious Robert Wood Foundation of current data indicates that the death rate for Indians aged fifteen to forty-four is over 300 percent higher than that of the overall U.S. population.[2] Since World War II, when reliable data began to be collected, alcoholism has registered as the single most serious health problem for American Indians, accounting for the four leading causes of death in that group: accidents, cirrhosis of the liver, suicide, and homicide. A fifth, more subtle causality of Indian alcoholism is fetal alcoholism, known as FAS (fetal alcohol syndrome). FAS is an especially problematic form of substance abuse, in that it tends to perpetuate a cycle whereby the compromised infants grow up with a host of physical and psychological problems that greatly increase their susceptibility toward alcohol and other substance abuse. The groups with the highest rates of FAS are the Sioux tribes residing within the Indian Health Service's (IHS) Aberdeen area (North and South Dakota, Nebraska, and Iowa).

FAS is also a common health problem among urban Indians, especially among these who are phenotypically Indian but are unaware of their native languages or traditional ways. Here, psychocultural marginality, a phenomenon Eric Erickson noted when studying American Indian disorganization a half-century ago, appears to play a major role in the intensity of FAS.[3] The more alienated the Indian mother is from both her traditional culture and the dominant U.S. society, the more likely she is to be afflicted with the combination of poor mental and physical health associated with fetal alcoholism.

The schism between our Western-oriented society and that of traditional Indian ways is illustrated by the competing epistemological methodologies. Western societies base their relative constructs of reality upon a secular version of the protestant ethic, while traditional (aboriginal) North American Indian groups based their world view on the *harmony ethos*.[4] Simply stated, the former engenders individual competition and culpability within a society, while the latter promotes cooperation and shared responsibility. It is rare for American Indians to be adequately socialized within both cultural orientations; they are forced to be primarily oriented to one or the other. American Indians socialized within the protestant ethic, regardless of their phenotype or blood degree, are commonly termed *white Indians* or, in derogatory terms, *apples* (red on the outside and white on the inside). American Indians adequately encultured (understanding both their language and customs) within their respective tribe are known as *traditional Indians*, while those who are not adequately socialized within either epistemological methodology are termed *marginal Indians*. Marginal Indians are those most susceptible to substance abuse.[5]

The book is divided into four parts: (1) Historical Perspectives on Native American Addictions; (2) The Nature of Substance Abuse among Native Americans; (3) Prevention, Intervention, and Cultural Treatment;

and (4) a special section on a new aspect of addiction within Indian country—Indian Gambling—the New Addiction.

Part I consists of two sections: Chapter 1 explores the pre-Columbian worldview of Native Americans and their aboriginal lifestyle, while Chapter 2 looks at Euro-American control processes and their impact on Indian marginality. In Part II, we review current research on the nature and extent of substance abuse among American Indians and Native Alaskans. Psychological factors are discussed in Chapter 3, followed by epidemiological studies of substance abuse and related health problems in Chapter 4, while Chapter 5 addresses one of the most serious health problems facing American Indians and Alaskan Natives—fetal alcoholism. Part III addresses treatment, intervention, and prevention issues facing therapists treating Native Americans addictions. Chapter 6 explores primary and secondary clinical diagnoses from the American Indian cultural perspective, while Chapter 7 looks at culture-specific prevention and treatment strategies for fetal alcoholism, with special focus on the efforts made by the three largest tribes: the Navajo, Cherokee, and Sioux. Chapter 8 provides current federal clinical standards and practice guidelines for Indian country. The last section, Part IV, Indian Gambling—the New Addiction, explores the current controversy over Indian gaming. In Chapter 9, the link between reduced federal funding and greater tribal autonomy under the U.S./Indian policies of self-determination and "New Federalism" is reviewed relevant to the gaming industry in Indian country, while Chapter 10 looks at prevention and treatment issues.

I

HISTORICAL
PERSPECTIVES ON
NATIVE AMERICAN
ADDICTIONS

1

THE ABORIGINAL
WORLDVIEW AND LIFESTYLE

During aboriginal times, North American Indians subscribed to a world-view that dictated intragroup cooperation. Intergroup conflicts existed between tribes, but archeological and anthropological studies indicate that these were sporadic and usually involved contested territories. Spectacular raids were not the norm, given that horses were not introduced until European contact. Considerable intracontinental interactions were evident, with well established foot trails and trading, especially between the eastern, plains, and southwestern tribes. The normative structure supporting this cooperative lifestyle is known as the *harmony ethos*. A common theme prevailed across tribal group despite variations in their creation myths, one that promoted respect for "Mother Earth" and "Father Sky." Mother Earth represented all that constitutes the earth, including water and all living creatures. Father Sky interacted with Mother Earth, providing wind, weather, the sun, stars, and moon.

Common to various aboriginal worldviews was the concept that humans are not considered superior to other living creatures. Nonetheless, aboriginal tribal groups did distinguish themselves from other elements within nature, including fellow humans, by referring to themselves as "the people." Clearly, this concept of a group identity separating it from other human groups connotes ethnocentrism, a common human phenomenon needed for psychocultural boundary maintenance. The role of ethnocentrism is to provide the group with a special identity relevant to individual, family, and clan responsibilities. Tribal identity per se was a loose concept during aboriginal times, with group linkage provided primarily through clan membership along with a shared worldview and normative structure (verbal folkways, mores, customs, sanctions, and taboos). Twelve tenets of the aboriginal harmony ethos are as follows:

1. The avoidance of overt hostilities regarding interpersonal matters and an emphasis on nonaggressiveness in intrafamilial/clan/tribe interactions.
2. The use of a neutral third person, or intermediary, for resolving personal altercations.
3. A high value placed on independence.
4. A resentment of authority.
5. A hesitance to command others.
6. Caution in interactions with other persons.
7. A reluctance to refuse favors and an emphasis on generosity.
8. A reluctance to voice opinions publicly.
9. Avoidance of eye and body contact (handshakes, back slapping, etc.) when interacting with others.
10. Emphasis placed on group cooperation and not on individual competition.
11. Deference to elders: old equals good equals honor.
12. Challenging life in the raw: "counting coup," "dog soldiering."[1]

Generally speaking, the aboriginal harmony ethos consisted of a complex social code whereby individual freedom was checked by the extended family and clan. Respect for, and cooperation with, nature was imperative for existence, according to this ethos. Accordingly, animals and plants were thanked for providing sustenance to the group. Elements of the harmony ethos have survived to the present and are represented in tribal traditionalism. Obviously, these tenets are quite different from, many opposite to, those promoted by the protestant ethic—the epistemological methodology guiding Western cultures, including the United States and Canada.[2] Psychocultural marginality occurs when American Indians and Alaskan Natives are denied their traditional enculturation or are forced to live in the larger dominant society without being adequately socialized in either mode. The combination of cultural alienation and personal disorganization (anomie) places these marginal individuals at high risk for self-medication and escapism, hence substance abuse.[3]

The key to group and self identity is an understanding of one's culture. The foundation of aboriginal culture is an understanding of the aboriginal ways; the ways that existed prior to the advent of Europeans, the horse as a mode of transportation, and the firearm.[4] The particular role of an individual native during aboriginal times was molded by the group's respective methodological epistemology, or worldview. Each of the major American Indian groups that have survived to the present knows variations of its creation myth.

The most widely studied group is the Cherokee. At the time of European contact, the Cherokee had a territory that included what is now western North Carolina, northwest South Carolina, eastern Tennessee, northwest Georgia, and northeast Alabama. They practiced a horticultural lifestyle, residing in some sixty permanent villages within this vast region. During aboriginal times, thousands of years prior to European contact and the introduction of the horse, they traded with other Indian groups throughout North America. Given that the western Pueblos established trade routes with Mexican and Central and South American tribes during aboriginal times, it is likely that the Cherokee and other eastern tribes shared in this trade when they traded tobacco with the Pueblo tribes in what is now west Texas, New Mexico, and Arizona. The diet that sustained these long-distance runners conducting this trade was composed of dried protein (fish and game meats), water, bean bread, a ball of cornmeal, and shell beans saturated in bear grease. Sugar, other than honey, was unknown to the aboriginal Cherokee. Mind-altering or psychoactive agents, other than tobacco, fermented corn, and the "black drink," were also unknown to the aboriginal Cherokee culture. The Cherokee's diet and lifestyle attested to their fitness at the time of contact with Europeans whose records presented the Cherokee as a tall, fit, and lean people, not obese and sickly as so many are today.[5]

The sense of being *Ani-yun-wiya* (real people, or principal people), as the Cherokee called themselves in their own language, welded this scattered group into a viable ethnocentric or culture-centric whole, through a clan system and a corresponding complex value system. Cherokee (*Chelaque, Chalaque, Cheraqui, Cherakees*) is a term given them by neighboring tribal groups, as interpreted by the early European explorer Hernando DeSoto and his group.[6] Their aboriginal worldview—that is, how they saw themselves vis-à-vis other elements within nature, was established within their creation myth.

In this myth, the earth is seen as a great island, floating in a sea of water and suspended from the sky by four cords that link Mother Earth with Father Sky. In the beginning, the world consisted entirely of water. The first creations were plants and other living things. They lived in a rock vault in the sky, high above the water. When it became crowded, the water-beetle went down and dove to the bottom and brought up mud until it had built an island. This island grew until it reached its present size and became Mother Earth. Initially the island was flat, soft, and wet, not ready to be inhabited by the living things residing in the sky vault. Then the Great Buzzard went down and began to sink in the mud. Fighting to stay airborne, he flapped his wings frantically, creating the mountains and valleys of what is now southern Appalachia, the home of the Cherokee Indians. This new surface relief allowed Mother Earth to drain, creating a variety of soils and bodies of water, including lakes and rivers. The living things now moved from the sky vault to Mother Earth.

Once they were all on Mother Earth, man emerged. Initially there was a single man and woman, who were brother and sister. The initial reproduction process involved the brother hitting his sister with a fish; she would bear a child every seven days. Fearful of overpopulation, the first humans decided that women should only reproduce once a year. These first full-sized humans coexisted with all the other living things on Mother Earth, including the "little people," who many still believe inhabit the secluded coves of southern Appalachia. The aboriginal Cherokee also viewed bears as emerging from these first humans: instead of creating a village lifestyle, they had gone off by themselves and adapted claws, fur, and big teeth for their survival. The other tribes the Cherokee encountered in trading and conflicts were also considered to be descendants of these first humans.

Cooperation, at least some form of balance, was the key ingredient for coexistence among all living things sharing Mother Earth. Correspondingly, cooperative interaction between Mother Earth and Father Sky was seen as vital to the continuation of life. Interestingly, the interaction between Mother Earth and Father Sky mimics the fertility rituals among other living things. Simply stated, water, sun, and wind from Father Sky represent the intercourse needed to keep Mother Earth fertile so that she can continue to sustain life for all her living things—plants, insects, birds, and animals.[7]

The scattered villages of tens of thousands of Cherokee were linked by a social system based on clan affiliation. Clearly, the seven aboriginal clans of the Ani-yun-wiya represented the major organizational and structural unit within their culture. This strong cultural network not only provided a sense of identity and social boundaries but gave the Cherokee a group identity, one that transcended villages and regions. Georg Simmel, the noted German social philosopher, attests to this phenomenon in his social psychological theorem regarding boundary maintenance: reciprocal antagonisms are a necessary component of group solidarity, and outgroup hostilities serve to maintain ingroup cohesion.[8] Indeed, the aboriginal Cherokee lifestyle accommodated these social psychological tenets. Horticulture dictated a divided year, with the important growing season from April until October and hunting and warfare the rest of the year. This division was such an integral component of Cherokee life that

there were separate chiefs for each season: the White Chief and his domestic council presiding over the growing season, and the Red Chief and
his war council ruling during the hunting and warring season. There is
little question that the White Chief and the domestic council were the
more significant, since the Cherokee farm (*gadugi*) provided the sustenance for the group's survival. This was reflected in customs and rituals.

Six festivals occurred during the year, all relating to the planting and
harvesting of the *gadugi*: the first new moon of spring, the new green
corn festival, the green corn festival, the first appearance of the October
new moon festival, establishment of friendship and brotherhood festival,
and the bouncing bush (*Eelah, Wahtah, Lay-Kee*) festival. These festivals
signified the importance of the year as an entity in itself. The bouncing
bush festival celebrated the yearly harvest and the need to prepare for
a new year. This was a cleansing festival, where old clothing, furniture,
and other artifacts representative of the past year were discarded and
burned in a large village bonfire. Moreover, the sacred fire in the village
Town House was extinguished, and all village dwellings were cleaned,
signifying a collective purge of past errors, sins, crimes, and mistakes for
all clan members. Adults within the village participated in the individual
purification ritual of the "black drink," a mild toxin that may have had
hallucinogenic effects and induced vomiting. The vomiting represented
an internal cleansing and purification, much as peyote did for their
Pueblo Indian counterparts in the Southwest. Following this collective
purification, wherein all personal transgressions were forgiven, the
buildings were whitewashed and a new fire ignited in the community
center—the Town House.

The hunting and warfare season allowed for expressive behaviors but
operated within the dictates of the harmony ethos. Accordingly, both
intragroup (domestic) and intergroup (with other Indian groups) conflicts were based on a simple formula of blood vengeance; excessive punishment and death were strictly forbidden. Intertribal wars were highly
regulated by custom. With this cultural perspective, the number of en-
emies killed equaled the number that the Cherokee had suffered in previous encounters with this outgroup. Excess victims were made up in
captives, and who often served as personal slaves of the clans of which
their captors were members. Even murder was treated as a clan, and not
village or tribal, matter; again, resolution was based on blood vengeance.
However, if the offender could hide or escape to a neutral community
(town of refuge) and avoid capture until the bouncing bush festival, he
or she was absolved of the offense.[9]

Another interesting element of the aboriginal Cherokee culture was
the role that women played in the clans and villages. The aboriginal
Cherokee were matrilineal and matrilocal, meaning that the clans were
female dominant; when a couple married, they moved into the wife's

home, and the children were raised within her clan. The head clan matriarch was known as a "Pretty Woman" and served in the councils of both the White and Red Chiefs. Clan matriarchs also served as judges over domestic disputes, including homicide.[10]

Under this matriarchal system of customs and rules, drunkenness and other forms of substance abuse, including excessive tobacco use, were unknown. This fits Rivers's contention that cultures that provide meaningful regulation of behaviors, including those related to substance use, have fewer social disruptions and less social disorganization resulting from these behaviors. Ironically, the Cherokee were forced to disenfranchise the females and discard the matriarchal system by the Euro-American administrations, in order to be considered *civilized*. In hopes of surviving their traditional homeland, the Cherokee, along with the Choctaw, Chickasaw, Creek, and Seminole, forsook their aboriginal ways and adopted the male-dominated Euro-American model—hence their recognition as the Five Civilized Tribes. Nonetheless, many attributes of their aboriginal harmony ethos survived over time and have been adapted to the present especially among the more traditional American Indian and Alaskan Natives.

Ironically, the survival of tenets of the harmony ethos can be seen as contributing factors in both substance abuse and the prevention and treatment of this problem among Native Americans. Clearly, challenging life in the raw—meaning that one learns for himself or herself, not by the experiences of others—can be a leading cause of excessive alcohol use among this population. This, coupled with a worldview that features an external locus of control, external forces and influences (third parties), a high value on independence, a reluctance to refuse favors among kin, and a resentment of authority, leads to a difficult prevention and treatment situation for traditional Native Americans. This is especially true when contemporary Euro-American interventions and techniques are attempted.

2

ABORIGINAL USES OF
PSYCHOACTIVE AGENTS

Many blame the Europeans for the introduction of alcohol, perhaps the most significant social ill associated with psychocultural marginality, but this is not the case: alcohol and other psychoactive agents have played a role among American Indians since aboriginal times, prior to Euro-American contact and influence. The major difference between aboriginal use and what transpired following the Euro-American influence was that, under the dictates of the harmony ethos, substance use was highly regulated and closely related to social customs and rituals. Another significant distinction was in the potency of the psychoactive agent in these rituals.

The New World had a number of indigenous psychoactive plants, in addition to corn, which had psychoactive properties. For the most part, it appears, the use of these psychoactive agents was linked to socially prescribed customs and rites. Fermented corn beer was perhaps the most common aboriginal substance used during the pre-Columbian era among North American native groups. We know today that alcohol was an integral component of Incan rites, including human sacrifices. Directly across the Mexican border in southern Arizona, the Tohono O'odham (formerly known as the Papago) traditionally made fermented wine by boiling the fruit of the saguaro cactus. This drinking ritual was most prominent during their fall festival, *Wihgita*, which occurred in August. Apparently, social license was allowed at this time, resulting in a communal bout drinking ritual, much like the Christian (Catholic) celebrations preceding Lent. Sanctioned aboriginal communal drinking bouts later gave way to collective binge drunks, commonly known throughout Indian country as "forty-niners."[1] The sacred role of corn is illustrated by its significance for the aboriginal Cherokee.

In former times the annual thanksgiving ceremony of the Green-Corn dance, preliminary to eating the first new corn, was the most solemn tribal function, a propitiation and expiation for the sins of the past year, an amnesty for public criminals, and a prayer for happiness and prosperity for the year to come. Only those who had properly prepared themselves by prayer, fasting, and purification were allowed to take part in this ceremony, and no one dared to taste the new corn until then. Seven ears from the last year's crop were always put carefully aside, in order to *attract the corn* until the new crop was ripened and it was time for the dance, when they were eaten with the rest. In eating the first new corn after the Green Corn dance, care was observed not to blow upon it to cool it, for fear of causing a wind storm to beat down the standing crop in the field.[2]

The indication here is that corn and other sources of fermented beers and wines were held in high regard by the aboriginal Native Americans and therefore would hardly be used outside prescribed rituals. Custom also prohibited their abuse, according the the dictates of the harmony ethos.

Tobacco was another psychoactive agent long associated with aboriginal customs and rituals. With its use dictated by customs and rituals rooted within versions of the harmony ethos, tobacco abuse was not widespread during pre-Columbian times. Indeed, lung disease was most likely to occur among those who had prolonged exposure to unvented or poorly vented pit fires—the most common sources of both cooking and heat. Tobacco during aboriginal times, according to the traditional ways of the three largest tribes today (Athapaskan, Sioux, and Cherokee), was used sparingly, due to its spiritual significance. Within the harmony ethos adaptations of these three linguistic groups, tobacco represented man's spiritual link with Father Sky. James Mooney, a noted ethnographer, wrote about the use of tobacco among the early Cherokee in his 1891 Bureau of American Ethnology publication, *Sacred Formulas of the Cherokee*.

Tobacco was used as a sacred incense or as the guarantee of a solemn oath in nearly every important function—in binding the warrior to take up the hatchet against the enemy, in ratifying the treaty of peace, in confirming sales or other engagements, in seeking omens for the hunter, in driving away witches or evil spirits, and in regular medical practice. It was either smoked in the pipe or sprinkled upon the fire, never rolled into cigarettes, as among the tribes of the Southwest, neither was it ever smoked for the mere pleasure of the sensation. Of late years white neighbors have taught the Indians to chew it, but the habit is not aboriginal. It is called *tsalu*, a name which has lost its meaning in the Cherokee language, but is explained from the cognate Tuscarora, in which *charhu*, "tobacco," can still be analyzed as "fire to hold in the mouth," showing that the use is as old as the knowledge of the plant. The tobacco originally in use among the Cherokee, Iroquois, and the eastern tribes was not the common tobacco of commerce (*Nicotiana tabacum*), which has been introduced from the West Indies, but the *Nicotiana rustica*, or wild tobacco, now distinguished by the Cherokee as *tsal-agayun'li*, "old tobacco," and by the Iroquois as "real tobacco."[3]

The most common tobacco ritual practiced by Native Americans today, notably within the pan-Indian movement, involves aboriginal adaptations of the Sioux sacred pipe sacrament. According to the aboriginal Siouan adaptation of the harmony ethos, the sacred pipe, with a bowl of pipestone, stem of wood, and adornments of twelve eagle feathers, shell fragments, and colored beads sewed into a buckskin wrap, is symbolic of the universe (Mother Earth and Father Sky). The bowl represents both Manka (Mother Earth) and man's blood, while the red beads represent the west, blue the north, green the east, and yellow the south. The north/south direction represents the red road, or good way, where north signifies purity and south the source of life. On the other hand, the east/west direction represents the blue or black road, the path of error and destruction. The sacred pipe rite was the most significant and common of the Sioux's seven sacred rituals, in that it provided a form of communion and purification so that the four virtues of bravery, fortitude, generosity, and wisdom could be maintained and reinforced on a regular basis. Specifically, the bowl represents Mother Earth and all the grandmothers (female ancestors) as well as all the "two-leggeds" (American Indians), who are red. It also is symbolic of the red road (good way) provided to the inhabitants of Mother Earth by Father Sky (the Great Spirit, or Wakan-Tanka). The wooden stem represent all that grows upon Earth, while the shell, leather, and feathers decorations represent respectively things of the water, the land, and the sky. The twelve feathers of the sacred pipe are taken from Wanbli Galeshka (the spotted eagle), which itself represents Wakan-Tanka. The sacred tobacco mix is offered up to Wakan-Tanka and placed into the bowl in a ritual that involves pointing the pipe bowl first to the heavens, then to the west, north, east, and south, and finally down toward Mother Earth. When not in use, the sacred pipe is wrapped in buckskin and kept by the medicine man (keeper of the sacred pipe).[4] The smoke itself is the medium of spiritual communication with Wakan-Tanka. Like their Cherokee counterparts, the aboriginal Sioux did not use tobacco casually.

Indeed, tobacco from the eastern tribes was a valued commodity, as was the pipestone, from the western quarries. According to Wilbert, shamans of the Warao Indians of Venezuela use tobacco as their primary vehicle for communication with their gods: "Tobacco may be one of several vehicles for ecstasy; it may be taken in combination with other plants, as we have seen, to induce narcotic trance states; or it may represent the sole psychoactive agent employed by shamans to transport themselves into the realm of the supernatural, as is the case among the Warao of the Orinoco Delta in Venezuela."[5] Wilbert noted that the Warao priests-shamans smoked enormous cigars, having done so since first contact with Europeans. Like their counterparts in North America, the Warao believed that the smoke from their cigars allowed communication with the supernatural, providing a celestial bridge with the Great Spirit (Bahana). Smoke communication with the spirits was used for both good and evil purposes. Accordingly, tobacco use among the traditional Warao was restricted to certain rituals and used only by the priest-shaman: "In the old days, ordinary mortals hesitated to smoke for fear of precipitating an undesirable encounter with tobacco-craving spirits."[6]

Peyote, like fermented alcohol (corn or cacti) and tobacco, played a special and sacred role within aboriginal cultures. However, peyote and other plant hallucinogens used during aboriginal times fall within the broad class of illicit drugs within contemporary U.S. society. Their use among Native Americans resulted in considerable litigation until passage of Public Law 103–344 by the 103d Congress on January 25, 1994, amending the American Indian Religious Freedom Act to provide for the traditional use of peyote by Indians for religious and other purposes. This act was approved by President William Clinton on October 6, 1994.[7]

Peyote is a small, spineless, round cactus with psychedelic properties; it contains more than fifty alkaloids, most notably mescaline. It grows naturally in the deserts of the southwestern United States (notably southern Texas) and northwestern Mexico. It was called *peyote* by the Aztecs, as it is today. "Dry whisky," "divine herb," "devil's root," and "medicine of the gods" are other names. This *cactaceae* plant species was first documented in 1651 by Hernandez, who called it *Peyote zacatecensis*. It was given its current name, *Lophophora Williamsii*, by John Coulter in 1984. Francisco Hernandez noted that it appeared to have a sweetish and hot taste and that when ground up it was used to alleviate joint pain. He also noted its hallucinogenic properties and its use in sacred rituals by medicine men to prophesy. It was also used by warriors, providing them with courage to fight and the ability to withstand thirst, hunger, and fear.

Its aboriginal use among Native Americans extends from the Yanomamma Indians of Venezuela to the Plains Indians of the United States. Today an estimated 250,000 members of the Native American Church in

the United States and Canada legally use peyote during religious ceremonies. Schultes notes that while the spread of the peyote sacred rituals
from Mexico is unknown, several routes at different periods were likely.

Raids into the Mescalero country may have been the principal method of ac-
quainting Plains Indians with the plant and its cult. Slow and gradual diffusion
northward almost certainly took place as well. At any rate, the cult was well
established among the Kiowas and Comanche between 1880 and 1885 and was
being spread with missionary zeal. By the late 1920's, the cult had been forced,
by the strong hostility and outright untruthful propaganda of many organized
Christian missionary groups, to incorporate itself into the Native American
Church—a legally constituted religious sect due the protection and respect enjoyed by any other religious group. In 1920 there were some 13,300 adherents in
about thirty tribes. At present, an estimated 250,000 Indians in tribes as far north
as Saskatchewan, Canada, practice this religion, which advocates brotherly love,
high moral principle, abstention from alcohol, and other admirable teachings.
There is still disagreement about the reasons peyote use spread so fast, edging
out other well-established Indian "nativistic" movements, such as the famous
Ghost Dance.[8]

The use of peyote among the Huichol Indians of Mexico illustrates a
ritual similar to the Siouan Sun Dance, considered to be the ultimate rite
of passage for adult males. Those who have completed four Sun Dances
are considered to have "counted coup," taking on the challenges of life
in the raw, having obtained the critical dimension of wisdom, and are
now considered respected elders ("grandfathers") among their people.
This status and ritual is also popular among pan-Indian groups in the
United States and Canada. The Huichol Indian rite of passage for its
respected elders, *Peyoteros*, is the peyote quest or pilgrimage. Furst describes the significance of this ritual: "The pilgrimage helps one attain
whatever one desires—health, children, rain, protection from lightning
and sorcerers, or diving intervention against the ever-troublesome veci-
nos ('neighbors,' Mestizos), who encroach illegally on the Huichol lands
with their cattle and sometimes employ force to drive the Indians from
their farms. Above all, one goes to attain visions of great beauty, to hear
the voices of the spirits, the divine ancestors, and to receive their guidance."[9]

Other psychoactive agents were used during aboriginal times including the Cherokee's black drink. Mooney hints that the concoction drunk
at the new year purification rite was a root the Cherokee called *unaste'
tstiyu*, or the Virginia or black snakeroots (*Aristolochia serpentaria*). It produces stimulation while inducing vomiting and sweating, the elements
required for internal cleansing.[10] Schultes later noted that the snake plant,
a member of the morning glory family, was used for its hallucinogenic
properties among Mexican Indian groups. The Aztecs used hallucino-

genic mushrooms, known as *teonanacat* (god's flesh), in their sacred rituals, as did the aboriginal Indians of western Mexico. Along the current Mexican/United States border, aboriginal Indians used the seeds of the *Sophora secundiflora* shrub for thousands of years prior to European contact. These tribes participated in what is known as the mescal, or Red Bean, cult. Archeological evidence also indicates pre-Columbian use of the morning glory, whose seeds have an hallucinogenic property. Indeed, dozens of plants, mushrooms, and tree barks were used for their psychoactive properties during aboriginal groups in the Americas, mainly in conjunction with sacred rituals. There is little evidence that any of these psychoactive agents were abused by these native populations.[11]

3

FEDERAL POLICIES AND MARGINALITY

❖

Euro-American contact and interactions contributed much to Indian marginality and the disruption and destruction of traditional customs and even the aboriginal use of psychoactive substances. This process was noted in the 1976 *Final Report to the American Indian Policy Review Commission, Task Force Eleven: Alcohol and Drug Abuse*. It noted the historical justification for the Snyder Act of 1921, which authorized appropriations for the Bureau of Indian Affairs (BIA). Despite anthropological and archeological evidence to the contrary, Congress held the false belief that alcohol had been alien to most Native American groups prior to white contact. Unfortunately, this misconception led to the stereotype that American Indians were childlike, requiring lifelong, paternalistic supervision.

The native people of North America (with the exception of a few tribes) before the coming of European settlers to the New World in the 15th and 16th centuries, were unacquainted with liquor in any form. The first Native Americans to come in contact with the substances were obviously those along the western seaboard, with the peoples further inland not experiencing contact until the 17th, 18th and 19th centuries in western-most regions.

Tribes such as the Pimas, Papagos, Apache and Havasupai, located along what is now the Mexican Border and somewhat to the north, were known to have a crude form of liquor used for religious ceremonies. Papagos used their crude form of liquor, cactus fruit wine, in a ceremonial context particularly to produce rain. These tribes and many in the same area, also came into early contact with Spanish explorers but there is no documented evidence available to show any ill effects in regards to alcohol use from this period. This was to occur later in their history from westward expansion of European settlers.

The initial avenue of contact of liquor to the Native Americans was to come from the fur trappers and traders moving westward in search of more game. At first used as a gesture of friendship or article of trade, the sharing of liquor soon degenerated into a powerful weapon which white entrepreneurs used to their distinct advantage and the Indians' disadvantage. Trading for the most part was preceded by drinking sessions after which the intoxicated Indians "blithely traded away valuable possessions to maintain their inebriated glow. Most of the respectable traders discouraged the use of alcohol as regular payment for furs, largely because drinking obviously lowered productivity but partly because they could see all too clearly how disruptive it could be in a society with no traditional means of coping with it."

It is from these traders, trappers and later miners and cowboys out of the western frontier that Indians formed a style of drinking. Because of having no contact with the substance before the invasion of the whites, they had no norms by which to regulate drinking sociably. They also had no one but these traders, trappers and other frontiersmen as examples upon which to base their drinking patterns.[1]

It has already been noted that American Indians used psychoactive agents during aboriginal times, but within the constraints and sanctions prescribed by custom and rituals. Pueblo Indians of the Southwest had a long history of making a fermented corn beer for their rituals. This practice is still evident among the Tarahumara Indians of northwest Mexico. Given the pre-Columbian interaction between southwestern tribes with plains and eastern Indians, it is likely that other aboriginal tribes made and used this corn beer as well. Many other native plants provided ritualistic euphoria; this is well documented by anthropological and archeological studies. These plants include mushrooms (*Conocybe, Panaoeolus, Psilocybe,* and *Stropharia*), cactus (*Ariocarpus, Epithelantha, Lophohora Williamsii, Neoraimondia, Pachycereus,* and *Trichocereus*), as well as tobacco and psychoactive plants from the morning glory and mint families. After alcohol, the most widely recognized of these aboriginal psycho-active agents is peyote *(Lophophora Williamsii)* which, now that it is legal in the United States, is widely used by followers of the Native American Church.

The historical research clearly indicates that it is not substance use per se by American Indians and Alaskan Natives that is the root cause of substance abuse but rather the context in which these substances are used. Obviously the potency of these agents plays a role here, as does the health of those ingesting them. Nonetheless, credence is given to Rivers's contention that cultural norms regulating the use and abuse of psychoactive substances are a major factor. Groups that provide approved circumstances for substance use and follow up with negative sanctions against excessive use are most likely to provide an enculturation process, with well-established norms relevant to the customs of substance use. In contrast, social, cultural or personal ambivalence regarding substance use, including simplistic social proscriptions such as prohibition, often creates situations where individuals are likely to abuse these agents. The Snyder Act of 1921 suggested that the frontier drinking patterns provided a poor model for Native Americans, who were otherwise unfamiliar with nonritualistic uses of alcohol.

Liquor was also given as a form of payment for services rendered. Military aid given by the Indians to both the British and French was paid for by quantities of liquor. Scouts enlisted by westward expeditions and later American military forces were reimbursed with "firewater."

Even the Indian Whiskey itself "was a vile potion that was usually drugged and diluted to best serve devious ends." Drugs such as strychnine and laudanum were added and justified on the grounds that aggression would be diminished. But this was not to be the case, as aggressive acts come to be the outcome of heavy drinking bouts. Men, women and even children drank huge quantities rapidly with the sole purpose of becoming totally inebriated. Other characteristic drinking patterns included:

No solitary drinking;

Food and alcohol were never mixed;

Drinking until the supply was exhausted or until the drinkers passed out;

The sharing of beverages if in short supply;

Breaches of Indian codes of good conduct excused while under the influence;

Development of a high cultural expectancy for the value and effects of alcohol; and

A marked release of hostilities.

It is from this last characteristic of drinking—a marked release of hostilities—which served to reinforce the white man's view of the savage Indian who, they thought, due to physiological differences, transformed upon drinking from stoical, reserved, circumspect behavior to that which was erratic, destructive and terrifying.[2]

This model of drinking came from colonial and early American society, which, for the most part, was a drunken one. Mancall saw the roots of American drunkenness as stemming from licentious drinking in Great Britain: "Given the wide acceptance of alcohol in English culture, it is not surprising that Americans made no serious efforts to control liquor consumption until after the Revolution, and then only because leading physicians, notably Benjamin Rush, began to identify what they believed were cases of actual addiction to alcohol." Prohibition later became a national imperative, not only for white Americans but for Native Americans as well.

The upshot of aboriginal traditional use of psychoactive agents, for those tribes that used these agents, and the pervasive ambiguity and subsequent high rate of substance abuse among American Indians was a series of U.S. Indian policies whose latent, and often manifested, mandate was the destruction of the Indian's traditional culture. Task Force Eleven noted the influence of federally enforced prohibition on Indian marginality.

As early as 1802, a verbal plea was made to President Thomas Jefferson from Chief Little Turtle to regulate the sale and traffic of intoxicants into Indian country. This plea culminated in the Act of March 30, 1802 (Sec. 21, Stat. 139) "to take such measures, from time to time, as to him may appear expedient to prevent or restrain the vending or distribution of spirituous liquors among all or any of said Indian tribes," but this Act alone did not suffice to effect general prohibition. This prohibition came about gradually with the passing of the Indian Intercourse Act of July 9, 1832, which made it *illegal* to sell liquor to Indians anywhere in the United States. "By 1844, traders were not allowed to enter Indian camps. By 1850, most American Indian tribes had become sufficiently disorganized in terms of social, political and religious organization, and of values and beliefs, to arrest the attention of health and welfare groups."

A more comprehensive system of prohibitions and enforcement measures evolved gradually, culminating in the Act of July 23, 1892 (27 Stat. 260), as amended in the Act of July 15, 1938 (52 Stat. 696), which was in effect until 1953. Under conditions of the law, any disposition of intoxicants to Indian country was made a federal offense punishable by imprisonment and heavy fines.

Many tribes forcibly relocated to reservations after defeats in war during the 1860s and those tribes already living on assigned tracts of land came under the control of both Indian agency superintendents and military commanders, some of whom "issued spirits to the Indians as part of their regular rations." The reservation, although defined by specific boundaries, was so vast and thinly populated that bootleggers and smugglers of liquor and other articles were never effectively controlled by enforcement officers, and therefore they flourished.

Prohibition for Indians was to continue past the repeal of the Eighteenth Amendment in 1933, even though they had been granted full citizenship in 1924. The bootlegger and smuggler continued to peddle their intoxicating wares, at great expense to the Indian people, both financially and legally. It is from this Prohibition era in Indian history that many of the patterns of drinking and causative factors for that drinking emerged. Gulp drinking and rapid ingestion of alcohol, as particular drinking patterns of the American Indian, are said to evolve particularly from this era. The very illegality of the drink "may have in fact increased its appeal, especially for the adolescents and young adults."

After repeal in 1953, a few tribal councils decided to continue the prohibition of liquor on certain reservations or to regulate strictly its sale. On some reservations the law remains in effect until the present day. It is thought by some that this discriminatory, if well meaning, prohibition of liquor to Indian tribes for over 120 years only made the problem of alcoholism among Indians even more rampant.[3]

A review of major U.S./Indian policies illustrates the disruption in Indian culture and traditionalism, factors that greatly contributed to psychocultural marginality. The late Reuben Snake, a noted Winnebago-Sioux and chairman of the Task Force Eleven Report on Alcohol and Drug Abuse, succinctly explained this phenomenon in his report.

The streamrolling effect of the "civilized society" upon Indian people has wreaked a havoc which extends far beyond that of loss of material possessions. The American Indian and Alaska Native are caught in a world wherein they are trying to find out who they are and where they are, and where they fit in. The land which was once their "mother," giving them food and clothing, was taken. Their spiritual strengths were decried as pagan, and familial ties were broken. Their own forms of education, i.e., that of legends, how to live, how to respect themselves and others, were torn asunder by the "white society's" reading, writing, and arithmetic. No culture could, or can be, expected to be thrust into a world different from its own and adapt without problems of cultural shock. Also, the Indian people were not even given citizenship until 1924. An 1832 federal Indian law prohibiting the sale of liquor to Indian people remained in effect until 1953 and could have been instrumental in the formation of the "hidden group," "drink until it's gone," and "quick" drinking patterns that Native American people exhibit. The Indian people of today are proud of their heritage and are fighting to maximize its influence upon their lives in a dominant white world. Many have succeeded. Many have not.[4]

In any case, destructive use of alcohol and drug misuse among Native American and Alaska Native individuals, families, and communities is inextricably interwoven into all aspects of their lives, and any effort to alleviate the problem must be comprehensive in scope and have the full commitment of the Indian people and of the federal government to support it in any way necessary.

A related factor was the deterioration of the health of Native Americans during the post-Columbian era. This is an important consideration, given that physical health problems are almost always comorbid conditions with Native American substance-use disorders. More significantly, outright attempts at physical genocide occurred from the earliest

European contact and were part of official policy until President U.S. Grant's peace policy in 1870. The focus now was predominantly on cultural genocide, although physical genocide continued to be inflicted on the Apache in the southwest United States and northwestern Mexico and on the Sioux, Crow, and Cheyenne in the plains and mountain states— Nebraska, Wyoming, Montana, Minnesota, and North and South Dakota. French notes that "outright slaughter, massacres at the hands of the military and civilians, slavery, wars, removal, treaty deceit, starvation, disease genocide, forced sterilization and cultural genocide are some of the methods used in the Euro-American effort to destroy the native peoples and their culture in the American hemisphere." Task Force Six of the 1976 American Indian Policy Review Commission, like Task Force Eleven, provided the first comprehensive analysis of health of Native Americans and the role colonial and U.S. policy played in the deterioration of the health of the indigenous people of America.

It is believed that the Indian race was remarkably disease free before European settlers came to the new world. But with the foreign invasion, Indian health began to deteriorate. The natives had no immunity to the disease germs carried by Europeans. Their health was further impaired when they were forcibly removed from their traditional habitat and denied the practice of their customs, one of which was the use of the medicine man and his herbs for healing.

The federal government made sporadic attempts over the years to attend to the poor health of Indians, but the cumulative effects of confining, unsanitary reservation life, combined with government rations, put the population into a cycle of deteriorating health and increasing susceptibility to still further illness. Nothing short of a comprehensive, coordinated health program could have corrected the situation at any given time.

But such a program was never designed. The health care which Indians actually received in the first 100 years was delivered in a piecemeal, inconsistent fashion, and the few appropriations made were never large enough to meet the overwhelming need. There was always on on-going shortage of hospitals, clinics, nursing homes, convalescent centers, equipment, doctors, nurses, dentists, technicians, administrative and maintenance personnel, and staff housing. Preventive or general health care was not possible under these circumstances. Generally, health service was solely of the crisis type.

A number of different agencies have been responsible for Indian health care, beginning with the War Department, in 1803; the Interior Department, 1849; and finally, in 1955, the Department of Health, Education and Welfare, the agency currently responsible. Each of these agencies was always limited by insufficient funding, inadequate statutory basis, and lack of commitment by the federal government. Moreover, each time a new agency assumed responsibility, it inherited a backlog of unmet needs and the unchanging, depressed environment in which dispossessed Indians lived.

The result today is an Indian race whose health is at a level below that of the general U.S. population.[5]

In 1849, with the establishment of the Department of the Interior, medical care for Native Americans was transferred from military control to the Bureau of Indian Affairs (BIA). In 1955, the Indian Health Services agency was established and placed directly under the authority of the U.S. Surgeon General and the Public Health Service. Task Force Six was instrumental in passage of Public Law 94–437 (94th Congress) in late 1976. The Indian Health Care Improvement Act was designed to improve the services and facilities of federal Indian health programs. It was the first major federal effort since the Snyder Act of 1921, which provided the primary authorization for Indian health programs via the Bureau of Indian Affairs. Nonetheless, Indian health continues to be a major problem within Indian country. A brief, sequential review of U.S./Indian policy is imperative for a better understanding of the current dilemma facing Native Americans and of the physical and mental health problems endemic both on the reservations (Indian country) and in the urban Indian ghettos. Since the colonial era, U.S./Indian policy has seen five basic eras: *removal, reorganization, termination/relocation,* and *self-determination/New Federalism.*

REMOVAL

Removal policies were first applied in the forcible displacement of the Five Civilized Tribes (Cherokees, Choctaw, Chickasaw, Creek, and Seminole) across the Mississippi River into Indian Territory, into what is now the state of Oklahoma. The removal policy was later extended to include Indians of the Southwest and the plains. Removal's strongest proponent was President Andrew Jackson, who made his sentiments clear in his first annual message to Congress:

As a means of effecting this end [removal] I suggest for your consideration the propriety of setting apart an ample district west of the Mississippi, and without the limit of any State or Territory now formed, to be guaranteed to the Indian tribes as long as they shall occupy it, each tribe having a distinct control over the portion designated for its use. There they may be secured in the enjoyment of governments of their own choice, subject to no other control from the United States than such as may be necessary to preserve peace on the frontier and between the several tribes. There the benevolent may endeavor to teach them the arts of civilization, and, by promoting union and harmony among them, to raise up an interesting commonwealth destined to perpetuate the race and to attest the humanity and justice of this Government.[6]

On May 28, 1830, Congress passed the Indian Removal Act, authorizing President Jackson to exchange lands in the West for those held by Indian tribes in any state or territory.

Be it enacted . . . ,That it shall and may be lawful for the President of the United States to cause so much of any territory belonging to the United States, west of the river Mississippi, not included in any state or organized territory, and to which the Indian tribe has been extinguished, as he may judge necessary, to be divided into a suitable number of districts, for the reception of such tribes nations of Indians as may choose to exchange the lands where they now reside, and remove there; and to cause each of said districts to be so described by natural or artificial marks, as to be easily distinguished from each other.

Section 2. And be it further enacted, That it shall and may be lawful for the President to exchange any or all of such districts, so to be laid off and described, with any tribe or nation of Indians now residing within the limits of any of the states of territories, and with which the United States have exiting treaties, for the whole or any part or portion of the territory claimed and occupied by such tribe or nation, within the bounds of any one or more of the states or territories where the land claimed and occupied by the Indians, is owned by the United States, or the United States are bound to the state within which it lies to extinguish the Indian claim thereto.

Section 3. And be it further enacted, That in the making of any such exchange or exchanges, it shall and may be be lawful for the President solemnly to assure the tribe or nation with which the exchange is made, that the United States will forever secure and guaranty to them, and their heirs or successors, the country so exchanged with them, and if they prefer it, that the United States will cause a patent or grant to be made and executed to them for the same: Provided always, That such lands shall revert to the United States, if the Indians become extinct, or abandon the same.[7]

There is little argument that this policy was designed to allow white expansion into the Cherokee Nation, especially by the state of Georgia. This act resulted in the removal of the Five Civilized Tribes into the Indian Territory. Some of the tribal members left voluntarily, but the bulk of the Cherokee Nation was forcibly removed during the dead of winter in 1838, in what became known as the infamous "Trail of Tears" in which a quarter of the sixteen thousand Cherokees perished.

Adding insult to injury, the suffering, exiled Indian groups were subjected to militant efforts to shift them from their traditional harmony ethos to the Protestant ethic. The philosophy of cultural genocide; the need to separate American Indians into concentrated areas, accommodated white settlers, who desired the lands protected by U.S./Indian treaties. A major justification for forced removal was the alleged inferiority of American Indians and the consequent need to kill their culture in order to save their souls. Essentially, the idea was twofold: first, providing desired tribal lands for white expansion, and second, subjecting American Indians to the superior Christian ways. This ethnocentric philosophy was articulated by Indian Commissioner William Medill in 1848:

Stolid and unyielding in his nature, and inveterately wedded to the savage habits, customs, and prejudices in which he has been reared and trained, it is seldom the case that the full blood Indian of our hemisphere can, in immediate juxta-position with a white population, be brought farther within the pale of civiliza-tion than to adopt its vices; under the corrupting influences of which, too indolent to labor, and too weak to resist, he soon sinks into misery and despair. The inequality of his position in all that secures dignity and respect is too glaring, and the contest he has to make with the superior race with which he is brought into contact, in all the avenues to success and prosperity in life, is too unequal to hope for a better result. The collision is to him a positive evil. He is unprepared and in all respects unfitted for it; and he necessarily soon sinks under it and perishes. It must be recollected, too, that our white population has rapidly in-creased and extended, and, with a widening contact, constantly pressed upon the Indian occupants of territory necessary for the accommodation of our own people; thus engendering prejudices and creating difficulties which have occa-sionally led to strife and bloodshed—inevitable between different races under such circumstances—in which the weaker party must suffer.[8]

Commissioner Medill's removal philosophy set the stage for subse-quent relocations to Oklahoma. In 1864, the removal of another major Indian group, the Navajo, was equally devastating, again resulting in a high death rate. The Navajo remember this as "the Long Walk." During the Reconstruction era following the Civil War, a number of plains tribes were removed to Indian Territory: Kaw, Osage, Pawnee, Tonkawa, Ponca, Oto-Missouri, Iowa, Sac and Fox, Kickapoo, Potawatomi, Shaw-nee, Cheyenne, Arapaho, Wichita, Caddo, Comanche, and Kiowa Apache. The plains Indians removal was specified by the 1868 Fort Lar-amie Treaty, similar to the Navajo treaty of that same year, which al-lowed the Indians to return to a portion of their traditional lands. In 1871, unable and unwilling to enforce these treaties, Congress outlawed further treaties with American Indians. Whites were allowed onto the Great Sioux Reservation when gold was found in the sacred Black Hills and Bad Lands of what is now western South Dakota and North Dakota. Again, a pattern emerged of Indians starving around the forts that were charged with feeding and caring for them. These conditions led to the Little Big Horn in 1876 and Wounded Knee in 1890. In the Southwest, the last of the Apache tribes—the Chiricahua, led by Geronimo—were forcibly removed to a concentration prison in the swamps of Florida. Even the Apache scouts in the Army were removed to this devastating prison. Once the "Indian problem" was seen to be under control, the U.S. government changed its policies, breaking its removal treaty prom-ise to secure and guarantee the tribal lands in Indian Territory. The new policy designed to cheat the American Indian of his land, was called "allotment." Like termination and relocation, it became a main tool for the United States' new imperialism, under the guise of Manifest Destiny, Again, the justification for these actions and the reversal of treaty prom-ises was the ethnocentric belief that Native Americans were inferior, both biologically and culturally. Ironically, the policies of the dominant U.S. society produced a self-fulfilling prophecy of psychocultural marginality and dependency among the Native Americans under their care.[9]

ALLOTMENT

Allotment was the general application of deeded homesteads to all Indians at the expense of their collectively held reservations in Indian Territory. In 1886, Indian Commissioner J.D.C. Atkins sowed the seeds of allotment in his annual report:

The Treaties of 1866, and other treaties also, guarantee to the five civilized tribes the possession of their lands; but, without the moral and physical power which is represented by the Army of the United States, what are these treaties worth as a protection against the rapacious greed of the homeless people of the States who seek homesteads within the borders of the Indian Territory? If the protecting power of this Government were withdrawn for thirty days, where would the treaties be, and the laws of the Indians and the Indians themselves?

If the Indians of the five civilized tribes would then put away tribal relations, and adopt the institutions common to our Territories or States, they would no longer be subjected to the jealousy, contention, and selfish greed of adventurous land-grabbers who now seem to regard the Indian a legitimate object of prey and plunder. These adventurers do not attempt to dislodge and drive from their domiciles the peaceful white settlers in their distant homes.

The great objection that is urged by the Indians to dissolve their tribal relations, allotting their lands, and merging their political form of government into an organized Territory of the United States, arises out of their excessive attachment to Indian tradition and nationality. I have great respect for those sentiments. They are patriotic and noble impulses and principles. But is it not asking too much of the American people to permit a political paradox to exist within their midst— nay, more, to ask and demand that the people of this country shall forever burden themselves with the responsibility and expense of maintaining and extending over these Indians its military arm, simply to gratify this sentimentality about a separate nationality?

Congress and the Executive of the United States are the supreme guardians of these mere wards, and can administer their affairs as any other guardian can. . . . Congress can sell their surplus lands and distribute the proceeds equally among the owners for the purposes of civilization and the education of their children, and the protection of the infirm, and the establishment of the poor upon homesteads with stock and implements of Husbandry.[10]

By the 1880s, Congress was moving toward ending tribal government and dividing Indian lands, despite what previous treaties had stated. In 1889, President Benjamin Harrison supported the aim of Congress to open up Indian Territory to white settlers. The vehicle was the Curtis Act of June 28, 1898. This act abolished tribal laws and tribal courts and mandated that all people in Indian Territory, regardless of race, were to come under U.S. authority. The Curtis Act authorized the earlier Dawes Act to proceed with the allotment of tribal lands, thus dissolving all tribes within Indian Territory. This process was completed in 1907, at which time Indian Territory became the state of Oklahoma. Unfortunately, Indians did not have due weight of law on their side under federal and state jurisdictions, and many Indian allotments were stolen due to a conspiracy of unsavory "boomers" and discriminatory courts.[11]

Ironically, Charles Curtis, the architect of tribal destruction in Indian Territory, was of mixed Indian heritage (white, Kaw, and Osage) and went on to serve four years as Herbert Hoover's vice president. Like many mixed-blood Indians who could pass within the larger dominant society, he was a strong advocate of cultural genocide and full assimilation of all American Indians. Curtis took it on himself to force change upon those he believed were less enlightened, traditional Indians. History attests to the misery inflicted upon American Indians by allotment, a policy strongly opposed by the majority of American Indians at the time. In 1901, Congress granted U.S. citizenship to Indians in Oklahoma. In 1919, Indian citizenship status was extended to Indian veterans of World War I who initiated this action. Finally, on June 2, 1924, nearly sixty years after all African Americans were granted citizenship, all Indians born in the United States were granted citizenship. The failed Indian policy required new strategies, and the Great Depression provided the vehicle for change.[12]

REORGANIZATION

Reorganization (under the Wheeler-Howard Act of 1934) was the master plan for the current reservation system. This represented a 180-degree reaction to allotment and the abuses associated with this failed effort at forced accommodation. The Indian Reorganization Act (IRA) was designed to provide federal protection to Indian groups. The corruption that existed during the time leading up to reorganization is illustrated by the actions of Albert Bacon Fall, who served as President Harding's secretary of the interior. Fall was instrumental in a scheme designed to divide the nineteen Pueblo tribes in New Mexico. The Pueblo tribes were exempt from allotment until 1912, when New Mexico became a state, thus bringing the Pueblo tribes under federal control. Fall's intent was to open up Pueblo territory to white ranchers. Fall's approach was first to outlaw, as an Indian offense, traditional dances and religious ceremonies of the Pueblo tribes. His next step was to initiate the Bursum Bill of 1922. The corruption associated with the Bursum Bill led to an investigation by the Brookings Institute known as the *Meriam Report*. The two-year Brookings Institute study, cosponsored by the American

Medical Association, resulted in a dismal portrayal of the shocking social and economic conditions among American Indians living under the federal guidelines of allotment. Fall was convicted and incarcerated for an unrelated act of corruption—the Tea Pot Dome scandal.[13]

The *Meriam Report* set the stage for the appointment of the first progressive Indian Commissioner, John Collier. Appointed by President Franklin Roosevelt in 1933, Commissioner Collier lost no time in initiating New Deal relief programs for American Indians. Another outgrowth of the *Meriam Report* was the 1934 Johnson-O'Malley Act (J-O'M). This act allowed for federal monies to be allocated to states and territories for the provision of educational, medical, and social welfare services to Indians living off protected Indian lands. J-O'M provided congressional support for Collier's progressive Indian education plan. By eliminating the Board of Indian Commissioners, a conservative group that supported allotment and a boarding school concept, and shifting the emphasis to near-reservation day schools, Collier set the stage for a unique form of mainstreaming. J-O'M established direct relationships between public schools and the Bureau of Indian Affairs, a relationship that continues to the present.[14]

The Indian Reorganization Act (IRA) provided annual funding for special Indian education, but its most significant element was the prohibition of allotment. The IRA offered funds and governmental assistance for the purpose of expanding Indian trust lands. Other provisions were relevant to tribal organization and incorporation. Tribes were encouraged to reorganize and to exercise their sovereignty, albeit in limited ways, through the vehicle of tribal governments based on tribal constitutions. Two years later, these acts were extended to Indians living in Oklahoma.[15]

Again, the nineteen Pueblo tribes of New Mexico were exempt from these policies. They had been organized in a loose structure for three centuries, from the 1690s until 1965. In 1965, they developed a constitution recognizing their traditional tribal structure, whereby each Pueblo continued to retain its own leadership and council, with an elected governor. The governors elected a president for the all-Pueblo group. Another Pueblo group, the Hopi, was selected for reorganization, with the underlying purpose of destroying its traditionalism. Toward this end, Commissioner Collier elicited the help of the Pulitzer Prize–winning anthropologist Oliver LaFarge. The idea was to both restrict the practice of traditional customs and to reduce tribal lands. This policy resulted in the Hopi reservation being reduced from the 2,499,588 acres decreed by President Chester A. Arthur to the present 631,194 acres. Thus the Hopi, in violation of the basic tenets of the IRA, were given a constitution they had neither written nor adopted. This has resulted in a long-standing conflict between the Hopi and the Navajo tribes over traditional lands, a conflict that still remains unresolved.[16]

TERMINATION/RELOCATION

The duality in United States policy toward American Indians resurfaced once more during the Eisenhower administration. This time an effort was made to reinstate the destructive policies associated with forced accommodation, like those of allotment. "Termination," the elimination of Federal protection and responsibility to tribes, began with House Concurrent Resolution 108. On August 1, 1953, Congress attempted to terminate federal supervision over American Indians, thereby subjecting them to the same laws as applied to other citizens of the states where the reservations were located, without the special class protection promised in previous treaties and policies.[17]

This sudden change in policy was strongly opposed by American Indians. In its pilot application, all Indian tribes in California, Florida, New York, and Texas, along with the Flathead tribe of Montana, the Lkamath tribe of Oregon, the Potowatami tribe of Kansas and Nebraska, the Chippewa tribe of Turtle Mountain Reservation in North Dakota, and the Menominee tribe of Wisconsin, were slated to be affected. The failure of this experiment came mainly at the expense of the Menominee tribe. Public Law 280 augmented termination by extending state jurisdiction over offenses committed by Indians in Indian country (reservations). Termination began and ended with the failed Menominee experiment. Attempts at making the tribe a corporate entity resulted in increased poverty and exploitation in the name of capitalism. A dire failure, termination ended with the Menominee Restoration Act of 1973, by which the tribe was restored to federal recognition and protection.[18]

"Relocation" was the companion policy to termination. The plan was to entice young adult Indians off the reservation into magnet urban areas. This process served to separate subsequent generations from their traditional language, culture, and customs. Beginning in 1954, thousands of Indians were relocated in what are now commonly known as "urban Indian ghettos." The American Indian Historical Society has assessed relocation as a very destructive policy, one that contributed greatly to the process of cultural genocide: "Finally, the federal government, jockeying precariously between policies of assimilation and the growing recognition that the tribes simply would not disappear together with their unique cultures, originated what has become known as the *Relocation Program*. The litany of that period provides the crassest example of government ignorance of the Indian situation. The *Indian problem* did not go away. It worsened."[19]

Relocation survived, creating large urban populations of marginal Indians, individuals who are Indians in appearance but not in culture or language. They hold membership in neither the larger dominant society nor their particular traditional culture. In 1996, the federal government estimated that urban Indians, the product of relocation, will suffer most from anticipated restrictions of Indian Health Service (IHS) monies. Ironically, IHS was transferred from the Bureau of Indian Affairs (BIA) to the Public Health Service the same year relocation was initiated.

The American Indian Policy Review Commission's series of reports in 1976 set the stage for the contemporary era in U.S./Indian policies, which attempt to form a partnership between U.S. government agencies (the Department of Interior, the Department of Health & Human Services, the Department of Education) and tribal governments.

SELF-DETERMINATION/NEW FEDERALISM

"Self-determination" was preceded by the American Indian Policy Review Commission, a congressional analysis of the historic and legal status of American Indians in the United States. The Review Commission was initiated by Senator James Abourezk (South Dakota) in January 1975. In its final report, the Review Commission made 206 recommendations, most favorable to the Indian perspective, such as those on Indian sovereignty and expanded federal trust responsibility. Certain of these recommendations were incorporated into the Self-Determination Act of 1975.

Sec. 2. (a) The Congress, after careful review of the Federal Government's historical and special legal relationship with, and resulting responsibilities to, American Indian people, finds that

(1) the prolonged Federal domination of Indian service programs has served to retard rather than enhance the progress of Indian people and their communities by depriving Indians of the full opportunity to develop leadership skills crucial to the realization of self-government, and has denied to the Indians people an effective voice in the planning and implementation of programs for the benefit of Indians which are responsive to the true needs of Indian communities; and

(2) the Indian people will never surrender their desire to control their relationships both among themselves and with non-Indian governments, organization, and persons.

(b) The Congress further finds that (1) true self-determination in any society of people is dependent upon an educational process which will insure the development of qualified people to fulfill meaningful leadership roles; (2) the Federal responsibility for and assistance to education of Indian children has not effected the desire level of educational achievement or created the diverse opportunities and personal satisfaction which education can and should provide;

and (3) parental and community control of the educational process is of crucial importance to the Indian people.[20]

The Self-Determination Act clearly stipulated that it does not termi- nate, modify, or diminish existing trust responsibilities of the United States with respect to tribes or Indian people. The most significant ele- ments of self-determination were tribal control over their schools and school boards, and improvements in health care. The latter was man- dated in 1976 by Public Law 94–437, the Indian Health Care Improve- ment Act, which declared: "The Congress hereby declares that it is the policy of this Nation, in fulfillment of its special responsibilities and legal obligation to the American Indian people, to meet the national goal of providing the highest possible health status to Indians and to provide existing Indian health services with all resources necessary to effect that policy."[21]

A preliminary to the current modification of Indian self-determination, known as "New Federalism," was passage of the Indian Alcohol and Substance Abuse Prevention and Treatment Act of 1986, Public Law 99– 570. This federal legislation was actually a subtitle of Public Law 99– 570—the Anti-Drug Abuse Act of 1986, "An Act to strengthen Federal efforts to encourage foreign cooperation in eradicating illicit drug crops and in halting international drug traffic, to improve enforcement of Fed- eral drug laws and enhance interdiction of illicit drug shipments, to pro- vide strong Federal leadership in establishing effective drug abuse prevention and education programs, to expand Federal support for drug abuse treatment and rehabilitation efforts, and for other purposes."[22]

Subtitle C of Public Law 99–570 described this significant health prob- lem within Indian country as follows:

The Congress finds and declares that
(1) the Federal government has a historical relationship and unique legal and moral responsibility to Indian tribes and their members;
(2) included in this responsibility is the treaty, statutory, and historical obli- gation to assist the Indian tribes in meeting the health and social needs of their members;
(3) alcoholism and alcohol and substance abuse is the most severe health and social problem facing Indian tribes and people today and nothing is more costly to Indian people than the consequences of alcohol and substance abuse measured in physical, mental, social and economic terms;
(4) alcohol and substance abuse is the leading generic risk factor among In- dians, and Indians die from alcoholism at over 4 times the age-adjusted rates for the United States population and alcohol and substance misuse results in a rate of years of potential life lost nearly 5 times that of the United States;
(5) 4 of the top 10 causes of death among Indians are alcohol and drug related

injuries (18 percent of all deaths), chronic liver disease and cirrhosis (5 percent, suicide (3 percent), and homicide (3 percent);

(6) primarily because deaths from unintentional injuries and violence occur disproportionately among young people, the age specific-death rate for Indians is approximately double the United States rate for the 15 to 45 age group;

(7) Indians between the ages of 15 to 24 years of age are more than 2 times as likely to commit suicide as the general populations and approximately 80 percent of those suicides are alcohol-related;

(8) Indians between the ages of 15 and 24 years of age are twice as likely as the general population to die in automobile accidents, 75 percent of which are alcohol-related;

(9) the Indian Health Services, which is charged with treatment and rehabilitation efforts, has directed only 1 percent of its budget for alcohol and substance abuse problems;

(10) the Bureau of Indian Affairs, which has responsibility for programs in education, social services, law enforcement, and other areas, has assumed little responsibility for coordinating its various efforts to focus on the epidemic of alcohol and substance abuse among Indian people;

(11) this lack of emphasis and priority continues despite the fact that Bureau of Indian Affairs and Indian Health Service officials publicly acknowledge that alcohol and substance abuse among Indians is the most serious health and social problem facing the Indian people; and

(12) the Indian tribes have the primary responsibility for protecting and ensuring the well-being of their members and the resources made available under this subtitle will assist Indian tribes in meeting that responsibility.

Section 4203: PURPOSE

It is the purpose of this subtitle to:

(1) Authorize and develop a comprehensive, coordinated attack upon the illegal narcotics traffic in Indian country and the deleterious impact of alcohol and substance abuse upon Indian tribes and their members;

(2) provide needed direction and guidance to those Federal agencies responsible for Indian programs to identify and focus existing programs and resources, including those made available by this subtitle, upon this problem;

(3) provide authority and opportunities for Indian tribes to develop and implement a coordinated program for the prevention and treatment of alcohol and substance abuse at the local level; and

(4) to modify or supplement existing programs and authorities in the areas of education, family and social services, law enforcement and judicial services, and health services to further the purposes of this subtitle.[23]

"New Federalism" (1989) emerged in a report of the Special Committee of Investigations of the Senate Select Committee on Indian Affairs. This plan, in contrast to self-determination, called for a reduction of federal programs but continued federal oversight. Improved oversight is needed, given the abuses within the existing federal oversight agencies, as indicated by The Principal Findings of the Special Committee on Investigations, in its executive summary, "A New Federalism for American Indians."

In exchange for the vast lands that now comprise most of the United States, the federal government promised the tribes permanent, self-government reservations, along with federal goods and services. Instead, government administrators, many of whom were corrupt, tired to substitute federal power for the Indians' own institutions by imposing changes in every aspect of native life. At its height, there seemed no limit to the government's paternalistic ambitions. It severed ties between parents and children by confining students in government boarding schools; it shattered the authority of religious leaders by prohibiting traditional rituals and jailing those who resisted; and it destroyed indigenous economies by seizing tribal territories and reneging on the promises it made for land, federal support and financial assistance. Finally, while the government offered Indians equal membership in the United States, it failed to grant them the basic freedom enjoyed by all other Americans: the right to choose their own form of government and live free from tyranny.

Only in the last two decades have federal policy makers taken some cautious steps toward renewing Indian self-rule. Pressed by a persistent and articulate American Indian leadership, as well as other concerned citizens, Congress has begun to return governmental authority to the tribes. Yet even as we near the end of the 20th century, American Indians remain largely trapped by 19th century poverty: 16 percent of reservation homes lack electricity, 21 percent an indoor toilet and 56 percent a telephone. And for the most part, federal policy makers and administrators are still held captive by the ghosts of paternalism and dependency.

Now is the time, on the 200th anniversary of both our constitutional democracy and its first Indian treaty, to reject the errors of our history and return to the high standards set by President Washington. Now is the time to embark on a new era of negotiated agreements between Indian tribes and the United States that abolish federal paternalism but ensure full federal support. By launching a New Federalism for American Indians, we will reaffirm our faith in the extraordinary vision of those who created this unique Republic, while redeeming the promise made long ago to its first people.

Paternalistic federal control over American Indians has created a federal bureaucracy ensnared in red tape and riddled with fraud, mismanagement and waste. Worse, the Committee found that federal officials in every agency know of the abuses but did little or nothing to stop them.

Federal agencies knew, for example, that hundreds of millions of dollars spent on the government's program to promote Indian economic development were largely drained by shell companies posing as legitimate Indian-owned firms. The Bureau of Indian Affairs (BIA) did not need the Committee to discover that 19 of the largest so-called Indian companies that garnered federal contracts were frauds: A BIA Division Chief warned his superiors in an internal memo over a year before the Committee's hearings that the entire program was a "massive fraud (and) financial scandal." Yet, in 31 years, the BIA only discovered two minor instances of possible fraud.

In federally-run schools for Indians, BIA officials knew that school administrators had hired teachers with prior offenses for child molestation. Moreover, BIA knew its employees had failed to report or investigate repeated allegations of sexual abuse by teachers, on one case for 14 years. Yet BIA promoted negligent school administrators and, unlike all 50 states, never fully adopted a system that required employees to report and investigate child abuse.

Federal agencies responsible for protecting natural resources also neglected known problems. For instance, federal officials in Oklahoma admitted that Indian land was "wide open" to oil theft, yet for the past thee years they uncovered none. They even ignored specific allegations against the nation's largest purchaser of Indian oil, which Committee investigators caught repeatedly stealing from Indians.

The federal budget for Indian programs equals $3.3 billion annually. Yet surprisingly little of these funds reach the Indian people. In fact, the total household income for American Indians from all sources, including the federal government, is actually less than the entire federal budget of $3.3 billion.[24]

These abuses, including sexual abuse of Indian students within the BIA school system, were conducted by non-Indians. In response to the New Federalism report, the Indian Child Abuse and Treatment Act was passed on November 6, 1989, compelling federal employees to comply with reporting laws similar to those of the fifty states. This history of U.S./Indian policy provides a clear picture of major social and cultural disorganization among American Indians and Alaska Natives. This chapter provides the link between cultural genocide, personal marginality, and substance abuse as these factors relate to federal policies, mainly those designed to destroy Native American traditionalism and their harmony ethos.

II

THE NATURE OF SUBSTANCE ABUSE AMONG NATIVE AMERICANS

4
PSYCHOCULTURAL FACTORS

Clearly, the psychocultural perspective best explains the dilemma of Native American addictions. Currently, the Bureau of Indian Affairs (BIA) is involved in coordinating services in Indian country for more than 1.2 million federally recognized American Indians and Alaska Natives in thirty-one states. These services include elementary, secondary, and post-secondary education; social services; law enforcement; courts; business loans; land and inheritance records; tribal government support; forestry; agriculture and range lands development; water resources; fish, wildlife, and parks; roads; housing; adult and juvenile detention facilities; and irrigation and power systems. Substance-use disorders within Indian country often involve law enforcement agencies. The BIA is responsible for law enforcement services on 224 reservations, comprising some 826,000 American Indians (Alaska Natives fall under Public Law 280 and local and state law enforcement). Since 1990, law enforcement obligations of the BIA include detention services, yet there are only seventy-three Indian jails in Indian country, on fifty-seven reservations located in nineteen states. Only ten are juvenile detention facilities, while thirty-six of the remaining sixty-three jails have juvenile beds. Hence there are only 256 juvenile beds within ten facilities within Indian country. Most of these facilities are in poor condition, with capacities of only ten to twenty inmates, and have few clinical intervention programs to serve the over six hundred thousand Native American youth.[1]

This profile points to both the inadequacy of current services and the complexity of the population of Indian country. This picture is made more complicated when nonrecognized American Indians and Alaska Natives are factored into the research equation. Urban Indians, a product of relocation during the 1950s, coupled with nonrecognized tribes, such as the Lumbee of North Carolina, and others who feel that they have Indian heritages, cloud any research on the nature of substance abuse among Native Americans. Phone surveys and the U.S. census take the respondents' word on race or ethnicity, and claiming to be part Indian is currently in vogue. French calls this phenomenon the "my grandmother was a Cherokee princess" syndrome. Another consideration when looking at Native American research is the recent tendency for tribes to reduce the minimum "blood degree" for enrollment. French notes that the blood-degree dilemma began in 1979 with the Hopi Pueblo of Arizona.[2] Prior to this, many tribes had a minimum of a quarter blood quantum, one-fourth Indian genetic heritage, according to some government rolls. Even then there is a problem: often the more traditional Indians refuse to enroll, while corrupt federal officials often allow whites to enroll. Among the Cherokee, the latter were known as "five dollar Indians."[3] Another factor is the interaction and interbreeding among indigenous Indians prior to and following Euro-American contact. This factor obviates any purity standard regarding tribal affiliation, even when it is obvious that a predominance of Indian blood exists.

Examples of aboriginal intertribal mixing are the Athapaskan group (Apache and Navajo) and the Cherokee. Today there is a physical distinction between full-blooded Navajo and their cousins, the Apache in the Southwest. This difference is due mainly to the fact that the Navajo adopted the agrarian lifestyle of their pueblo neighbors, thereby creating a larger intertribal genopool. The Apache, up until the late 1800s, pursued a nomadic existence and therefore maintained their gene pool and a distinctive phenotype. Later the Spanish, and then Anglo-Americans, mixed with the Navajo, Pueblo Indians, and Apache. Nonetheless, Euro-American interactions appear to have occurred at a lower rate in the southwestern tribes than among many other Indian groups. The aboriginal Cherokee, although from the Iroquois linguistic family, mixed with their Muskhogean-speaking and Algonquian linguistic neighbors, either through trade or through the adoption of captives.[4] Following European contact, white and African genetic influences began to emerge. Indeed, the interaction between Indian slaves and their African counterparts has resulted in the largest Indian group in the Southeast—the forty-thousand-strong Lumbee Indians of North Carolina. All of these factors effect research relevant to biological factors distinguishing American

Indians and Alaska Natives from other peoples the United States. Therefore, it is imperative that any study of Native Americans involve both biological and sociocultural factors.[5]

Clearly, a combination of sudden cultural disruption (cultural genocide) and dramatic lifestyle changes (diet, disease, level of activity) contributed to the array of health problems plaguing American Indians and Alaska Natives today. A profile of these health and social ills was articulated in 1976 by Task Force Six (in its *Report on Indian Health*) of the American Indian Policy Review Commission. The report noted that one of the most comprehensive studies on the devastation of Indian health resulting from decades of both physical and cultural genocide was prepared by a joint study by the Brookings Institute and the American Medical Association, known as the *Meriam Report*, in the late 1920s.

Some of its findings are as follows: High general death rates; high infant death rates; high childhood death rates; high tuberculosis death rates; high incidence of blindness—causing trachoma; low level of general health at all ages; inadequate health facilities and equipment; shortage of health facilities and equipment; improperly qualified health personnel; shortage of health personnel; inadequate salaries and housing for personnel; inadequate and incomplete vital statistics; no comprehensive preventive-medicine program; inaccessibility of health facilities; deficient diets among Indians; ignorance of preventive health among Indians; poor general health, deficient diets, overcrowding in Indian schools; lack of conventional utilities (running water, sewage disposal, waste disposal, flushing toilets) in Indian homes; and substandard overall living conditions in Indian homes.[6]

These findings were similar to those articulated in the Snyder Act of 1921.[7] Even then it took Congress another twenty-six years to authorize the Indian Health Service, and thirty-seven years to pass the Indian Health Care Improvement Act (Public Law 94–437), in 1976.[8] Nonetheless, many of these conditions continue today. The implication here is that to understand Native American addictions, especially when looking at preventive and interventive strategies, one has to first understand these glaring systemic factors.

Systemic factors play a significant role in the combined biological/sociocultural etiology of Native American addictions, and they need to be placed within the appropriate perspective whenever reviewing postfactor (i.e., after the fact) data banks and analyses. A compromised health profile, especially among American Indians and Alaska Natives who have the highest Native American blood degree and live under improverished socioeconomic conditions, emerges from the available data. Psychocultural marginality, the major product of cultural genocide, also plays a significant role in the physical and mental health profile of Native Americans. Rivers argues that substance use and abuse is usually culturally based. Drawing on Mizruchi and Perrucci's model of culturally relevant proscriptive and prescriptive drinking norms (where proscriptive norms are those that foster abstinence and prescriptive norms provide controlled drinking situations), Rivers concludes, "Members of the groups with high rates of alcoholism (Irish-Americans, French, and Protestants from abstinence backgrounds) share some common characteristics, although the agreement among all groups is not always consistent." These factors are: high social pressure to drink; inconsistent or nonexistent social sanctions against drunkenness; utilitarian or convivial goals of drinking; and ambivalent attitudes and feeling toward moderate drinking. Interestingly, the aboriginal substance-use context fit Rivers's low-risk groups: gradual socialization of children in the use of psychoactive agents; relatively low social pressure to abuse these substances; sanctions against excessive use of these agents; positive, accepting attitudes toward moderation and the nondestructive use of these agents; a well-established consensus on the customs of substance use; and ambivalence about the substance-use situation.[9]

Cultural ambivalence regarding drinking was institutionalized in U.S./Indian policy by the Indian Intercourse Act of July 9, 1832, which made it illegal to sell liquor to Indians anywhere in the United States. The Indian Intercourse Act was actually part of a congressional authorization for a Commissioner of Indian Affairs.

Be it enacted . . . , That the President shall appoint, by and with the advice and consent of the Senate, a commissioner of Indian affairs, who shall under the direction of the Secretary of War, and agreeably to such regulations as the President may, from time to time, prescribe, have the direction and management of all Indian affairs, and of all matters arising out of Indian relation, and shall receive a salary of three thousand dollars per annum. . . .

Section 4. And be it further enacted, That no ardent spirits shall be hereafter introduction, under any pretense, into the Indian country.[10]

Intended as a mechanism for control over Native Americans, not as a humanitarian or benevolent act, this federal intervention remained in effect until repealed in 1953. Even thereafter, federal influence was exercised to keep Indian country dry. This process inadvertently led to two highly profitable non-Indian enterprises in and around Indian country—bootlegging and "drunk towns."[11] Task Force Eleven (Alcohol and Drug Abuse) of the American Indian Policy Review Commission substantiated the manifest intent (cultural genocide and psychocultural marginality) of the Indian Intercourse Act: "By 1850, most American Indian tribes had become sufficiently disorganized in terms of social, political and religious organizations, and of values and beliefs, to arrest the attention of health and welfare groups."[12]

Removal and other elements of the federal policy of cultural genocide and paternalism contributed greatly to the difficulties associated with the Indian Intercourse Act as well.

The reservation, although encased by specific boundaries, was still so vast and thinly populated that bootleggers and smugglers of liquor and other articles were never effectively controlled by the available enforcement officers and therefore left to flourish. Prohibition for Indians was to continue past the repeal of the 18th Amendment in 1933 even though they were granted full citizenship in 1924. The bootlegger and smuggler continued to peddle their intoxicating wares at great expense to the Indian people, both financially and legally. It is from this prohibition era in Indian history that both the patterns of drinking and causative factors for that drinking can be seen emerging. Gulp drinking and rapid ingestion of alcohol, as particular drinking patterns of the American Indian, are said to evolve strongly from this era. The very illegality of the drink "may have in fact increased its appeal, especially for the adolescent and young adults."[13]

Indian drinking outside culturally-approved rituals and other substance abuse falls into Jellinek's "epsilon alcoholism" category.[14] Jellinek postulates five types of alcoholism: "alpha alcoholism," the social drinker; "beta alcoholism," alcohol dependence relevant to intoxication complications and related health problems, according to the latest *Diagnostic and Statistical Manual of Mental Disorders* (DSM-IV); "gamma alcoholism," alcohol dependence with both intoxication and withdrawal features and associated health related problems according to DSM-IV; "delta alcoholism," alcohol abuse according to DSM-IV; and "epsilon alcoholism," periodic heavy consumption.[15]

Jellinek argues that the last is the least understood form of alcoholism. It is enigmatic, in that these individuals can abstain but still have a history of periodic binges in which they manifest the symptoms of a continuously alcohol-dependent individual. The epsilon category clearly fits the traditional Indian drinking pattern known as "bout drinking." Paradoxically, traditional Indians, those who have the highest blood degrees, know their native languages, and customs, and who are often respected members of their tribes, are the ones most likely to engage solely in bout drinking—sometimes with devastating results, such as accidents, assault, homicide, or suicide. A form of bout drinking popular in Indian country and within urban Indian ghettos is the forty-niner, celebrations with some form of pan-Indian rituals (drums, singers, and dancers) but with the predominant activity of binge drinking. The binge drinkers also are found in off-reservation drunk towns (see Chapter 5).

Native American drinking patterns can be linked to psychocultural orientation. The contemporary American Indians spectrum consists of three categories: *traditional Indians, middle-class Indians,* and *marginal Indians.* Traditional Indians are also known as full bloods, real Indians, and conservative Indians. This group accounts only for about 20 percent of the 1.2 million enrolled Native Americans. Often their blood degree and phenotype is close to that of their pre-Columbian ancestors. They usually know their native language and those customs that have survived. They are adherents of their adaptation of the harmony ethos. Basically, traditional Indians feel that their destiny is intricately and intimately related to, and dependent upon, natural phenomena. This is their assumptive world, one where life operates in accordance with nature (Mother Earth, Father Sky) and its cycles. Tension management among traditionalists is based upon prescriptive norms, by which considerable personal license is accepted (counting coup) during the active adult years. While counting coup, a traditionalist male often engages in bout drinking, without suffering tribal reproach.[16]

The middle-class Indian category is estimated to be even smaller than the traditional Indian, with the actual proportions of these two groups varying according to tribe. These are the affluent Native Americans, regardless of blood degree and phenotype. They subscribe to the dominant U.S. societal norms and adhere to the protestant ethic. This group was groomed by federal control agents to play a brokering role within Indian country. Accordingly, this group of Native Americans is most favored by the larger dominant society, and its members are most likely to hold important tribal and agency positions within the white-dominated Indian regulatory structure. They do not generally enjoy the respect of their Indian peers. This disdain for the middle-class Indian is evident in the derogatory labels other Indians have for them—white Indians, apples, five-dollar Indians, and Uncle Tomahawks. Their drinking patterns and problems are similar to those of their non-Indian middle-class mentors.[17]

Marginal Indians account for the majority of Native Americans. Included in this category are those who identify with, and often are enrolled as, tribal members but do not share the traditional phenotype (Euro-American or African-American traits may predominate). Those who are phenotypically Indian but do not know either their native language or traditional customs also fall into this category. Most would agree that this is the major product of the major focus of U.S./Indian policy—cultural genocide. These individuals are caught between two worlds, the dominant U.S. society and their Native American heritage, without fully belonging to either. These individuals are prone toward what Erik Erikson calls cultural identity crises.[18] French has termed this process psychocultural ambiguity or marginality.[19] Many marginal Indians suffer the dilemma of looking Indian and wanting to be Indian but do not know their traditional cultural ways or how to learn their heritage—a phenomenon that attests to the success of relocation and other forms of cultural genocide. The emergence of pan-Indianism during the early 1960s provided a generic Native American role model, one now acceptable throughout Indian country. Nonetheless, avenues to either traditional or middle-class enculturation are greatly limited, making this group the most vulnerable Native American category. They are the ones most likely to be arrested for public drunkenness and alcohol-related offenses as well as to victimized by substance abuse–related mental and physical health problems, including fetal alcoholism.

Coined in 1973, the term fetal alcohol syndrome (FAS) describes the cluster of defects associated with alcohol abuse during pregnancy, the most preventable form of mental retardation in the United States, FAS often represents comorbidity between two or more DSM-IV classifications: mental retardation (axes II and III); substance-related disorders (axes I and III); and posttraumatic stress disorder (PTSD) (axes I and III). The basic physiological features of FAS include facial anomalies, heart defects, low birth weight, behavioral problems, and in many cases, mental retardation. Other physical problems include hearing deficits, poor fine and gross motor coordination, short stature, malformed or misaligned teeth, spinal deformity (scoliosis), sensory awareness problems (hypersensitivity or hyposensitivity), small head (microcephaly), altered palm crease patterns, poor visual-motor coordination, and seizures.[20] Many of these individuals, if not diagnosed as mentally retarded during infancy, present attention-deficit/hyperactivity disorder (ADHD) during childhood and adolescence. This may be a misdiagnosis, according to the DSM-IV, which cautions that the term ADHD not be used if "the symptoms do not occur exclusively during the course of a Pervasive Developmental Disorder, Schizophrenia, or other psychotic disorder and are not better accounted for by another mental disorder (e.g., Mood Disorder, Anxiety Disorder, Dissociative Disorder, or a Personality Disorder)."[21]

Finkelstein associates a number of stress factors with substance-abusing women and hence their susceptibility to FAS. These include a poor self-image, notably their sexual image; feelings of powerlessness and learned helplessness; stormy relationships with men, including violence and abuse; and labile affect (anger, depression, guilt, shame, stigma, dependence).[22] Weiner and her team of researchers at Boston University School of Medicine finds that the effects of alcohol are not equal among women and that their susceptibility is related to a number of biopsychocultural factors: gestational stage at time of exposure, fetal susceptibility to alcohol and viability of both the blood brain barrier and placenta, maternal nutrition, chronicity of the mother's alcohol abuse, and the prevalence of stress and anxiety in the mother's life. These factors account for the wide variability of women who do drink during pregnancy, ranging from less than 2 percent to up to 85 percent. The implication of this research is that well-nourished and mentally and physically healthy women who drink moderately have only a slight chance of producing a FAS birth, while those with a poor biopsycho-cultural profile are most at risk. Marginal American Indians and Alaska Natives fall into the at-risk category.[23]

French notes that with marginal Native Americans, posttraumatic stress may be comorbid with FAS birth.[24] The relationship between PTSD and FAS emerged with the inclusion of the posttraumatic stress disorder in the *Diagnostic and Statistical Manual of Mental Disorders*, third edition, in 1980.[25] Posttraumatic stress is an unresolved traumatic experience that results in autonomic nervous system responses, such as hypervigilance and prolonged sympathetic responses of the endocrine and limbic systems, resulting in untargeted and extreme anxiety and a correspondingly compromised immune system. It is now clearly established that substance-use disorder, notably alcohol-related self-medication is linked to PTSD. At an international conference known as "Addictions '98: Comorbidity across the Addictions," held in the United Kingdom, a majority of the presentations addressed this phenomenon. Correspondingly, a special issue of *Addictive Behaviors* (November/December 1998) presented research based on the Addictions '98 conference. The majority of these articles addressed comorbidity between substance-related disorders and posttraumatic stress disorder. An important outcome of this international conference was the finding that substance-related disorder is easier to treat than PTSD.[26]

A problem in Indian country, notably among marginalized Native Americans, is the cycle of abuse. A FAS teenager gets pregnant while under the influence of alcohol, continues to drink and neglects her health during the pregnancy, and gives birth to yet another FAS baby. Cognitive interventions do not seem to work in these cases, mainly due to the fact that the FAS is often comorbid with PTSD. This relationship was only detected within the past decade, at neuropsychiatric treatment centers for youth in New England. This relationship between FAS and PTSD was discovered in aggressive/suicidal adolescents who were idiosyncratic substance abusers, an unusual phenomenon among teens.[27] Clinical background investigations found that these youth had experienced trauma in the prenatal or neonatal stages or during infancy or early childhood, prior to the establishment of an "autobiographic memory."[28] Autobiographical memory is the measure of long-term or remote memory relevant to the individual's personal history. A prerequisite for this memory of self is a sufficient acquisition of the language employed in the cultural milieu where one is socialized. Amnesia and other organic insults to the central nervous system (CNS), conditions that are exacerbated by substance abuse, notably alcohol, can also contribute to an impairment of one's autobiographic memory. The FAS fetus is compromised at the neonatal stage, with the trauma going unregistered by the cognitive part of the brain. Yet the emotional insult is registered within the CNS, activating the greater limbic system of the reptilian brain, triggering a pervasive state of unresolved anxiety and hypervigilance.

These conditions, in turn, compromise the immune system and set the stage for comorbid clinical conditions that usually are exacerbated at the onset of puberty and its increased activation of the endocrine system. Alcohol generally becomes the self-medication of choice for these conditions. Dorris, in his National Book Critic's Circle Award–winning book, *The Broken Cord*, perhaps more than anyone else has brought to the public's attention the severe social and behavioral challenges associated with Native American marginality and fetal alcoholism.[29] Nelson and Wright address the issue of PTSD by association in their study of female partners of veterans with PTSD: "This paper addresses the fact that women in long-term relationships with veterans suffering from PTSD commonly experience PTSD-like psychiatric symptoms themselves."[30] This phenomenon certainly pertains to marginal Indians and is a contributing factor in the FAS/PTSD cycle of abuse. Clearly, any viable solution to the Indian FAS/PTSD problem plaguing marginal Native Americans must transcend simple cognitive, well-intended but ineffective, intervention and treatment approaches—such as those whose message is: just say no to alcohol, sex, and drugs.

5

STUDIES ON SUBSTANCE ABUSE IN INDIAN COUNTRY

❖

THE DRUNK TOWN PHENOMENON

Anyone who has worked extensively in Indian country knows about the "drunk town" phenomenon. White Clay, Nebraska, just across the border from the dry Pine Ridge Oglala Sioux Reservation; Waynesville, Bryson City, and Robinsville in North Carolina, adjacent to the Eastern Band of Cherokee Indians; and Macy, Nebraska, just outside the Omaha/Winnebago Reservation—these are just a few examples of the fallacy of the Indian Intercourse Act and Euro-American exploitation of marginal Native Americans. Unfortunately, every American Indian and Alaska Native family has a tale of death and destruction associated with a drunk-town tragedy.

Weibel-Orlando, in a 1990 article, described this problem as it afflicted the Navajo Indian reservation, with the largest Native American population: "Bordertowns such as Flagstaff, Arizona, at the southwest corner, Holbrook and Winslow to the south, and Gallup to the east of the reservation are all long-established legal drinking sites for reservation Navahos. It has been argued that the 'drunken Indian' stereotype was generated by non-Indian observation of the highly public and raucous payday binges that characterized Indian drinking behavior in border towns well frequented by both Indians and non-Indian tourists."[1] She went on to describe the situation at the second-most-populous U.S. Indian reservation, Pine Ridge: "The road that runs directly south of Pine Ridge Village and into White Clay, Nebraska, is studded with crosses commemorating the car crash deaths of loved ones who did not return from their last 'border run.' The hard-bitten towns of Gordon, Rushville, and Scenic can all claim an economic stake in legally providing alcoholic beverages to Indians who have the cash resources to pay for such services."[2] Two of the most studied drunk towns are those adjacent to the largest U.S. reservation, in both physical size and population—the Navajo Nation of the Diné. Two off-reservation New Mexico counties towns, Gallup and Farmington, have come to illustrate the magnitude of the drunk-town problem among the Navajo.

About the same time the American Indian Policy Review Commission was conducting its study for Congress, a series of brutal murders occurred in Farmington, New Mexico. A federal investigation of these atrocities found that a pervasive hostility among the "Anglo" (Euro-American) population toward Native Americans had been a major factor in these murders. The report of the New Mexico Advisory Committee to the United States Commission on Civil Rights, *The Farmington Report: A Conflict of Cultures*, used Philip Reno's quote to articulate this hostile environment.

The towns just beyond the borders of Indian reservations have historically served as middlemen between whites and Indians. Border town trading posts and stores bought from and sold to Indian agencies, and as time went on, border towns also became the local headquarters of corporations exploiting Indian resources. These various services have bound Indians and border towns together in the same "relentless reciprocity" that Jean-Paul Sartre saw binding colonized to colonizer in Africa. Now, the old reciprocity, which was based on inequality and dependency, is breaking down and a new reciprocity, based on more equal rights and power must be established.[3]

Peter MacDonald, the Navajo tribal chairperson at this time, noted that the reciprocity that binds Navajos to Anglos in Farmington is oppressively unequal, with the Navajo suffering from injustice. What spurred this investigation and the resulting twenty-year federal supervision of Farmington was the murder of three inebriated Navajo men by three Anglo youth.

In April 1974 the bodies of three Navajo men were found in separate locations in the rugged canyon country near Farmington, their bodies severely beaten, tortured, and burned. The brutality of these three crimes provoked immediate and angry outrage from the Navajo community. The tranquility which had seemed a way of life in Farmington was to be abruptly ended. The slayings proved the catalyst for bringing the civil rights movement to Farmington. Much of the Anglo community in Farmington found itself not only ill-prepared to deal with the ensuing crisis, but indeed confused, threatened, and frightened.[4]

Three Anglo teenagers from Farmington were carrying out a time-honored tradition among local white teenagers, "rolling" and beating Navajo drunks. This father-to-son rite of passage was clearly tolerated by the Anglo community and produced an environment for the escalation of violence toward American Indian victims. In 1974, the three white teenagers, Vernon Crawford, Peter Burke, and Oren Thacker, went looking for "Subs" to roll, beat, torture, and kill (the Anglo teenagers referred to the inebriated Navajo as subhuman, hence the derogatory Subs). They picked up their victims under the pretense of befriending them, drove them to a remote area in Chokecherry Canyon, where they beat them, stripped them, and burned plastic cups and bottles in their body openings while they were still alive. They finished the job by pouring gasoline on their beaten and tortured bodies and setting it on fire. These were acts of pure racial hatred, a sentiment prevalent in this region of northwestern New Mexico among Anglos who were reaping the benefits of lands that had once belonged to the Navajo. The U.S. Civil Rights Commission became involved following the outcry among Indian groups against the light sentences the teenagers received (two years at the New Mexico Boys School in Springer).[5]

At the Civil Rights Commission hearings, many of the Navajos stated that alcoholism was the major problem affecting their people and that it was fueled by the non-Indian, off-reservation business community, which deliberately took advantage of this social ill for its profit. There was a call for closing all local Indian bars.

The New Mexico Advisory Committee heard extensive testimony describing alcoholism and alcohol abuse as being a pervasive and profound problem affecting the Navajo people. In the city of Farmington, the Advisory Committee finds the situation especially critical. Arrest patterns among Navajo in Farmington, indicate that the vast proportion of all Navajos arrested are incarcerated for alcohol-related crimes. An analysis of police records in Farmington undertaken by Commission staff reveals the extent and severity of the alcohol-abuse problem among Navajos. Over a 5 year period (1969–1973), approximately 15,000 Navajos have been arrested for alcohol-related offenses. Since the passage of the Detoxification Act by the New Mexico State Legislature in 1973, more than 3,800 Navajos have been placed into protective custody by the Farmington Police Department. During 1973 Indian arrests constituted more than 80 percent of all arrests in Farmington; approximately 90 percent of these arrests were alcohol-related. Moreover, testimony indicated that at the time of the open meeting there were no facilities or treatment programs in Farmington, San Juan Country, or on the Navajo Reservation.[6]

Looking at the related area of health and medical services, the New Mexico Advisory Committee to the U.S. Commission on Civil Rights noted:

The New Mexico Advisory Committee finds that the health care situation for Navajos living in the northwestern part of New Mexico is at a crisis stage. The present Public health Service/Indian Health Service (PHS/IHS) Hospital located in Shiprock is inadequate to meet the needs of the Navajo people living in its service area. Private medical facilities in the region are very limited. Moreover, there appears to be little cooperation between the medical facilities and staff on the reservation and the private medical community in Farmington. The Advisory Committee also finds that there is no coordinated health planning in the region which involves the PHS/IHS facility in Shiprock and the San Juan Hospital in Farmington.

The New Mexico Advisory Committee finds that the problem of securing medical and health services is acute for low-income people and for Navajos living off the reservation. The Advisory Committee also heard testimony alleging that San Juan Hospital has refused services to some Navajos in need of medical attention, and has instead transferred them to the PHS/IHS Hospital in Shiprock for medical care. This situation is aggravated by the complex jurisdictional problems in providing health and medical care to Indians living off the reservation.[7]

Despite federal intervention and supervision by the U.S. Civil Rights Commission, alcoholism and Anglo exploitation of Native Americans continued in northwestern New Mexico (McKinley and San Juan Counties). The Gallup phenomenon was described in 1990 by the *Arizona Republic*:

Truckers rolling through on Interstate 40 refer to this city of 20,000 on their CBS as "Drunk City, USA." The label reflects Gallup's long-established reputation as a place where people—most of them from the nearby Navajo reservation—come to get drunk. Along Route 66 and its assortment of bars and package outlets, drunks slump against buildings a block from the Sante Fe train yard, where passenger trains bound for Los Angles and Chicago stop each day. The National Institute of Alcohol Abuse and Alcoholism estimates that surrounding McKinley County has the worst alcoholism problem in the nation.[8]

In the fall of 1994, twenty years after the torture/murders of three Navajo in Farmington, another report, *Taking the Long View: A Review of Substance Abuse-Related Social Indicators in McKinley County, New Mexico*, was disseminated. This is the executive summary of a Northwest New Mexico Council of Governments document reflecting their efforts to correct this problem (with the assistance of the Robert Wood Johnson Foundation). In its 1989 grant proposal, the Council offered the following scenario of northwest New Mexico and its Anglo/Indian relations:

Northwest New Mexico is unique. What distinguishes this region from other parts of the country is the impact which residents of the "dry" (Navajo Nation) have on the border towns where alcohol is legal. This is particularly true of Gallup, which has received a national reputation as "Drunk Town." Gallup and the surrounding region are faced with an epidemic of alcohol abuse which has received national exposure after the *Albuquerque Tribune* did a six-part expose (October 26–November 1, 1988). The broadcast media followed up on the story, and segments on Gallup have since been aired on NBC's "Today Show," ABC's "20/20," PBS's "On Assignment," and the syndicated "Inside Edition." Gallup is the major border town of the region, and is the most heavily impacted by alcohol abuse. Gallup's population on weekends expands from its 21,000 residents to well over 100,000 people. Gallup has 61 liquor outlets, which exceeds New Mexico's quota system by 50. Individuals who become intoxicated are picked up by the police to protect them from injury and death, such as might result from staggering onto the highway or freezing. More than 30,000 people are taken into "protective custody" (incarcerating the individual without criminal offense for up to 12 hours) each year in Gallup. More than one-third of these individuals are Arizona residents.

The National Institute on Alcoholism and Alcohol Abuse "U.S. Alcohol Epidemiological County Problem Indicators" found McKinley County had the highest composite index of alcohol-related problems of all 3,107 counties in the United States (for the 1975–1980 time period). Death rates from cirrhosis of the liver in McKinley County were three times higher than the national average, alcohol-related traffic accidents were seven times higher, chronic alcoholism rates were 19 times higher, and deaths from all alcohol-related causes were four times higher.

During the last year (1988), 164 deaths, which represents 40% of all deaths in McKinley and San Juan counties, were alcohol-related. The carnage includes deaths from exposure, pedestrians run over by trucks and trains, acute alcohol poisoning, child abuse, automobile collisions, drownings, suicides and homicides.[9]

In a 1994 report, the Northwest New Mexico Fighting Back Regional Council reported: "Substance abuse remains a serious threat to the health, safety and well-being of McKinley County residents. This county still ranks high on many indicators of substance abuse, in comparison with the remainder of New Mexico."[10] In an Associated Press release in the October 25, 1998, *Albuquerque Journal*, Senator John McCain, who serves on the Senate Indian Affairs Committee, is quoted as saying, "Some members of Congress are led to believe the standard of living for Indian people is improving due to the economic success enjoyed by a few Indian tribes. Unfortunately, the statistics prove otherwise. Reports of Indian child abuse continue to increase and unemployment rates are perpetual high. American Indians still suffer the highest mortality rates for any group in the nation due to alcoholism, tuberculosis, diabetes, pneumonia and influenza."[11] Another 1998 *Albuquerque Journal* article focused on the increased number of deaths in Gallup of drunk Indians by being run over by trains.[12]

Another environment of marginal Indians where there is a high concentration of substance abuse is the urban Indian ghettos, created (as noted above) by the federal policies of termination and relocation in the 1950s.[13] As Weibel-Orlando notes, the termination/relocation policy contributed to California's large Indian population. Prior to these policies, California's Native American population consisted of a number of small reservations with a total population of less than twenty thousand. Today it has about a quarter-million Native Americans, of whom less than fifty thousand are indigenous California Indians. The nonreservation urban ghettos suffer from problems similar to those that plague the off reservation border towns.[14]

REVIEW OF CONTEMPORARY RESEARCH

Two U.S. Department of Health and Human Services agencies, the National Institute on Drug Abuse (NIDA) and the National Institute of Alcohol Abuse and Alcoholism (NIAAA), publish research monographs on etiology, assessment/evaluation, diagnoses, prevention/intervention, and treatment relevant to substance-related issues and disorders. NIAAA's director also issues a timely periodical, *Alcohol Alert*, with thematic research results. Four of its issues offer general information germane to Native American addictions: alcohol and the liver (no. 19, PH 329), alcohol and nutrition (no. 22, PH 346), alcohol and hormones (no. 26, PH 352), and alcohol and tolerance (no. 28, PH 356),[15] Two NIDA monographs and one NIAAA paper look at paternal substance-use research: *Consequences of Maternal Drug Abuse* (NIDA no. 59), *Methodological Issues in Epidemiological Prevention and Treatment Research on Drug-Exposed Women and Their Children* (NIDA no. 117), and *Stress, Gender, and Alcohol-Seeking Behavior* (NIAAA no. 29).[16] Other related monographs include: *Alcohol and Glial Cells* (NIAAA no. 27), *Alcohol-Induced Brain Damage* (NIAAA no. 22), *Inhalant Abuse* (NIDA no. 129), *Alcohol and Interpersonal Violence* (NIAAA no. 24), *The Development of Alcohol Problems* (NIAAA no. 26), and *Drug Abuse among Minority Youth* (NIDA no. 130).[17]

The last has a section on American Indian youth. Here King and Thayer note that American Indian youth use substances like alcohol, inhalants, and marijuana at an earlier age than whites. The authors' research shows that much of this early experimentation occurs during the boarding school years. King and Thayer tested two causal models that purport to explain the high incidence of addictions among American Indian youth:

The life stress and social support theory identified life stress as a significant influence on levels of family support and drug use. That it did not *predict* levels of alcohol use is surprising, and why it did not remains unclear. Apparently, reasons for alcohol use differ from those for using other drugs. Family support moderates rates of alcohol use and is also itself influenced by life stress factors. Overall, life stress appears to be a major influence on factors related to substance use.

The peer cluster theory also identified factors significant to substance use. Family strength or, in the case of this analysis, parental expectations were found to influence levels of friend support, family support, and school adjustment. Adolescents who received greater friend support and had better school adjustment chose same-age peers to drink with. These drinking arrangements seem categorically different from those adolescents who drink with older peers. Further analyses may reveal the specific distinctions between these peer cluster groups.[18]

A review of the current literature can be placed into a number of categories: general overviews of the problem, fetal alcohol syndrome/fetal alcohol effect, research and theories on the cause of Native American addictions, inhalant abuse, and such other related topics as drunk driving and Native American veterans.

The National Institute on Alcohol Abuse and Alcoholism, in a 1994 *Alcohol Alert*, looked at alcohol and minorities. Its research concluded that blacks and Hispanics had higher rates of mortality from alcoholic cirrhosis than did whites or Asian-Americans, even though a higher percentage of blacks than whites abstain from using alcohol. More compelling was the results for American Indians: "Although highly variable among tribes, alcohol abuse is a factor in five leading causes of death for American Indians, including motor vehicle crashes, alcoholism, cirrhosis, suicide, and homicide. . . . Among tribes with high rates of alcoholism, reports estimate that 75 percent of all accidents, the leading cause of death among American Indians, are alcohol related."[19] Regarding fetal alcoholism, the study reported that among two populations of Southwestern Plains Indians, from birth to age fourteen, the FAS rate was 10.7 per thousand births. This compares with 2.2 per thousand for Pueblo Indians and 1.6 for Navajo Indians, supporting the views that the rates of alcohol dependence and abuse are variable among Native American groups.[20]

A substantial article on American Indian and Alaska Native adolescent health appeared in the March issues of the *Journal of the American Medical Association*. Blum and others surveyed 13,454 Native Americans in the seventh through the twelfth grades attending nonurban schools serving eight Indian Health Service areas. The findings indicated that "the majority of American Indian youth are not faced with significant health risks. . . . While the majority of youths do not experience significant risks, a sizable minority do, and it is a larger minority than for other groups of teenagers in the United States." The authors concluded that "American Indian and Alaska Natives reported high rates of health-compromising behaviors and risk factors related to unintentional injury, substance use, poor self-assessed health status, emotional distress and suicide." They call for cultural sensitive and culture—specific interventions.[21]

Burd and Moffatt, in a 1994 publication, conducted a critical review of research articles on the epidemiology of FAS among American Indians, Alaska Natives, and Canadian Aboriginals. Reviewing ten studies, the authors concluded, "The papers included in this review suggest that the rate of FAS among Indian or Aboriginal peoples in the United States and Canada may be greatly increased compared with rates for whites." However, due to methodological flaws, Burd and Moffatt suggest, more research is needed on this topic: "Future studies should include four features: (a) the cohorts should include people with both FAS and developmental disorders other than FAS, (b) the cohorts should be stratified by ethnic status, (c) the blinding of diagnosticians to the history of maternal alcohol use during pregnancy, and (d) the expansion of study designs to allow for identification of sensitivity and specificity of both screening methods and diagnostic criteria."[22]

Beauvais's longitudinal study of substance use among American Indian students is another valuable contribution to the literature. In 1996, Beauvais presented the results of his twenty-year (1975–1994) surveillance project involving American Indian youth residing on or near reservations. Anonymous substance-use surveys were administered annually to a nationally representative sample of Indian youth in the seventh to twelfth grades. The results indicate that "Indian youth continue to show very high rates of drug use compared with their non-Indian peers. The trends in rates during the last 20 years parallel those of non-Indian youth. While overall drug use may be decreasing, about 20% of Indian adolescents continue to be heavily involved with drugs, a proportion that has not changed since 1980."[23] Beauvais also found that Indian youth, especially those who drop out of school, are at high risk for substance use and abuse.

In his 1994 article on the epidemiology of alcohol abuse among American Indians, May questioned any genetic differences between Native Americans and others relevant to the metabolism of alcohol, stating that "no basis at all for this myth is found in the scientific literature, and it should not be a consideration in current prevention and intervention programs." Looking at drinking rates and styles, drunk-driving rates, gender differences, and the prevalence of FAS, May concluded, "Many of the myths and common understandings about alcohol use among American Indians are gross oversimplifications. . . . As this paper has demonstrated, the truth about Indian drinking is indeed complicated and quite different from the myths. But the insights and explanations that emerge from seeking the facts are those that will help create meaningful improvement."[24]

Most students of Native American social and health issues agree that indeed this is a complex field. Native Americans are no more homogeneous than are Anglo-Americans, Asian-Americans, Hispanics, or African Americans. A major variable here is the blood degree and cultural integration of those who claim to be American Indian or Alaska Native. Given these complexities, the scientific method of statistically significant causal relationships may in itself prove too simplistic to provide meaningful answers. May and other raw empiricists; may manifest a form of ethnocentrism that clouds their objectivity with respect to the uniqueness of traditional/aboriginal Native American cultures. Clearly, a more holistic approach is indicated. Multiple data sources and an understanding of the cultures being studied are imperative. Ex post facto analysis of survey data and secondary analysis of canned data at a university research center, especially where self-aggrandizement through publication and grants may be the primary motive, are hardly the roads to either the understanding or resolution of Native American addictions.

Recent studies on fetal alcoholism provide insights into the nature of this complex problem and its relationship to other health and social problems plaguing Native Americans. Kaufman, a Scottish medical researcher, wrote in 1997 an article on the teratogenic effects of alcohol following exposure during pregnancy and its genetic influence on the pre-ovulatory egg.

Much information has emerged over the years concerning the teratogenicity of acute and chronic alcohol exposure during pregnancy. Both alcohol and its primary metabolite, acetaldehyde, are teratogenic. Exposure during pregnancy may lead to fetal alcohol syndrome (FAS), and this is said to occur in a substantial proportion of infants born to mothers who are chronic, heavy daily drinkers. Such infants usually survive to birth but are mentally retarded, often display growth retardation and additionally display a characteristic range of clinical features, principally craniofacila abnormalities and neurological damage. . . . The author's experimental findings indicated that the potential hazard of exposure of preovulatory human eggs and, but to a lesser extent, recently fertilized embryos, to alcohol is at least as harmful as exposure to this agent during pregnancy, and consequently this should be an equal cause for concern.[25]

An international group of researchers, Kopera-Frye, Dehaene, and Streissguth, administered eleven neuropsychological assessments to twenty-nine adolescent and adult clients diagnosed with either fetal alcohol syndrome or fetal alcohol effect. Their research on FAS/FAE cognitive deficits, published in a 1996 article, indicated that the cognition estimation test, which is sensitive to frontal lobe insults, indicated the greatest level of impairment: "The patterns of deficit described may reflect either the diffuseness of brain damage incurred from prenatal alcohol exposure, or a cumulative deficit in comprehension which may be important for the acquisition of higher-order mathematical abilities."[26]

Two other articles address central nervous system damage secondary to FAS. Mattson et al. used magnetic resonance imaging to study six FAS clients and a control of seven matched, normal individuals. Their research indicated a decrease in the size of the basal ganglia in children with FAS. The basal ganglia is the neuronetwork located at the base of the cerebral hemispheres; its function is to connect sensory input to the frontal lobe. It play a role in procedural learning, language, attention, and personality. A compromised basal ganglia can result in movement disorders. Mattson's group found, "When basal ganglia were divided into the caudate and lenticular nuclei, both of these regions were significantly reduced in the children with fetal alcohol syndrome. Finally, when the overall reduction in brain size was controlled, the proportional volume of the basal ganglia and, more specifically, the caudate nucleus was reduced in the children with fetal alcohol syndrome."[27]

Church and Kaltenbach, in a 1997 article, linked FAS to hearing, speech, language, and vestibular (anatomical structure of acoustic nerve) disorders. Their review of human and animal research indicated four types of hearing disorder associated with FAS: "(1) a developmental delay in auditory maturation, (2) sensorineural hearing loss, (3) intermittent conductive hearing losses due to recurrent serious otitis media, and (4) central hearing loss."[28]

Along similar lines, Kaneko et al. devised a screening method for discerning between FAS and Down's syndrome, the two most common etiologies of mental retardation in the Western world: "The present study is the first to characterize auditory event-related potentials (ERPs) in children with FAS and contrast them to subjects with Down's Syndrome and controls." Their findings again indicated neurophysiological differences between FAS and Down's etiologies: "A discriminant function analysis also revealed that these children could be correctly classified as being either Down's Syndrome, FAS, or normal controls using measures of latency and amplitude of the P300. These data suggest that an evaluation of ERP characteristics may provide a better understanding of the differences between FAS and Down's Syndrome children."[29]

Research and theories on Native American addictions cover a range of topics, including the prevalence of substance abuse among children, youth, and women as well as such associated features as abuse, trauma, mental and physical illnesses, familial issues, education, peer influences, and delinquency. More information relevant to early abuse and trauma among Native Americans is emerging in clinical publications. Candice Fleming, of the National Center for American Indian and Alaska Native

Mental Health Research at the University of Colorado, presented a comprehensive case study of a young adult American Indian women whose clinical diagnosis included double depression (dysthymia with bouts of major depression), alcoholism, and childhood trauma. In this case, it is evident that PTSD should have been an Axis I primary diagnosis.[30]

Irwin and Roll have assessed the psychological impact of sexual abuse of American Indian boys attending boarding schools. As noted earlier, this type of abuse, if not immediately treated, is a prime source of PTSD and subsequent substance abuse in the form of self-medication. The authors, in their 1995 article, noted, "Although there is a small but growing literature about the presence and prevalence of sexual abuse of Native American children and about the difficulties in determining the range and extent of such abuse, there is almost no literature about the diagnosis or evaluation of the impact of sexual abuse on Native American children."[31] In their analysis of twelve Native American boys from two boarding schools, Irwin and Roll concluded that these abused youth experienced a broad range of severe disruptions of drive, functioning of ego, objective relations, inhibition of sexual drive, increased aggression, and substance abuse.

French, in his 1997 book *Counseling American Indians*, addressed the issue of pedophilia government-run Indian schools. He notes, "The fact that Indian children and youth were systematically abused by non-Indians—notably those employed by the federal government—first came evident in *The Executive Summary: A New Federalism for American Indians*."[32] The Select Committee on Indian Affairs illustrated two Anglo pedophiles who were career teachers in Bureau of Indian Affairs schools. Between them, they molested hundreds of prepubic Indian children, mostly males, with the knowledge of their superiors. Punitive action from the BIA was merely to transfer these pedophilic teachers to another, unsuspecting tribe and BIA school. Thus, sex abuse is yet another variable in the complex picture of trauma to American Indian infants and youth relevant to their autobiographical memory, self-identity, and subsequent mental disorders, including substance-related disorders and PTSD.

Five recent studies look at the nature of drinking patterns among Native American youth. King and his group examined adolescent substance use in an American Indian boarding-school population. Their results showed that 87 percent of the students had tried alcohol with 25 percent using alcohol weekly. Nearly three-quarters of the students (73 percent) claimed that they drank until they were high or drunk. Another 74 percent indicated that they had tried marijuana, while 31 percent reported that they had tried inhalants.[33] The other four studies compared Native American youth substance use and abuse with non-Indian groups, with equally alarming results. Gfellner, in her 1994 article, presents the results of her matched-group comparison of substance use and problem behavior among urban Canadian Indian and white adolescents. She notes that her data base of 3,523 students from grades five through twelve indicated higher rates of use for cigarettes, marijuana, and solvents (inhalants) for Indian youth; overall, with the exception of alcohol, the results portrayed the higher rates of substance abuse among Native American youth. Interestingly, Gfellner found that the white youth reported more liberal parental attitudes toward adolescent drinking, and greater alcohol use by their parents, then was the case among the American Indian youth, whose parents generally did not aprove use of alcohol by their children.[34]

In another Indian/white youth study, Roski et al. studied the prevalence of heavy alcohol use among sixth and eighth-graders in northeastern Minnesota. The data indicated widespread alcohol use and heavy drinking among both white and Indian youth. However, the alcohol abuse rates for the American Indian youth were between 50 percent and 100 percent higher than their white counterparts. This rate also exceeded drinking rates of eighth-graders in a nationally representative sample comprising all ethnic groups. Features of this profile of Indian drinking patterns were that Indians tend to begin their drinking experience at a younger age and drop out of school due to their drinking problems.[35] Finley, in her study of 2,234 students in grades six through twelve in Montana, also found significant differences between Indian and non-Indian students. Unlike Gfellner, Finley found a greater tolerance for drinking among the Indian sample, with Indian parents more likely than non-Indian parents to be sources, of alcohol. Also, drinking and driving was more prevalent among the Native American youth.[36]

The author and Nancy Picthall-French assessed 468 rural Anglo-American, African-American, Mexican-American, Mexican, and Navajo adolescents according to a number of related functional areas: substance use/abuse, physical health, mental health, family relationships, peer relationships, educational and vocational status, social skills, leisure and recreation, and aggressive behavior/delinquency. Using the National Institute on Drug Abuse's Problem-Oriented Screening Instrument for Teenagers (POSIT), the authors developed aggregate profiles for these samples. A minimum score of thirty-eight for the ten areas indicated clinical pathology. Their data found the Navajo to be at highest risk.

When looking at the individual functional items the Navajo adolescent females scored highest in Mental Health, Family Relations and Education status. Navajo adolescent males scored highest in Substance Use/Abuse, Peer Relations, and Leisure & Recreation. Caucasian adolescent males scored highest in Aggressive Behavior/Delinquency. African American adolescent males scored highest in Social Skills and Physical Health, while Mexican adolescent females scored highest in Vocational Status. All of these scores were above the item scale score for pathology. Clearly, Peer Relations, Substance Use/Abuse, and Mental Health appear to be interrelated functional items for all groups in this study.[37]

Inhalant abuse is seen by many as a critical problem among Native Americans. Fred Beauvais's research highlights the seriousness of this phenomenon. The prevalence of inhalant abuse first emerged from his yearly substance-use/abuse survey of a large sample of Native American youth. He noted that inhalant abuse rates were markedly higher than that for non-Indian youth and that there was a corresponding dramatic rate of increase for Indian youth from 1975 through 1981.[38] This alarmed tribal officials, who were thus alerted to the potential for intense, often irreversible physiological and neurological disorders associated with the toxic effects of inhalants, especially agents composed of volatile hydrocarbons, such as gasoline, paint solvents, and glues. In a 1992 National Institute on Drug Abuse (NIDA) research monograph, *Inhalant Abuse*, Pamela Jumper-Thruman and Fred Beauvais discussed the damage caused by inhalant use.

Unfortunately, not a great deal is known about the extent and duration of neurological damage caused by solvents. There are a number of studies that reveal that heavy solvent users do indeed incur damage; however, the duration and/or reversibility of this damage is unclear. The majority of volatile solvents are lipophilic, meaning that they are stored in fatty tissue in the body and are eliminated much more slowly than most other drugs. One consequence of this is that solvent users may be experiencing residual effects from the drugs for quite some time (due to the deposit of solvents in the white matter of the brain), including altered affect and dullness of intellectual functioning. The implication for treatment is that the period of detoxification for solvent abusers may need to be longer than that of other drugs of abuse. It is quite possible that much of the frustration with treating solvent users is that very few short-term treatment gains can be achieved. Solvent abusers simply are not able to capitalize on the therapies that are typically used in treatment programs until the abusers have recovered sufficient cognitive and emotional functioning.[39]

However, Pamela Jumper-Thurman, in a presentation at Portland, Oregon sponsored by the National Institute of Justice in October 1998, reported that data gathered at the Tri-Ethnic Center for Prevention Research at Colorado State University showed a decline in the rate of inhalant abuse among Native American youth.

As many of you know, inhalant use has been gradually increasing every year among non-Indian youth ever since the Monitoring the Future study began. The pattern for Indian youth is quite different. Their use of inhalants in the early 80's was higher than that of other kinds and continued to increase up to 1985. At that point, however, it began to decline and our last data point indicates that Indian youth are now lower than non-Indian youth on inhalant use.[40]

Other related studies provide additional insight into the nature and extent of Native American addictions. Adrian, Laune, and Williams compared the absolute alcohol consumption per person aged fifteen and over for Ontario, Canada. An interesting element of their study was the inclusion of Linklater's ten styles of Indian drinking:

1. Drinking for drinking's sake
2. Gang drinking
3. Occasion for drinking (anniversaries, memorials)
4. Set days for drinking (welfare days, family allowance days, paydays)
5. Binge drinking
6. Traveling drinking (table or bar-hopping, house-to-house)
7. Drinking to get drunk
8. Coaxing or shaming others to drink
9. Explorative behavior (loud talking, singing, dancing, fighting)
10. Drinking up all there is.

Their data indicated that "average alcohol consumption is significantly higher for counties with reserves than for those without reserves."[41] (American Indian reservations are called "reserves" in Canada.) The author's also noted that:

"Binge Drinking" is likely to occur when access to alcohol is not sanctioned officially and the drinking supply is irregular. Reserves are said to represent emotional and psychological security for the Indian, but they have also been described as bleak, remote, dilapidated, and poor.... Native reserves are generally geographically isolated, which can lead to an experience of psychological isolation that increases with lack of proximity to other settlements and urban areas. Residents on a reserve experience boredom which increases with lack of occupational and community activities. It has been claimed that alcohol has become the Indians' chief source of recreation.[42]

Two studies reviewed the relationship between Native American addictions, criminal and juvenile arrests, and incarceration. Duclos et al., in a 1998 article, looked at 150 American Indian adolescent detainees in a reservation-based juvenile facility over a year (1995–1996). The results showed that 49 percent had at least one alcohol, drug, or mental health disorder, while 13 percent had two disorders, and 9 percent had three or more. The most common were substance abuse/dependence, conduct disorder, anxiety, and major depression; female Indian youth were significantly more likely to suffer from multiple disorders, including major depression and anxiety.[43] Similarly, Elizabeth Grobsmith, in her applied anthropological analysis of the American Indian inmates at the Nebraska Department of Corrections, found a pattern of substance abuse similar to those already described:

Inmates indicated that they began to abuse substances at an extremely early age: the average age of beginning use was 11.6, with a mode of 13. A number of individuals indicated that they began to drink or smoke marijuana by the time they were seven or eight years old. . . . The most commonly abused substance among children, however, were inhalants, which were cheaper and easier to obtain. . . . While today, Lysol and correction fluid seem to be the inhalants of choice, in these inmate's childhood, spray paint, lighter fluid, nasal inhalers, glue, and gas were more readily available. It has been suggested that repeated use of inhalants produces exceptional temporary strength, particularly aggressive and even violent behaviors. . . . Inmates indicated that they frequently were abused by foster parents and step-parents and to a lesser extent by biological parents.[44]

Howard and his group found a simpler pattern among Native American veterans treated in a regional Veterans Administration (VA) hospital in Austin, Texas. They found that a disproportionately large number of Native American veterans were diagnosed with a substance-use disorder. They also reported that the Native American veterans were more likely to be diagnosed with both substance-related disorders and the posttraumatic stress disorder but were less likely to be diagnosed with drug-use disorders and other psychiatric disorders than were their non-Indian counterparts.[45]

Lastly, Chang, Lapham, and Barton studied the relationship of drinking environment and sociodemographic factors relevant to driving while intoxicated (DWI) in New Mexico. Their data indicated that both Hispanics (Mexican-Americans and Mexican nationals) and Native Americans were disproportionately represented among those arrested for DWI, with Native Americans having higher blood-alcohol concentrations and more alcohol-related problems.[46]

It is important to note that New Mexico has the highest Hispanic proportion (38 percent) of any state and is home to twenty-two different Indian tribes. Moreover, these tribes have a high degree of blooded (aboriginal phenotypes) members, while a great proportion of the Hispanics, both Mexican-Americans and Mexican nationals, are *mestizo*—mixed Spanish and Indian. Both the Hispanic and Native American populations also suffer disproportionately from diabetes and hypertension. Perhaps this is why New Mexico leads the nation in alcohol-related social, criminal, and health problems.

French conducted a five-year study on risk taking among 277 police academy candidates in New Mexico, using the Minnesota Multiphasic Personality Inventory (MMPI). His results indicated an overall greater risk taking for both sexes among all groups—Anglo-Americans, Mexican-Americans, and American Indians. He concluded that risk taking appears to be a cultural element of the Southwest, one borrowed from the indigenous Native Americans. This lifestyle had influenced both the Spanish and Anglo-American invaders.[47] This behavior is a consequence of the risk-taking tenet of the harmony ethos, where young adults are expected to experience life in the raw. This aboriginal concept of counting coup has survived to the present and is part and parcel of traditional enculturation, especially among tribes with a high proportion of blooded members, such as in the Southwest (New Mexico, Arizona, Nevada, and Utah).

Granted, enculturation is only one factor; a shared genopool, especially among high-blooded American Indians (aboriginal phenotypes), is another important variable, despite May's contention to the contrary. Two recent research findings lend credence to the genetic factor. In November 1998, the Center for Disease Control and Prevention released findings indicating that American Indians may have genetic differences that put them at greater risk for diabetes.[48] Another recent study, by Nowak et al., published in the October 1998 *Clinical Pharmacology & Therapeutics*, found cytochrome P450 (CYP) differences among Canadian Native Indians. CYP 450 is essential for the metabolism of a wide array of endogenous (neurotransmitters, neuroregulators, neuropeptites, hormones) and exogenous compounds, such as drugs/medications, steroids, prostaglandins, and pheromones in the liver and gut. This study indicated that "analysis of the Canadian Native Indian data suggested that there may be an association between the presence of the CYP2C19 and CYP2A6 mutant alleles such that the co-occurrence of these 2 alleles is higher than would be predicted on the basis of their individual frequencies in this population."[49] Diet, alcohol and other substance use, and medications all would be affected by this metabolic (pharmacokinetics) disregulation.

In the October 1998 NIAAA *Alcohol Alert*, Gordis noted that the current research on alcohol-induced liver disease indicates that the free radical acetadehyde, a by-product of alcohol metabolism, is more toxic than the alcohol itself: "In addition, a group of metabolic products called free radicals can damage liver cells and promote inflammation, impairing vital functions such as energy production. The body's natural defenses against free radicals (e.g., antioxidants) can be inhibited by alcohol consumption, leading to increased liver damage."[50] Not only does alcohol promote heptic inflammation, cell death, and scarring, dietary fat and carbohydrate levels also influence the progression of liver disease. The report lists four significant factors relevant to the alcohol liver disease (ALD) susceptibility: genetic factors, dietary factors, gender, and hepatitis C. All of these factors are significant for Native American FAS.

III

PREVENTION, INTERVENTION, AND CULTURAL TREATMENT

6

UNDERSTANDING CULTURE-SPECIFIC PRIMARY AND SECONDARY CLINICAL DIAGNOSES

INTRODUCTION

Calls by many researchers for a scientific approach to the study of Native American addictions also apply to the clinical/treatment arena. The scientist practitioner model has done much to bring substance-related disorders into the scientific medical/clinical realm. In this model, objective (reliable, valid, and standardized) assessments and evaluations are used to determine viable diagnosis (primary, secondary, comorbidity), which in turn drive the treatment plan. New technologies, such as the CT (computerized tomography), MRI (magnetic resonance imaging), and PET (positron emission tomography) scans, have provided more insight into the functioning of the brain and central nervous system (CNS) in the past twenty years than has all previous research in this area. This research into the structure and function of the CNS and its relationship to the peripheral nervous system (PNS), endocrine system (EC), and autonomic nervous system (ANS) has resulted in new insights into human neurophysiology, which have greatly enhanced our knowledge of the effect of substance-related disorders.

By the same token, culture specific treatment modalities have proven equally successful. Indeed, a recent edition of the *Diagnostic and Statistical*

Manual of Mental Disorders, fourth edition (DSM-IV) addressed the need for cultural sensitivity. Indeed, the DSM-IV warns against ethnocentrism and the tendency to presume that Western-style therapies and treatments are superior merely because they are based upon the philosophy of science.

Special efforts have been made in the preparation of DSM-IV to incorporate an awareness that the manual is used in culturally diverse populations in the United States and internationally. Clinicians are called on to evaluate individuals from numerous different ethnic groups and cultural backgrounds (including many who are recent immigrants). Diagnostic assessment can be especially challenging when a clinician from one ethnic or cultural group uses the DSM-IV Classification to evaluate an individual from a different ethnic or cultural group. A clinician who is unfamiliar with the nuances of an individual's cultural frame of reference may incorrectly judge as psychopathology those normal variations in behavior, belief, or experience that are particular to the individual's culture.[1]

Efforts were made to make the DSM-IV international and cross-cultural in the assessment of behaviors necessary to determine a definitive clinical diagnosis. It even provides an appendix addressing culture-bound syndromes.[2] Toward this end, tribal-centric training for addiction counselors has emerged in Indian country. Trained in the DSM, these Native clinicians forge culture-relevant prevention, intervention, and treatment strategies for their clients. The Navajo beauty way; the Peacemaker model, the purification sweat treatment, Sun Dance training for Sioux counselors; and the Cherokee harmony ethos unity model are examples of cultural treatment models. Even then, however obstructions to the implementation of cultural-specific treatment remain.

One of the most prominent is Public Law 280, enacted in 1953, which is a contemporary reminder of the long history of the majority society's attempt to destroy Native American cultures. It is an extension of the force-fed, external control mechanism designed to curtail traditional customs and rituals. In 1883, the Secretary of the Interior, Henry M. Teller, was concerned that traditional Indian customs would continue even once the tribes were confined to reservations. Secretary Teller wanted Western-style legal controls enforced within Indian country. That is, Teller wanted to enforce the dominant white, Anglo-Saxon, protestant norms, those that produced the protestant ethic, as against traditional harmony ethos customs, among these newly designated "dependent aliens." This led to the creation of Courts of Indian Offenses.

If it is the purpose of the Government to civilize the Indians, they must be compelled to desist from the savage and barbarous practices that are calculated to continue them in savagery, no matter what exterior influences are brought to bear on them. . . . The Government furnishes the teachers, and the charitable people contribute to the support of missionaries, and much time, labor, and money is yearly expended for their elevation, and yet a few non-progressive, degraded Indians are allowed to exhibit before the young and susceptible children all the debauchery, diabolism, and savagery of the worst state of the Indian race. Every man familiar with Indian life will bear witness to the pernicious influence of these savage rites and heathenish customs.[3]

A month later, on December 17, 1883, the Supreme Court overturned the death sentence handed down by the First Judicial District Court of Dakota to a Brule Sioux leader, Crow Dog, for the 1881 murder of another Brule leader, Spotted Tail. Crow Dog's appeal was based on the grounds that the federal courts had no jurisdiction over crimes committee in Indian country by one Indian against another. An angry Congress retaliated and on March 3, 1885, passed the Major Crimes Act, which provided exclusive federal jurisdiction for what were then the seven major crimes (murder, manslaughter, rape, aggravated assault, arson, burglary, and larceny) within any territory of the United States. This law, with the advent of the establishment of the Bureau of Investigation in 1908, placed FBI agents throughout Indian country, much like an occupational police force. The FBI augmented the cultural police force in Indian country while contributing to the sense of alienation among Native Americans residing under these conditions.[4]

Public Law 280, passed on August 15, 1953, was part and parcel of the termination policy of the Eisenhower administration. Public Law 280, which extended state jurisdiction over offenses committed in Indian country, was passed two weeks after House Concurrent Resolution 108, which initiated termination. PL 280 expanded the forces of cultural genocide to include state control agencies, in addition to the federal control, which already existed in the Courts of Indian Offenses and the Major Crimes Act. Snyder-Joy explains this attempt at cultural genocide and forced accommodation.

The Major Crimes Act made substantial inroads into American Indian sovereignty to define and enforce criminal law on their own lands. The imposition of federal jurisdiction over Indian country was further expanded to include state authority in some areas. Public Law 280 (67 Stat. 588), passed in 1953, granted some states criminal and civil jurisdiction over Indian lands. . . . Public Law 280 also provided that any states that wished to gain jurisdiction over tribes could do so by state law or by amending the state constitution. This latter activity could be done *without* the consent of the affected tribes. The passage of the Indian Civil Rights Act of 1968 modified state jurisdiction on Indian lands.[5]

Those working in Indian country realize that some of the most intense hatred, prejudice, and discrimination against Native Americans is harbored by non-Indians living adjacent to Indian country. This appears to be a collective defense mechanism, a reaction formation, against the people from whom they or their ancestors stole the prime Indian lands.

From 1953 until 1968 the government expanded this local authority, without the consent of the tribes involved. In 1968, Public Law 280 was amended to require tribal consent to state jurisdiction. No tribe has ever consented to this obvious hostile police action; more significantly, no existing PL 280 jurisdiction has been revoked. Today, PL 280 involves 23 percent of Indian country in the lower forty-eight states and all Alaska Native communities, with an overall influence of 75 percent of all recognized tribes. This is a major obstacle to clinical/legal efforts to combat substance abuse within Indian country, in that it is a major source of protestant ethic ethnocentrism.

Today, federal operational procedures are determined by either the Bureau of Indian Affairs or the Indian Health Service. The BIA provides for the safety, housing, and educational needs of the nearly two million Native Americans residing within Indian country (535 tribal governments), while IHS provides medical services within Indian country. The Administration of Native Americans (ANA) provides similar services within urban Indian communities. Federal policies and procedures, and their relevance to culture-sensitive clinical interventions, are explored in Chapter 8.

THE HISTORY OF THE ICD, DSM, AND PTSD

Psychiatry was made popular by the works of Sigmund Freud in the late 1800s. In 1840, the medical profession in the United States had recognized one combined, basic mental health category—that of *idiocy/insanity*. The Civil War brought a new term into the realm of clinical classifications, *nonpsychotic nostalgia*, which later became known as battle fatigue. St. Elizabeth's Hospital also emerged during this era, becoming the first Veterans Administration (VA) hospital. Freud and his new discipline of psychiatry influenced the mental health classification scheme with his new term, *neurosis*. Neurosis was presented as a clinical-specific alternative to the older gender-specific disorder, *hysteria*. Seven mental health classifications existed during the World War I era.

Drawing on Freud's contribution to clinical classification, the term *traumatic war neurosis* emerged during the Russo-Japanese War, at the turn of the twentieth century. The impact of this classification on the U.S. medical profession was likely due more to the fact that President Theodore Roosevelt negotiated the Russo-Japanese treaty in New Hampshire and won the Nobel Peace Prize for this effort than to Freud's having coined the term neurosis. Another turn-of-the-century classification pertained to the mentally retarded. In 1910, the medical profession developed three classifications for these individuals—*idiots, imbeciles,* and *morons.* The stigma these terms have accumulated over time is quite evident.

World War I, and its ensuing medical and clinical challenges, brought a dramatic increase in the classification of mental disorders. Fifty-nine disorders were now classified, including *shell shock.* Freud also became aware of posttraumatic stress, when his friend and colleague, Victor Tausk, committed suicide because of what he had witnessed as a physician in wartime. Nonetheless, the foundations for the contemporary classification of mental disorders were established in reaction to the needs presented by World War II.

Two factors came into play here, the combined efforts of the U.S. Army and the VA, and the establishment of the World Health Organization (WHO). WHO was established as a specialized agency of the United Nations in 1948. The World Health Organization is responsible for the development of a universal codification and classification of diseases—the *International Classification of Diseases* (ICD). The World War II forerunner of PTSD was termed *combat fatigue.* Freud's student Erik Erikson became aware of the effects of war-related posttraumatic stress when working with veterans in the 1940s. Erikson, in his work with Native Americans in Indian country, noted a similar process occurring among this population. Thus, while PTSD has a history that extends back to the Civil War, both Freud and Erikson recognized the devastation of delayed acute stress, with Erikson equating the intensity of reservation marginality with that of combat trauma.[6]

The *Diagnostic and Statistical Manual* (DSM) first appeared in 1952, in response to the VA's work with veterans of World War II and the Korean conflict. The DSM was presented as a specific area within the ICD. Indeed, its mental disorders corresponded with the sixth edition of the *International Classification of Diseases* (ICD-6). The first DSM, crude in comparison to the current version, represented the first effort to codify mental diseases. The DSM listed 106 mental disorders, including the PTSD forerunner, *physio-neurosis*, which was used to explain war trauma during the Korean conflict. In 1968, again in response to the demands of combat, DSM-II appeared. It corresponded with ICD-8 and used the term *transient situational disturbances* to describe the psychological impact of combat trauma. A more accurate clinical classification for delayed psychological combat trauma did not emerge until 1980, with DSM-III. This revision was due to the high number of Vietnam veterans suffering from combat trauma. *Posttraumatic stress disorder* appeared along with 264 other clinical diagnoses in DSM-III, which corresponded with the U.S. version of the ICD—the *International Classification of Diseases, 9th Edition, Clinical Modification* (ICD-9-CM).

DSM-III marked the first edition in which scientific data replaced the previous theoretical bases of psychiatry. It corresponds with the science-practitioner clinical model, while previous clinical diagnoses had been based on the Freudian logic of psychoanalysis. The demise of the Freudian and neo-Freudian influence was evident in the changes in both the document's structure and the terms it used to describe mental disorders. Neurosis became obsolete, while a multiaxial format replaced the idiosyncratic logical deduction promoted by psychoanalysis. Advanced medical technology (notably the CT scan) and new more effective psychotropic medications had laid the foundation for this new scientific approach to mental disorders. DSM-III listed 265 diagnoses, many determined through American medical graduate programs and their affiliated teaching/research hospitals, including IHS and VA facilities.

The new format included a numerical code and corresponding clinical classification, whereby clinical disorders, including mental retardation, and the V-codes (Other Conditions That May Be a Focus of Clinical Attention) were listed on Axis I. Axis II was reserved for personality disorders viewed as due more to socialization and enculturation than to clinical conditions. Axis III was reserved for general medical conditions (etiologies and Axes I and II–associated features) and used ICD-9-CM codes. Axis IV provided a scale for psychosocial and environmental problems, while Axis V was a Likert-type scale for global assessment of functioning (GAF). Axes IV and V are subjective scales and therefore are generally matters of case management by the practitioner who follows the client from admission to discharge. With slight variations in format, this DSM format continues to the present.

DSM-III was revised in 1987, due mainly to new research and a 1985 U.S. Supreme Court decision, *City of Cleburne v. Cleburne Living Center* (84 S. Ct. 468 U.S. Supreme Court), that the mentally retarded (MR) did not constitute a special class like the mentally ill. Clients with just an MR diagnosis could not present this classification as mitigating circumstances in a court of law. (This is why the United States is the only Western nation that death-certifies MR offenders.) This change resulted in the MR classification being relegated to Axis II, along with personality disorders, another classification that cannot be used to determine a special class situation relevant to mitigating circumstances in court, even in death-sentence cases. DSM-III-R and its 292 diagnoses and corresponded to ICD-9-CM. In 1992, WHO released the ICD-10; two years later, DSM-IV appeared.

Diagnostic and Statistical Manual of Mental Disorders, Fourth Edition (DSM-IV) made significant internal changes but did not alter the multiaxial format. The new edition, which brought the number of diagnoses up to 297, corresponded with both the U.S. ICD-9-CM and the WHO ICD-10. The internal changes resulted in two less categories, from eighteen to sixteen, but the same codes (numerical designation for diagnoses) for similar diagnoses in the DSM-IV. Axis IV was simplified, eliminating the numerical scale, while the GAF scale on Axis V was extended in range from 1 to 100. "Passive-aggressive" was eliminated from the Axis II personality disorders, since it seemed to represent a common transitory defense mechanism in high-stress social environments. Non V-code additions to the Axis I nonclinical diagnoses (Conditions Not Attributable to a Mental Disorder) were also added, the better to reflect psychotropic and other medicine side effects.

The most significant changes, however, involved substance-related disorders and organic disorders, such as delirium, dementia, amnestic disorders, and other cognitive disorders. This finally brought the areas of substance-related disorders into parity with other mental disorders. Also included in the DSM-IV are six decision trees for differential diagnosis; substance-induced disorders are on one of the decision trees. DSM-IV provides specific cultural, age, and gender features of the mental disorders as well as the prevalence, course, and familial pattern where relevant. Generally speaking, DSM-IV and other science-practitioner (reliable and valid) measures of neuropsychological and psychopathological impairments appear to be culture-free instruments for determining viable diagnoses.

Accordingly, the DSM-IV format is as follows:

Axis I:	Clinical Disorders.
	Other Conditions That May Be a Focus of Clinical Attention (V-Codes, Psychological Factors Affecting Medical Condition, Medication-Induced Movement Disorders, Other Medication-Induced Disorders)
Axis II:	Mental Retardation
	Personality Disorders
	Borderline Intellectual Functioning (V-code)
Axis III:	General Medical Conditions (etiologies/associated features)
Axis IV:	Psychosocial and Environmental Problems (associated features of the V-codes)
Axis V:	Global Assessment of Functioning (100-point Likert-type scale, with 100 = good/1 = poor).[7]

The DSM is a self-contained assessment tool, with specific criteria listed under relevant categories for each diagnosis. The most common assessment protocol for clinical diagnoses is the combination of the DSM criteria and the mental status exam (MSE).[8] Additional scales can be used to augment the clinical protocol. The Minnesota Multiphasic Personality Inventory (MMPI) is the most widely used assessment supplement to the DSM and MSE, especially in forensic cases.[9] DSM-IV provides a comprehensive assessment tool for substance-related disorders, discerning between substance abuse, substance dependence, polysubstance dependence, and substance-related organic disorders that present themselves as other mental disorders: delirium, dementia, amnestic disorders, psychotic disorders (with or without delusions or hallucinations), mood disorders, anxiety disorders, sexual dysfunctions, and sleep disorders. Further distinctions are made relevant if these associated features occur during intoxication or withdrawal.[10]

A number of supplementary assessment scales are also available, in addition to the DSM, MMPI, and MSE, for detecting substance abuse: the Comprehensive Drinker Profile (CDP), the Michigan Alcoholism Screening Test (MAST), the Questionnaire on Drinking and Drug Use, and the Substance Abuse Subtle Screening Inventory (SASSI).[11] The U.S. Department of Health and Human Services also provides a number of screening instruments under its Treatment Improvement Protocol (TIP) series: Volumes 9 and 16 illustrate this endeavor: *Assessment and Treatment of Patients with Coexisting Mental Illness and Alcohol and Other Drug Abuse*, and *Alcohol and Other Drug Screening of Hospitalized Trauma Patients*. Additionally, the NIAAA, in its Treatment Handbook series, provides a comprehensive resource in its Series 4 handbook *Assessing Alcohol Problems: A Guide for Clinicians and Researchers*.[12] A valuable section is the Quick-Reference Instrument Guide, which rates the available instruments according to their utility: screening, diagnosis, assessment of drinking behavior, treatment planning, treatment and process assessment, and outcome evaluation.

Since first listed in the DSM-III, PTSD has been recognized in situations other than combat, including traumatized children, police officers, emergency medical technicians, firemen, and victims of disasters and rape. One of the most reliable instruments used to augment the DSM, MMPI, and MSE is the *Structured Clinical Interview for DSM-IV, Patient Edition* (SCID-P). The SCID-P, developed by the American Psychiatric Association, is specialized, differential diagnostic tool for the determination of primary, secondary, and comorbid diagnoses.[13] Another widely used instrument for PTSD assessment is the Mississippi Scale for Posttraumatic Stress Disorder, which has both combat and civilian adaptations. Other self-rating scales include the Davidson Trauma Scale (DTS), the *Structured Interview for PTSD* (SI-PTSD), the Clinician Administered PTSD Scale (CAPS), and the Harvard Trauma Questionnaire (HTQ).[14] These instruments, unlike the SCID, are used not so much for definitive diagnosis of PTSD as for assessing symptom severity.

One of these instruments, the HTQ, was found to be adaptable to non-Western cultural populations, making it a likely instrument for measuring PTSD among traditional Native Americans.[15] In contrast, the Composite International Diagnostic Interview PTSD Module (CIPI-

PTSD), which was designed to correspond with ICD-10 diagnoses, correlated poorly with the DSM diagnoses. However, future revision may make it a more reliable instrument, especially given that the internal consistency of its scales, composed of questions selected from both the DSM and the ICD-10, suggested that these diagnostic criteria describe a similar set of symptoms.[16] The challenge is to produce a scale that addresses the severity of symptoms for Native Americans diagnosed with PTSD comorbid with FAS.

THE NEUROPHYSIOLOGY OF ADDICTIONS

A prerequisite to understanding Native American addictions is awareness of what these substances do to the human body. The interactions between the nervous system and the endocrine system are especially relevant to substance abuse, psychopharmachological interventions (medicines), metabolism, stress, and comorbidity with other mental and physical disorders. Generally speaking, the nervous system consists of the central nervous system (CNS) and peripheral nervous system (PNS). The CNS includes the brain (neurons and glia) and the spinal cord. The PNS, which includes the sensory neurons, is divided into the *somatic* (voluntary) component the *autonomic* (involuntary) system. The autonomic component of the PNS includes two modes, the *sympathetic* (arousal) and the *parasympathetic* (recovery). The arousal component of the autonomic nervous system (ANS), in crises situations, is commonly referred to as the "fight or flight stage." The CNS plays a major role in this stress response, in that the hypothalamus, a critical component of the limbic system (LS) the emotional component of the brain, drives the endocrine system (ES) during periods of both crisis and recovery. The endocrine system and CNS work in concert to direct the needed stress hormones and neurotransmitters into the blood and brain neurons so that the body can instantly respond to a high-stress, crisis situation. This combined interaction between the CNS, PNS, and endocrine system is known as the *neuroendocrine system process*.[17]

The cerebral cortex perceives the stressor from PNS neuronal responses and activates the limbic system (hypothalamus), which directs the endocrine system (pituitary gland) to respond by releasing epinephrine (E) and norepinephrine (NE) from nerve endings in the inner part of the adrenal glands. This automatic process obviates frontal lobe deliberation for the sake of quick action, resulting in the following physiological responses: the pupils dilate, salivation decreases, respiration increases, heart rate accelerates, digestion is inhibited, adrenal gland activity increases, palms become dry, and the bladder relaxes. Once the body has responded to a crisis, parasympathetic recovery is needed to replenish the depleted hormones and neurotransmitters. During this stage the pupils constrict, salivation increases, respiration decreases, heart rate slows, digestion is stimulated, adrenal gland activity decreases, the palms become sweaty, and the bladder contracts.

If the body is in a constant state of stress, as is often the case with PTSD, the body never has a chance to recover, leading to what the late Hans Selye termed the general adaptation syndrome (GAS).

GAS has three stages. The first is the alarm stage, which leads to the initial activation of the sympathetic mode of the autonomic nervous system. Stage two is the resistance stage, where the body continues to respond to the stress situation at an abnormal level, without ever fully recovering. This continuous stress residual continues to tap the body's vital reserves of hormones, minerals, and glucose, compromising the body's metabolism and making the body more susceptible to illness. The last stage is exhaustion, the body's reaction to long-term, continuous stress. At this stage there is a marked deterioration of internal organs within the endocrine system, weakening the infection-fighting immune system.

The combination of FAS/PTSD in an American Indian or Alaska Native, along with already high susceptibility to compromised genetic and metabolic features, made worse by a poor diet and environment, certainly fits the GAS profile. Clearly, the criteria associated with posttraumatic stress disorder certainly indicate GAS: recurrent, intrusive, and distressing recollections of events, recurrent distressing dreams, feelings that the traumatic event(s) are recurring, intense psychological distress, physiological reactivity on exposure to internal or external stimuli, cognitive impairment, difficulty concentrating, hypervigilance, exaggerated startle response, and irritability or outburst of anger.[18]

Another critical area of understanding is how the body responds to substances, licit or illicit. A basic understanding to the nervous system at the cellular level is needed when discussing neurotransmission. Neurons function by means of electrochemical energy. Simply stated, when the neuron is at rest, positive (sodium, potassium, calcium, magnesium) and negative (chloride, phosphate, and other complex acids) ions neutralize each other. At rest the neuron is slightly negatively polarized. However, the neuron is stimulated to fire by chemical signals at excitatory synapses, conducting an impulse. This shift toward a positive charge causes the sodium cell gates to open, reversing the interior membrane's state from negative to positive, causing depolarization, or an *action potential*. In CNS neurons, this action potential allows for the release of neurotransmitters from the soma via synaptic vesicles (presynaptic neurons). The neurotransmitter is now in the synaptic gap and ready to attach itself to receptor sites located on the receiving neuron (postsynaptic neuron)—all CNS neurons are directional.

The structure of the CNS neuron includes the long axon, with a terminal on one end and the cell body (soma) on the other. Dendrites, or branches, are located at the ends of the neuron. The synaptic vesicles, containing neurotransmitters, are located in the sending soma. CNS neurons are separated by the synaptic gap, which, like the entire CNS, is insulated by protective glia cells. (The myelin sheath that protects portions of CNS neurons is one example of glia cells.) The astrocyte is the most common type of glial cell; one of its functions is to scavenge excess neurotransmitters and ions in the synaptic gap following an action potential. This is an important function, given that more of the neurotransmitters may be released from the synaptic vesicles than there are binding sites available on the receiving neuron. Transmitter molecules that are not reabsorbed back into the presynaptic neuron (a process known as "reuptake") are destroyed by astrocytes. Astrocytes are also thought to provide glucose and redirect blood flow to active neurons during excitement and stress.

CNS nerve impulses can be inhibited. The chemical signal at inhibitory synapses can cause the voltage inside the neuron to become even more negative than at the resting state, thereby causing the neuron to fire under normal excitatory stimulation (reducing its *firing threshold*). Neurotransmitters (NT) are generally thought of as being either excitatory or inhibitory, although some can be either, depending on the combination of neurotransmission; these NTs are considered *conditional*. Indeed, serotonin (5-HT) is considered to be a modulating, or regulatory NT instead of exclusively an excitatory NT.

The simplest and most common neurotransmitters are amino acid transmitters, such as glutamate and aspartate, which act as excitatory NTs, and glycine and GABA (gamma-aminobutyric acid), which act as inhibitory NTs. A little more complex are the monoamine transmitters (MOA), like acetylcholine (ACh), dopamine (D), norepinephrine, epinephrine, and serotonin. Acetycholine (ACh), the first NT identified, is the main NT that carries the messages to and from the CNS and PNS. It is the major NT associated with Alzheimer's type of dementia. The loss of ACh in Alzheimer's contributes to the progressive physical deterioration, resulting in death seven to eight years following onset. Dopamine, norepinephrine, and epinephrine are all synthesized from the amino acid tyrosine. They are also referred to as catecholamines. All three follow distinct neural pathways and are considered to be primarily excitatory. Serotonin, found only in the brain, plays a critical role in frontal lobe NT regulation. Peptides, such as substance P in the gut, are another source of neural transmission, although more needs to be known about their exact role in the CNS. Endorphins (endogenous morphine) are powerful NTs, also known as brain opioids. Enkephalin is considered to be the functional NT, while beta-endorphin is seen as a bloodborne hormone.

The neurotransmitters follow certain pathways within the brain. These neuronal pathways involve the three basic units of the brain: the brain stem and related structures, the central core, and the cerebral cortex. The greater brain stem region provides the link for PNS messages to the forebrain and controls autonomic functions, such as respiration and heart rhythms. The central core, often referred to as the reptilian, emotional, or primitive brain, is a major factor in emotional dysregulation and stress reaction. It includes the limbic system (amygdala, septum, cingulate, hippocampus), the diencephalon (thalamus and hypothalamus), and the basal ganglia, which relay impulses from the motor cortex and interrelated cerebellum-thalamic neuronetwork and take over motor skills that have been routinized and relegated to the automatic response system. Together, the limbic system and diencephalon form the greater limbic system. The cerebral cortex, on the other hand, is the thinking and reasoning component of the brain. Mental illnesses, including substance-related disorders, involve neurochemical dysregulation within the subcortical areas, notably the limbic system, basal ganglia, reticular system, and the brain stem. The cerebral cortex attempts to confer meaning to these dysregulations.[19]

All the substances listed in the DSM-IV under substance-related disorders have their psychoactive effects by interacting with one of the endogenous neurotransmitters, doing so along an established NT neuropathway. Psychotropic medications work in a similar way, though they need not provide a desired psychoactive reaction. The neuropathways that provide the desired psychoactive-results when stimulated by alcohol or other drugs are known as the brain's drug-reward systems. According to the National Institute on Drug Addictions (NIDA), the cocaine, amphetamine, and opiate reward systems involve neurons using dopamine found in the ventral tegmental area (VTA), which is connected to the nucleus accumbens and related areas in the prefrontal lobe. The opiate reward system also activates the arcuate nucleus, amygdala, locus coeruleus and the periaqueductal gray area. By the same token, the alcohol reward system includes the VTA and nucleus accumbens but affects the structures that use gamma-amino butyric acid (GABA), which is distributed throughout the brain—the cortex, cerebellum, hippocampus, superior and inferior colliculi, amygdala, and nucleus accumbens.

From this research, NIDA concludes that the VTA and the nucleus accumbens are the two basic structures involved in the reward system for all psychoactive agents, including alcohol, tobacco, and other drugs. Kandel et al. notes this reaction as well: "In animals that are trained to self-reinforce by electrical stimulation, dopaminergic neurons in the ventral tegmental area are indirectly activated, thereby increasing the level of dopamine at the synapses of the mesocorticolimbic projection. Psychoactive drugs that are reinforcing also increase the level of dopamine in the neurons of the ventral tegmental area."[20] In prolonged or cata-strophic stress situations, such as PTSD, three brain circuits are effected and altered: the locus ceruleus, which regulates brain hormones that pre-pare for sympathic responses from the autonomic nervous System (ANA); the hypothalamus and pituitary gland and their regulation of stress hormones; and the opioid system, locus ceruleus, hypothalamus, and amygdala, which blunt pains and emotions.[21]

Any mention of the neurophysiology of addictions, however brief, needs to include basic types of neuronal malfunctioning, given that substance-related disorders include self-medication with alcohol and il-licit drugs as a reaction to physical or mental disorders. This discussion is also relevant to a general understanding of psychopharmacology, es-pecially drug/drug interactions, in particular between prescribed medi-cations and alcohol and street drugs. Abnormalities in the presynaptic neuron include an inability to produce the neurotransmitting chemical, resulting in an insufficient amount for release into the synaptic gap. This can be due to an inhibition of the initial synthesis of these chemicals, or to biological disorders, or to the introduction of other agents into the system that inhibit the release of neurotransmitters. This process has been illustrated recently by research on medications designed to reduce serum cholesterol. Studies showed an increase in violence by these pa-tients, apparently due to the medication-induced decrease of brain-cell membrane cholesterol, which lowered lipid microviscosity, which greatly reduced the availability of protein serotonin (5-HT) receptors on the pre-synaptic neuron. This process resulted in a poorer uptake of serotonin from the blood and less serotonin entry into the sending neuron.[22]

Biological disorders or introduced agents can also facilitate the release of neurotransmitters by the presynaptic neuron. Panic disorder, one of the worst of the anxiety disorders, provides an example of this neuronal dysregulation. In panic attacks the normal braking function of the pre-synaptic neurons, those located in the locus coeruleus, malfunction and do not produce their normal inhibitory functions, allowing norepineph-rine to run rampant, thus falsely alerting the limbic/neuroendocrine sys-tem of a crises requiring an ANS sympathetic mode response. Another problem originating at the presynaptic neuron is the reuptake function. Again, biological disorders or introduced agents can either overstimulate or inhibit this function.

Interactive problems between the pre- and postsynaptic neurons can act in such a fashion that the receptors act as brakes, reducing the sen-sitivity of the neuron and making it less likely to fire. Paradoxically, an increase of inhibitory receptors can decrease neuronal excitability, caus-ing a process known as *up-regulation*. By the same token, the inhibitory receptors may result in increased sensitivity, *down-regulation*. Either pro-cess effects the normal synaptic interaction and CNS message process, with serious implications for mental and physical health homeostatsis. Another presynaptic and synaptic gap dysregulation involves excessive biodegradation of the neurotransmitter, resulting in an abnormal depletion of these NTs. This is believed to be the mechanism of clinical depression.

Problems at the postsynaptic neuron explain psychosis. It is believed that thought disorders, like schizophrenia, are caused by problems with postsynaptic binding sites for certain NTs, notably dopamine. Here, not only is an excess of dopamine received at the postsynaptic neuron but these NTs apparently attach themselves to the wrong receptor sites, causing the thought disorder. Chemical interventions (neuroleptics/ antipsychotic medications) keep the postsynaptic receptor sites from accepting the messenger NT transmitted from the presynaptic neuron. Another postsynaptic neural action is the stimulation of the receiving neurons via false neurotransmitters, such as mescaline. Lastly, neural membrane instability may cause greater limbic and neuroendocrine dysregulation, such as that which occurs with hyper- and hypomania, obsessive-compulsive disorders, and impulse control disorders. Accordingly, lithium carbonate, valporic acid, and carbamazapine are used to stabilize the neural membranes, protecting them from the excessive messages from the emotional brain (greater limbic system), while SSRIs (select serotonin reuptake inhibitors) keep this regulatory NT in the synaptic gap longer, so it can better interact with other relevant NTs, protecting the frontal lobe filter from excessive limbic messages.[23]

Plotnik has illustrated these processes, relevant to certain culturally based drugs. He noted that although cocaine has been used at low levels of psychoactivity for nearly 3,500 years by South American Indians, its mechanism of action has only recently been determined. Cocaine's activity at the synaptic gap is to block the reuptake of norepinephrine by the presynaptic neuron, allowing NE to activate the receiving neuron continually, beyond its normal arousal state. At lower levels, those traditionally reached by South American Indians who chew the coca leave, the cocaine acts to reduce fatigue and hunger, allowing the Indians to function at high altitudes that otherwise would be untenable for most humans. South American Indians also used curare on the ends of blowgun darts. Its mechanism of action is to block the receiving (postsynaptic) neuron from receiving the acetylcholine (ACh) presented to the synaptic gap by the presynaptic (sending) neuron, leading to muscle paralysis. A third example cited involves mescaline, the psychoactive agent of peyote, now legal for use in the United States by American Indian members of the Native American Church. Peyote's mechanism of action, that which causes the desired visions (physiological arousal and visual hallucinations), is that it augments NE by opening the same chemical keys on receiving neurons.[24]

A basic understanding of psychopharmacology requires a fundamental knowledge of both *pharmacokinetics* and *pharacodynamics*. Pharmacokinetics describes what the body does to drugs, while pharmacodynamics looks at what the drug does to the body. There are four basic components of pharmacokinetics: absorption, distribution, biotransformation (metabolism), and elimination (excretion). Absorption refers to intake of a drug, molecule, or substance into the body's cells, including neurons. There are various routes of administration of these exogenous agents: oral (PO), sublingular (under the tongue), rectal (PR), intravenous (IV), intramuscular (IM), subcutaneous (SC, under the skin), inhalation (via nasal passage), topical (rubbed on the skin), transdermal (skin patches), and intratracheal (within a sheath, for example a spinal tap). Most of the substances related to Native American addictions use the oral route, although inhalation and IV drug use also applies. Medications, a serious consideration with respect to drug/drug interactions, can use any of these routes. The focus of this brief overview of pharmacokinetics is on oral administration, used for alcohol and most medications.

Once an exogenous agent has been introduced to the body, it needs to be distributed if it is to have any psychoactive effect. This usually involves introduction to the bloodstream, where it may be distributed to cellular or interstitial fluids. Organs with highly perfused tissue, such as the heart, liver, kidney, and brain, receive a good portion of the agent during the first few minutes following absorption, while delivery to muscle, viscera, skin, and fat is slower. Highly perfused organs have a separate protection known as *membrane barriers* (BBB or blood-brain barrier, blood-testes barrier, and blood-placenta barrier). Once in the bloodstream, agents are usually (lithium is the psychotropic exception) first processed through the liver, where a portion of the agent is bound to blood protein, such as albumin. Only the portion that is not bound is active. Unbound agents can also be stored in reservoirs, where they are carried by the bloodstream—muscles or organs (cellular reservoirs), body fat (lipid reservoirs), and bone and teeth (calcium-binding agents). Metabolism involves a degradation process whereby these exogenous agents are generally converted into less active or inactive forms. However, a few agents are biotransformed into more active forms, known as prodrugs. Liver enzymes, notably the cytochrome P-450 series, are responsible for the greatest proportion of biotransformation.

Lastly, exogenous agents, once biotransformed by the liver, are eliminated from the body via the kidney. Fecal excretion usually includes unabsorbed orally administered agents or their metabolites, which are concentrated in the bile and are not reabsorbed from the intestinal tract. In addition to feces and urine, elimination involves sweat, tears, saliva, hair, skin, and milk. Also pertinent to elimination is the half-life of the agent. This refers to the amount of time required for plasma concentrations of the agent to decrease by 50 percent after the agent was taken. This is the measure of the rate of distribution, metabolism, and excretion of the agent, and it is crucial to dosing formulas for medications as well as to the rate of titration.

Pharmacodynamics, what these exogenous agents do to the body, was already discussed in part in the section on neuronal dysregulations. The first things to consider are side effects. The blood carries these exogenous agents everywhere the bloodstream travels, not only to the desired areas, such as the CNS. Side effects represent the body's reaction to these alien agents. Intolerance to the agent can result in serious reactions, but in most instances the side effects diminish in about two weeks, following the body's compensation to these agents. In some instances, side effects persist as long as the agent is in the body. At the neuronal level, these exogenous psychoactive agents influence the existing endogenous neurotransmitters, either through activation, facilitation, or alteration. When these processes occur, the exogenous agent is known as an *agonistic agent*; however, if these agents interfere with the unaltered neuronal process, they are known as *antagonistic agents*. The margin of safety of an exogenous agent is determined by the *therapeutic index*, which is the measure of the agent's effective concentration divided by its lethal dose. This formula is especially significant for lithium. Other pharmacodynamic considerations are tolerance, cross tolerance, dependence, and withdrawal—clinical conditions listed in the DSM-IV.

Drug/drug interactions can have serious consequences. Commonly, they occur when individuals inadvertently mix over-the-counter medications or herbal remedies with prescription medications, including psychotropics. Add alcohol and street drugs to this formula, and the process becomes even more complicated. A number of reactions can occur in drug/drug interactions, including altered absorption, metabolism, and excretion, as well as competition for blood-binding sites.[25] Additionally, it is important to note that cultural and genetic factors play a significant role in psychopharmacology, especially in the treatment of mental and physical illness among American Indians and Native Alaskans.[26]

7

CULTURAL TREATMENT CONSIDERATIONS

--- ❖ ---

INTRODUCTION

Few would dispute that federal and state endeavors in the prevention and treatment of substance abuse in Indian country have failed. The American Psychological Association urged Congress in 1998 to develop programs to train more Native Americans in the area of behavioral medicine. McDonald noted that the APA's "Indians into Psychology" program, although a good model for cooperative efforts between the Department of Veterans Affairs, Indian Health Services, and Tribal colleges, falls far short of meeting the current primary health care needs within Indian country, especially when the four leading causes of death among American Indians and Alaska Natives (accidents, alcohol and drug use, stress-related cardiovascular disease, and diabetes) are preventable.[1]

The Department of Health and Human Services has published volumes about substance abuse treatment services during the past decade through the National Institute on Drug Abuse, the National Institute on Alcohol Abuse and Alcoholism, and the Substance Abuse and Mental Health Services Administration. Recently, NIDA published its *Research Monograph Series No. 172*, addressing the "treatment of drug-dependent individuals with comorbid mental disorders," while NIAAA produced a substantial volume, "Assessing Alcohol Problems" as its *NIAAA Treatment Handbook Series No. 4.* SAMHSA has offered "National Admissions to Substance Abuse Treatment Services: The Treatment Episode Data Set (TEDS) 1992–1996" under its *Drug and Alcohol Services Information System Series: S-5.*[2]

Few of these otherwise valuable resources address culture-centric treatment approaches. Weibel-Orlando, in a 1989 article in *Human Organization*, reviewed more than fifty Native American substance-abuse treatment programs for a ten-year period, concluding that the best programs shared four factors: (1) they were all generated by natives themselves; (2) they all had charismatic role models, who provided direction to the program; (3) they all involved the recovering native in therapy and interaction with the group, both as clients and healers; and (4) they all saw themselves as social entities—a community structure alternative to the drinking culture.[3] Successful tribal-centric treatment programs include the traditional purification sweat, vision quest, and Sun Dance rituals, especially for the Sioux and other Plains Indians; the peyote rituals of the Native American Church; the peacemaking process of the Diné; and the American Indian Alcoholics Anonymous programs.

Unfortunately, not all proclaimed tribal-centric treatment programs are what they appear to be. With passage of Public Law 99–570, the Anti-Drug Abuse Act of 1986, and its provision for "Indian youth programs," federal monies have been available for treatment programs.[4] This act led to the development by the BIA of ten regional youth treatment centers (RYTC). However, numerous non-Indian, for-profit enterprises have attempted to encroach into what they feel is a lucrative, federally supported treatment market. These non-Indian groups usually hire a few phenotypical (visible) Native Americans, thus making a pretense of being an authentic aboriginal treatment program. Indian professionals hired just for their appearance may know little about traditional customs and rites. Indeed, Christian groups have made concerted efforts over the years to convert phenotypical Indians, training them as paraprofessionals and professionals who then recruit other Native Americans to the Christian cause. This process reflects the contemporary effort at cultural genocide and most likely contributes to psychocultural ambiguity and marginality, and not to effective treatment.

Narconon (though non-Christian) is an example of this conversion process. Narconon International offered a drug treatment program for school-aged children without disclosing that it was a recruitment arm of the Church of Scientology. Although the terms "Scientology" and "Dianetics" are absent from the Narconon literature, its "New Life" program is essentially an eight-part introduction to Scientology, a religious orientation that denies the existence of psychiatric illness. These components—"Therapeutic TR" (Scientology training routines), "Clear Body/Clear Mind" (controversial laxative, exercise, mega-vitamin routine), "Learning Improvement" (introduction to Scientology jargon), "Communication & Perception," "Ups & Downs in Life," "Personal Values and Integrity" (Scientology ethics), "Changing Conditions in Life Course," and "The Way to Happiness Course" (Scientology's take on the Ten Commandments)—all serve to orient the patient suffering from substance-related disorders to the cult's perspective.

Scientology's connection with Indian country began when it attempted to take over Chilocco Indian School property declared surplus by the BIA and turned over to the five tribes it had once served, the Ponca, Kaw, Pawnee, Oto-Missouri, and Tonkawa. This seventy-five bed inpatient facility would have greatly expanded the Scientologist clinical services program, which then consisted only of a twelve-bed facility in Los Angeles. In its application to the Oklahoma Board of Mental Health in October and December 1991 for certification for the program at Chilocco, it became clear that Narconon International did not subscribe to the scientist-practitioner model of mental or physical health, let alone being culturally sensitive to the Native Americans it hoped to treat. Its concept of "purification sweats" was five-hour sessions, seven days a week for a month, followed with mega-vitamin and mineral doses and cessation of any psychotropic or other forms of medications, regardless of comorbid diagnoses.

These dangerous practices not only did not protect patients from seizures, delirium, or psychiatric decompensation but often caused these adverse considerations. Instead of properly trained and licensed or certified clinicians, former patients were recruited as staff, in order to control the curriculum and promote the conversion process at Narconon-Chilocco. After reviewing the Narconon-Chilocco program, the Oklahoma Board of Mental Health concluded that the Narconon program was ineffective in the treatment of chemical dependency for anyone, certainly not Native Americans. Its certification was denied, but the program continued to operate.

Given these examples, it is imperative that treatment programs proposed for Native Americans be reviewed critically for both their tribalcentric application and for more subtle forms of cultural genocide disguised as clinical treatment.

REVIEW OF THE TREATMENT LITERATURE

A significant treatment consideration when looking at Native American addictions is that of fetal alcoholism (FAS) and such related disorders as posttraumatic stress. The most common links are between substanceinduced disorders, like FAS and FAE (fetal alcohol effect), PTSD, and depression. Clarren, Bowden, and Astley noted that fetal alcoholism can impair the developing CNS, causing pervasive neurological deficits without external signs of FAS.[5] A number of other studies have indicated similar pervasive neurological problems with both FAS and PTSD cases. Connor and Steissguth refer to these problems with FAS/FAE individuals as "alcohol-related neurodevelopmental disorder," or ARND. FAS/ARND, according to these researchers, manifests itself in memory and learning problems, attention deficits, poor motor coordination, and difficulties with problem solving, conditions that often result in disturbances in work, school, family, and social functioning.[6] Barrett et al. examined the relationship of cognitive impairment with PTSD and found that cognitive and related neurological problems are likely to be associated with comorbid mental disorders such as substance abuse, depression, and anxiety.[7] Bleich et al. drew similar conclusions from their study on PTSD and depression, while Deykin and Buka's study supported the contention that early trauma manifests itself in both PTSD and chemical dependence during adolescence.[8]

Three NIAAA *Alcohol Alert* issues specifically address alcohol and race and gender issues. In its 1990 issue on the theme "Alcohol and Women," it noted that "increasing evidence suggests that the detrimental effects of alcohol on the liver are more severe for women than for men. Women develop alcoholic liver disease, particularly alcoholic cirrhosis and hepatitis, after a comparatively shorter period of heavy drinking and at a lower level of daily drinking than men. Proportionately more alcoholic women die from cirrhosis than do alcoholic men."[9] In the NIAAA 1991 issue on "Fetal Alcohol Syndrome," it stated that the FAS rate per ten thousand total births for different ethnic groups in the United States was as follows: Asians 0.3, Hispanics 0.8, whites 0.9, blacks 6.0, and Native Americans 29.9. The article also specified, "Among Native Americans, the incidence of FAS varies among different cultures. Health units serving principally Navajo and Pueblo tribes report a FAS prevalence similar to that of the overall U.S. population, while for Southwest Plains Indians, a much higher prevalence was reported (1 case per 102 live births)."[10] These figures reappeared in the 1994 issue, on "Alcohol and Minorities," where NIAAA again looked at the prevalence of FAS among selected groups: "Among two populations of Southwestern Plains Indians ages newborn to 14 years, 10.7 of every 1,000 children were born with FAS. This was compared with 2.2 per 1,000 for Pueblo Indians and 1.6 for Navajo. Overall rates for FAS in the United States range from 1 to 3 per 1,000. Cultural influences, patterns of alcohol consumption, nutrition, and differing rates of alcohol metabolism or other innate physiological differences may account for the varying FAS rates among Indian communities."[11]

These differential rates appear to follow Erikson's cultural trauma concept, which he applies to tribes most impacted by harsh U.S. policies, cultural genocide. While most tribes were subjected to varying degrees of cultural genocide, the Plains Indians and Apache experienced the most intense punitive efforts. They also were the last American Indian groups to be aggressively pursued by the U.S. military. Within other tribal groups, like the Cherokee and Navajo, marginal members seem to target off-reservation communities, where alcohol for drunk Indians is a major economic factor. Another economic resource is the tribal bootlegger. At any rate, pockets of high FAS birth rates are likely to be found in these areas and among marginal Indians. Most treatment efforts addressing Native American FAS focus on prevention measures.

May, in an 1992 article, suggested three levels of prevention and intervention in which the primary preventive measure would be to eliminate the root causes of FAS/FAE within the native community. He sees this as involving public education and structural changes within the community. Secondary prevention efforts, for those requiring early detection and prompt, effective intervention, include accurate diagnoses and health interventions efforts. Tertiary prevention efforts, according to May, are measures designed to reduce the level of impairment and disability among tribal members afflicted with FAS/FAE.[12] These preventive responses are similar to those Prugh articulated in 1985. Prugh also suggested that IHS create a national Indian fetal alcohol syndrome prevention program and train local Native Americans as clinicians and prevention specialists to work with at-risk members of the tribe or pueblo.[13] This concept was again articulated by LaDue and O'Hara in their testimony given before the House Committee on Internal and Insular Affairs on March 5, 1992. Noting the high prevalence of FAS among Native Americans, they recommended passage of the Comprehensive Indian Fetal Alcohol Syndrome Prevention and Treatment Act. Passage would, according to the authors, address FAS in Indian country by focusing on culture-specific prevention for an underserved population.[14]

Treatment problems for Native Americans are complicated by research showing that substance-abusing women are less receptive than men to intervention. NIAAA, in its 1990 *Alcohol Alert* issue on "Alcohol and Women," noted, "Women alcoholics may encounter motivators and barriers to seeking treatment that differ from those encountered by men."[15] Weiner, Morse, and Garrido, however, provide encouraging data regarding the efficacy of treatment even following a diagnosis of FAS.

The efficacy of supportive therapy as a preventive strategy is underscored by the benefits observed in infants born to women who stopped drinking heavily before the third trimester. There was a significant reduction in the number of babies who were growth retarded and fewer abnormalities were observed among newborns. In early childhood, these children demonstrated fewer morphologic and

developmental abnormalities than children born to women who drank throughout pregnancy.[16]

The difficulty of reaching Native American mothers with substance
abuse problems is often increased by the effects of psychocultural marginality and the likelihood that the women themselves may be products
of FAS/FAE births and hence neurologically impaired and very likely
suffering from PTSD and bouts of depression. Louise Erdrich's recent
book *The Antelope Wife* is a sad postscript to her late ex-husband's book
The Broken Cord. Both works address the difficulties associated with living with a native FAS child. French (this author) in his study *Little Hawk*
documented the life of an adopted native infant who was afflicted by
FAS. Little Hawk was raised in New Hampshire and was about the same
age as the adopted child of Dorris and Erdrich, Abel, who was killed by
a car in 1991.[17]

The rest of this section reviews culture-centric treatment approaches
proposed for Native Americans afflicted with clinical illness. An underlying theme is the need for culture-sensitive treatment approaches, especially approaches that have the support of tribal communities. Articles
by Novins et al. and Robin et al. looked at gender differences among
Native Americans suffering from substance abuse. The Novins group
noted that from its sample, females reported greater substance use and
were more likely to seek mental health treatment than were their male
counterparts. Its results also indicated a high degree of comorbidity between substance abuse and other mental and physical disorders. Females, however, were more likely to be victims of abuse than Native
American males.[18] Robin's group found similar gender differences
among substance-abusing Native Americans regarding comorbidity, sexual abuse, among substance-abusing Native Americans and the likelihood of seeking treatment. It concluded that "gender, number of
psychiatric diagnoses, and childhood sexual abuse are strong predictors
of utilization of mental health and substance abuse treatment services."[19]

Calls for community-based culture-centric treatment programs, especially those that reflect contemporary versions of the harmony ethos, are
common. Brant warns that insensitivity to Native American cultural
traits can lead to misdiagnoses. Western-trained clinicians tend to view
traditional harmony ethos traits as manifestations of psychopathology.[20]
Garrett and Garrett, two enrolled members of the Eastern Band of Cherokee Indians, reinforced the harmony ethos healing tradition as addressing the need for a horizontal, circular milieu and a process rich in ritual
and low in confrontation and verbal expectations. Humor is also an important element in traditional healing processes. They recommend the
following guidelines: never interrupt, be patient, use silence as a therapeutic tool, use descriptive statements rather than direct questions,

model self-disclosure through the oral history tradition, and make use of metaphors and imagery.[21] Anderson postulates a similar healing process when describing the Kakawis treatment center, an interfaith Christian program in Vancouver Island, Canada, designed for Native Americans suffering from substance-abuse disorders. Apparently, Kakawis bases its treatment program on the tenets of the harmony ethos, much as does another Christian/aboriginal religious-based treatment program, the peyote rite of the Native American Church.[22] Clearly, however, non–Indian based treatment programs, especially those sponsored by Christian denominations, must be considered suspect until both their manifest and latent intentions are fully disclosed.

Community-based treatment programs face another obstacle, that of tribal politics. Anyone who has worked or lived in Indian country is aware of this phenomenon. Walker's group alludes to this factor in its article on treatment implications of comorbid psychopathology among American Indians and Alaska Natives.[23] This is one reason federally funded programs, especially those with external control, are more stable than tribally run programs. This tribal fact of life challenges the basic foundation of Indian self-determination; until tribal stability is demonstrated in this area, the politics of Native American mental health will only contribute to the problem of marginality instead of providing lasting, viable treatment solutions. Looking at the marginal Indian, Nofz suggests a task-centered group format: "The group-work approach proposed here is one that (1) recognizes that culturally marginal Native Americans must often cope with the pressures created by conflicting values, (2) views the use of alcohol as a likely means for short-term coping, and (3) considers task-centered treatment more promising than that which is based upon an existing theory of client personality."[24] These groups, according to Nofz, take up organized tasks based on gaining insight into common marginality-based conflicts and working collectively on sobriety.

Terrell spells out the foundations of culturally sensitive treatment models among American minorities. Regarding Native American youth she has noted, "Cultural-specific competence enhancement efforts may also increase self-esteem and ethnocultural pride in targeted groups. Building self-esteem is a widely recognized preventive strategy in substance abuse intervention and it may be particularly important for groups who face discrimination and negative stereotyping."[25] A number of other studies echo this sentiment. Dolan, in her Canadian study of First Nation youth, identified five counseling needs articulated by these youth: an opportunity to validate their cultural identity, personal and substance-abuse counseling, support in transition to provincial schools, academic support, and improved access to counseling services.[26] In another Canadian study, Wiebe and Huebert advocate the community mobile treatment model. A prerequisite for this program is full community support, thereby obviating the conflict often created by tribal politics. The authors noted that once a community is mobilized, an intense alcohol and drug treatment program, twenty-one to twenty-eight days long, is brought into the community. Since its inception in 1984, the program has been implemented in seventeen Canadian native communities, with good results.[27]

Similar programs have emerged in the United States. Dorpat has written the PRIDE program, instituted in the Chief Leschi schools of the Puyallup Tribe in Tacoma, Washington. Positive Reinforcement in Drug Education was instituted in 1988 as part of a schoolwide program. It involved four components: cultural aspects of the Indian student's identity, curriculum development focusing on health awareness, drug/alcohol awareness, refusal skills, and life skills; building and program security including policy designed to reduce in-school substance abuse; and intervention and social service access to counseling, case management services, and referral/after-care programs.[28] The Family Circles Program, used with high-risk Native American youth on the Lac du Flambeau Indian Reservation, also provides a culturally oriented curriculum that emphasizes traditional native values, beliefs, and practices. Van Stelle, Allen, and Moberg explain the three different curricula provided by the Family Circles Program: a twenty-four-week program designed for either adults or adolescents; a twenty-four-week children's curriculum; and an Ojibwa language curriculum. Community involvement in the curriculum is critical to its success and involves respected tribal elders.[29] The Substance Abuse and Spirituality Program initiated at the Institute for American Indian Arts in Sante Fe, New Mexico, also draws on the expertise of respected tribal (Pueblo) leaders in the performance of traditional rituals, ceremonies, and artistic practices.[30] This program differs from many others in that the majority of its curriculum is culturally based and engages already highly motivated Native American youths and young adults. Nonetheless, it can be a feeder school to needed graduate programs in clinical studies—something that is dire need in Indian country.[31]

THE NATIVE RESPONSE

A recent success story in Indian country involves the efforts of the Tri-Ethnic Center for Preventive Research at Colorado State University. One of its projects has been community and tribal awareness of the rise of inhalant abuse in Indian country. According to Pamela Jumper Thurman, the Tri-Ethnic Center initiated an awareness program in Indian communities across the United States focusing on preventive efforts, including school curricula, posters, and multimedia campaigns. At a 1998 Portland, Oregon, "Strategic Planning Meeting on Crime and Justice," Thurman reported:

As many of you know, inhalant use has been gradually increasing every year among non-Indian youth ever since the Monitoring the Future study began. The pattern for Indian youth is quite different. Their use of inhalants in the early 80s was higher than that of other kids and continued to increase up to 1985. At that point, however, it began to decline and our last data point indicates that Indian youth are now lower than non-Indian youth on inhalant use.[32]

Native American variations on Alcoholics Anonymous (AA) are yet another set of native responses to substance-abuse treatment. These modified AA sessions are usually circular and incorporate elements of the medicine wheel, purification sweat, and sacred pipe as healing devices. Within this therapeutic millieu, the abuse of alcoholism and other substances is viewed as a broken-hoop or broken-circle issue. The AA healing takes on the values of the harmony ethos as against the traditional AA values, rooted in the protestant ethic.

American Indian AA	*Traditional AA*
Uncritical attitude	Critical Attitude
Cooperation	Competition
Sharing	Ownership
Humble presentation	Outgoing/Self-righteous
Happiness	Success
Honor elders	Honor self
Silence	Verbalism
Tribal values	Individualism
Simplicity	Complexity
Tradition	Innovation
Spiritual values	Material values
Learning from elders	Formal education
Few rules	Many rules
Mysticism	Empiricism
Smallness	Bigness
Natural medicine	Synthetic drugs
Unity with nature	Separateness with nature
Accept others as they are	Change others

Indian AA Steps	*Traditional AA Steps*
We come to believe that the power of the Pipe is greater than ourselves and can restore us to our Culture and Heritage.	We come to believe that a Power greater than ourselves can restore us to sanity. (Step 2)
We acknowledge to the Great Spirit, to ourselves, and to the Native American Brotherhood, our struggles against the tide and its manifest destiny.	We admit to God, to ourselves, and to another human being, the exact nature of our wrongs. (Step 5)
Be entirely ready for the Great Spirit to remove all the defects of an alien culture.	We are entirely ready to have God remove all these defects of character. (Step 6)
Make a list of all the harm that come to our people from Demon Alcohol, and become willing to make amends to them all.	Make a list of all persons we have harmed and become willing to make amends to them all. (Step 8)
Seek through prayer and meditation to improve our conscious contact with the Equality and Brotherhood of all Mother Earth's children and the Great Balancing Harmony of the Total Universe.[33]	Seek through prayer and meditation to improve our conscious contact with God as we understand Him, praying only for knowledge of His will for us and the power to carry that out. (Step 11)

Another successful native response to substance abuse is the Native American Church. Weibel-Orlando, in her 1989 article, found, "The Native American Church (NAC) is, far and away, the most often mentioned of the indigenous curing strategies that have captured the imagination of anthropologists as possible alternatives to conventional alcohol addiction interventions. The list of proponents of the Native American Church's efficacy as a deterrent in the battle against alcohol abuse in American Indian populations reads like the roster of the inner circle of American anthropological dons."[34] Weibel-Orlando mentioned Warren LaBarre and Carl Menninger as supporting the work of the Native American Church in providing a viable native approach to Native American substance-abuse treatment and prevention. The NAC is also associated with the use of peyote; this led to considerable conflict within Indian country until peyote was recognized federally as a legitimate component of the Native American Church in 1994. A prescribed use of peyote and abstinence from alcohol or other drugs is a strict tenet of the NAC. The NAC and its peyote ritual represent a blend of aboriginal and Christian customs. Nonetheless, the historical link of the peyote rite and the Ghost Dance movement during the late 1800s once led to strict laws against its use.

The 1978 American Indian Religious Freedom Act did not in itself provide protection for NAC practitioners. The peyote issue intensified, reaching its peak in 1990, when the Supreme Court heard *Employment Division, Oregon v. Smith*, involving the firing of two recovering substance-abuse counselors for using peyote in a Native American Church ceremony. In its decision the Supreme Court ruled that the First Amendment does not protect the sacramental use of peyote by Indians, allowing states to outlaw its use. Following this decision, the Omaha and Winnebago NAC organizations asked the noted Winnebago leader Reuben Snake to help them preserve this custom from hostile state action. Reuben Snake formed the American Indian Religious Freedom Project. In 1991 Senator Daniel Inouye, chairman of the Senate Committee on Indian Affairs (SCIA), joined this endeavor, as did Peterson Zah, president of the Navajo Nation, and Pat Lefthand of the Flathead Nation. Zah and Lefthand became cochairs of the newly founded American Indian Religious Freedom Coalition. Early in 1994, the NAC received the support of the Native American Rights Fund (NARF), and their efforts were coordinated to support a bill sponsored by Senator Inouye, in Public Law 103–344 (H.R. 4230). It was passed on January 25, 1994. In Zah's words:

H.R. 4230 amends the 1978 American Indian Religious Freedom Act to provide the legal protection for the use, possession, or the transportation of the sacrament peyote and also provides protection against discrimination for such use, possession or transportation. The new law provides a uniform protection in all of the 50 states including the District of Columbia. The legislation preserves the authority of the U.S. Drug Enforcement Administration and State of Texas for the cultivation, harvest and distribution of peyote by Indians for religious purposes; does not require prison authorities to permit the use of peyote by inmates; authorize the Federal and State agencies to pass reasonable public safety regulations; and preserves the existing State traffic safety regulatory authority.[35]

The NAC peyote problem and its historical link to policies of cultural genocide were apparently resolved in Indian country on October 6, 1994, when President Clinton signed the American Indian Religious Freedom Act Amendment of 1994 into law. But, as usually is the case regarding U.S./Indian policy, qualifiers in this act keep the door open for further non-Indian interventions into the peyote debate.

The Navajo Nation has instituted its own traditional way of fighting marginality and substance abuse among its people. It is the Peacemaker's Court, which is based on the traditional harmony ethos of the Dine, known as the "Beauty Way." The Navajo Peacemaker Court process, a voluntary system existing in the Navajo district courts, is diametrically opposed to the adversarial, due-process system of the U.S. judiciary. The desired outcome of the peacemaker process is a return to community balance and harmony. Reconciliation and compromise replace the due-process concept of *mens rea*, with its expectation of a clear determination of accountability and corresponding labels of innocence or guilt, as prescribed under the protestant ethic. *K'e* is the basis of the peacemaking process. It is a Navajo word representing clanship, respect, friendliness, unselfishness, security, self-awareness, accountability, mutual dependency and other harmonious concepts within the Diné version of the harmony ethos.

Another departure from the Euro-American form of justice is the use of a respected community leader (*naat'aanii*) to guide the peacemaker process instead of a judge. Lawyers are not involved in this process at all. The *naat'aanii* is not neutral; therefore, this process is not to be confused with mediation. The *naat'aanii* invokes the rich oral tradition of the Navajo to guide the parties toward reconciliation, compromise, and ultimately harmony. These decisions cannot be appealed, since all parties must agree if the process is to be effective. Moreover, each decision is unique to each situation, and decisions are not documented as case law to be used as precedents. The Navajo peacemaker process of restorative justice has gained international attention since it began in 1982. It has been expanded to juvenile cases and has shown considerable success in treating domestic violence and substance abuse.[36]

The Sioux traditions of the sacred pipe, purification sweat, vision quest, and Sun Dance, all once outlawed and their practitioners severely punished, have emerged as treatment and training processes for native healers among both the Plains Indians and pan-Indians. An early success using a variation of this native treatment model was established at the Nebraska Penal Complex in the mid-1970s as a reaction to the incarceration of American Indian Movement warriors. The treatment program grew out of a class-action suit filed in 1972 in U.S. District Court. The Nebraska Penal Complex held a significant number of Indian inmates most of them from Siouan tribes of both Nebraska and South Dakota. The Native American Rights Fund (NARF) represented the Indian inmate class in this suit, which was strongly opposed by the white-dominated correctional officials, who historically had treated these inmates in an oppressive manner. The consent decree of *Indian inmates of the Nebraska Penitentiary v. Joseph Vitex* was signed on October 31, 1974. An essential component of the decree pertained to the religious freedom for Indian inmates:

In order to meet the religious and spiritual needs of the plaintiff class, defendants shall allow inmates access to Indian medicine men and spiritual leaders and provide facilities for spiritual and religious services, including but not limited to the Native American Church. . . . Upon agreement of the parties that a sweat lodge is a "facility" for the worship of Indian religion, and upon the pleadings, depositions and all proceedings heretofore and herein, and upon agreement of the parties represented by counsel and upon the Court's findings that the interests of the class have been fairly represented, it is: ORDERED, ADJUDGED AND DECREED that the defendants, their agents, servants, employees and their successors in office are hereby permanently enjoined and ordered to:

1. Permit the construction of a sweat lodge, within a reasonable time, at the Medium Security Unit of the Nebraska Penal and Correctional Complex, by an Indian medicine man to be agreed upon by the parties. The plaintiffs will bear all costs and expenses of building the sweat lodge, which would be a dome-like structure, approximately six feet in circumference, constructed with a sapling frame and covered by blankets; the interior will contain a small pit for the sacred rocks, along with a water bucket; the floor of said sweat lodge will be covered with pine or cedar branches, or other material as designated by the parties' medicine man.

2. The defendants will permit routine access to this sweat lodge at reasonable times to be agreed upon by the parties. The use of the sweat lodge will be available to all inmates subject to the same rules and regulations as govern other religious services, recreational clubs and similar facilities at the Nebraska Penal and Correctional Complex.[37]

These religious activities were coordinated through the newly created Native American Spiritual and Cultural Awareness (NASCA) association at the Nebraska Penal and Correctional Complex. In the 1970s, these events included services by Emerson Jackson of the Native American Church and Leonard Crow Dog, Jr., of the Sioux Council of Medicine Men. Jackson came from his headquarters in Wisconsin, while Crow Dog came down from the Rosebud (Brule Sioux) Reservation in South Dakota. This author spelled out the nature of this healing process in *Counseling American Indians*:

Sweat lodges were erected at the various penal sites and purification sweats and the smoking of the sacred pipe were two of the first of the long abandoned traditional rituals reintroduced to the Contemporary Warriors (incarcerated American Indian males). Soon other customs and rituals were added including traditional meals with buffalo meat and powwows with drumming, singing, dancing and hand games. Both the University of Nebraska and Southeast Community College faculty and staff joined in assisting the implementation of the Consent Decree, much to the chagrin of the extremely conservative correctional personnel.[38]

This effort over a quarter of century ago was a native attempt to turn the tide against the high level of substance abuse and psychocultural marginality among the Plains Indians. The teaching of the aboriginal values of bravery, fortitude, generosity, and wisdom was conducted within the traditional Siouan healing customs: the purification rite within the sweat lodge (*Initi*), communion via the sacred pipe, and Indian identification through the vision quest. Those who were initiated to these traditional customs while incarcerated at the Nebraska Penal Complex later became traditional healers among their people at the tribal level and within the urban Indian centers. Native substance abuse counseling training later included Indian-specific certification provided through the National Certification Reciprocity Consortium (NCRC). Native American NCRC certification (Certified Alcohol and Drug Abuse Counselor—CADAC) began in Oklahoma and soon spread to other states with high concentrations of Native Americans. In 1988, the native group with the highest fetal alcohol rate in the United States, the Sioux of the Aberdeen Area (North Dakota, South Dakota, Nebraska, and Iowa), created its own culture specific alcohol and drug abuse counseling training and certification program: the Northern Plains Native American Chemical Dependency Association (NPNACDA). New Mexico and the Nashville Area (including the Eastern Band of Cherokee Indians) are also involved in this culture specific addiction-counselor training and accreditation.

The Plains Indians took this native counselor training to a higher level with the reintroduction of the Sun Dance. This intense ritual, which lasts twelve days, is divided into three four-day segments. The first segment is dedicated to preparing the sacred grounds and constructing the Sun Dance Lodge while preliminary purification occurs during the second segment. It is during the final stage, known as the "holy days," that the ritual is conducted. During the first holy day, the cottonwood tree (a symbolic enemy) is hunted, marked, and reported to the dance leader. Next there is a celebration composed of a buffalo dance and a feast. The second holy day is devoted to the capture of the enemy—the designated tree. Four warriors count coup on the tree in order to neutralize its spirits. The Honored Woman then cuts the tree, and this act is celebrated. The tree is now prepared (painted and decorated with the enlarged genitalia symbolic of a member of the mythical evil family) and erected as a ritual pole on the third holy day. This is a licentious period, which allows jokes and discussion on otherwise taboo sexual topics. Later that day the men perform a war dance, in which warriors bring down the genitalia with their arrows, thus destroying the mystical evil family. On the fourth day candidates are painted and prepared for the Gaze at the Sun ritual. They are fastened to the cottonwood pole by leather thongs, which are fastened to their flesh with wooden pins. In the Sun Dance itself they dance about the pole, their heads raised to the sun, dancing until they tear themselves from the leather thongs. Warriors today, especially those who are recognized in Indian country as qualified native healers, undergo four Sun Dance ceremonies, usually in successive years. Some Native Americans see parallels between the Sioux Sun Dance and Jesus Christ's sacrifice upon the cross, with both constituting rituals of torturous self-sacrifice for purposes of spiritual recognition.

Once certified alcohol and drug abuse counselor (CADAC) native healers have completed this Sun Dance training, they conduct purification/healing sweats, sacred pipe ceremonies, and often direct healing circle AA meetings among their people. Once a purification sweat has been conducted, the blessed sweat lodge is used for group or individual therapy, which can include females. Men who completed the sweat lodge ritual stand silently about the fire until all the sessions are done; everyone involved, sweat participants and clients alike, then smoke the sacred pipe until its bowl is empty. The sacred pipe is then wrapped, and the ceremony is concluded. This process is popular in the treatment of substance abuse for both men and women, including pregnant women.[39]

8

THE FEDERAL RESPONSE: STANDARDS AND PRACTICE GUIDELINES

---◈---

IHS GUIDELINES

The latest Indian Health Service (IHS) standards for substance abuse and mental health programs are articulated in its *Indian Health Manual*. The 1991 *Indian Health Manual*, Part 3, Chapter 18, addresses alcoholism/substance abuse programs:

PURPOSE

This Chapter establishes general policy, staff responsibilities, operating relationships, standards, and guidelines for the development of alcoholism/substance abuse treatment and prevention services supported or administered by Indian Health Service (IHS). These programs may be administered by contracts or grants with Indian tribal governments of urban Indian authorities, or administered through an IHS Area Office or Service Unit. Included within the scope of this Chapter are policies and guidelines for the development and operation of Youth Primary Residential Treatment Centers (YPRT) authorized by Public Law (P.L.) 99–570, the Anti-Drug Abuse Act of 1986" October 27, 1986, as amended.

GOALS

(1) In accordance with the IHS goal of elevating the health status of the American Indian and Alaska native to the highest level possible, the Alcoholism and

Substance Abuse Program Branch (ASAPB) will attempt to lower the incidence and prevalence of alcohol abuse and alcoholism among American Indians and Alaska Natives to a level at or below that of the general population in the U.S. within a 15-year period.

(2) The ASAPB will assist American Indian and Alaska Native groups through school/community-based planning to establish effective programs of prevention, treatment, and rehabilitation for persons suffering from or afflicted with problems arising from alcoholism/substance abuse. Included is the development of YPRTs in each IHS Area.

OBJECTIVES

(1) Reduce years of productive life lost due to alcoholism/substance abuse by 5 percent per year (5 year goal is 25 percent).

(2) Guide the development of a comprehensive, effective prevention and intervention program with emphasis on Indian youth and family.

(3) Guide the development of a comprehensive effective network of Indian community-based *treatment* services for the alcohol/substance abuser and his/her family. Such a network will include emergency, inpatient, and outpatient services.

(4) Guide the development of a comprehensive, effective network of Indian community-based *rehabilitative* services for the alcohol/substance abuser and his/her family. Such a network will include quarter-way, halfway, and domiciliary facilities as well as outreach and aftercare services.

(5) Develop a series of well-designed, culturally relevant, appropriate research projects on alcoholism/substance abuse among American Indians and Alaska Natives.

(6) Promote medical and social detoxification services within each Area serviced by IHS.[1]

A number of IHS Areas responded to Public Law 99–570, the Anti-Drug Abuse Act of 1986, by establishing IHS-funded Regional Youth Treatment Centers (RYTCs). Ten facilities are currently in operation: the Unity Regional Treatment Center, located on the Eastern Band of Cherokee Indians; Raven's Way in Sitka, Alaska; the Nanitch Sahallie Program in Keizer, Oregon; the Jack Brown Treatment Center on the Cherokee Nation of Oklahoma (Tahlequah); the Phoenix/Tucson Regional Treatment Center in Sacaton, Arizona; the FNA/TCC Adolescent Treatment Program in Fairbanks, Alaska; the New Sunrise Regional Treatment Center in San Fidel, New Mexico; the Four Corners Adolescent Treatment Center, located on the Navajo Nation (Shiprock, New Mexico); the Indian Tribal Consortium Treatment Center in Spokane, Washington; and the California Youth Treatment Center, located in Sacramento, California. The Unity program in North Carolina is the only program accredited by the Joint Commission on Accreditation of Healthcare Organizations (JCAHO), and it receives the failures of many of the other IHS RYTCs.[2]

The 1993 *Indian Health Manual*, Part 3 (Professional Services), Chapter

14, addresses mental health programs, including treatment expectations. The treatment process standards include the expected core functions, including: patient rights/orientation, criteria for referral, policies and procedures, referrals, and documentation. Patient assessment also follows the standard clinical format: purpose, formal assessment, content of patient assessment, review of records, content of the patient interview, additional assessment procedures, diagnosis, treatment planning, and documentation. It is the area of therapeutic techniques that raises serious questions concerning a lack of cultural sensitivity.

(1) *Purpose*. It is the responsibility of each mental health program to provide a range of treatment modalities which are appropriate to the cultural tradition and mental health problems of the local population. A broad spectrum of treatment modalities available in the field of mental health is appropriate to Native American patients.

(2) *Standards*.

a. The therapeutic approach selected shall be within the provider's expertise and shall be selected based on the needs of the patients.

b. The program should provide a range of treatment modalities appropriate to the needs of adults and children, couples, families and groups which may be delivered in different settings and may require consultation and referral.

c. Referral to cultural, spiritual, and traditional practitioners may be appropriate when consistent with a patient's belief system.

d. Individual treatment modalities employed may include: crisis intervention; supportive therapy utilizing ventilation, active listening, reflection, problem redefinition, and others; insight oriented therapy utilizing, in general terms, ventilation, clarification, interpretation, problem definition, enhancement of self esteem and examination of alternative coping strategies, motivational techniques, dream analysis, education and others; behavioral modification utilizing progressive relaxation, cognitive therapy, hypnotherapy, desensitization, biofeedback, stress management, and some forms of aversive conditioning; and pharmacotherapy.

e. Couple and family treatment may include: identification of communication patterns, teaching of communication skills such as assertiveness, role playing, active listening, feeling statements, assessment of family roles; transactional analysis; and extended family meetings, social networks, and others as required by JCAHO standards.

f. Group treatment may include: self-help groups for special focus groups such as adult children of alcoholics, adult survivors of childhood sexual abuse, victims of family violence, and suicide attempters; self-help groups for the chronically mentally ill, parents of chemically dependent children, Narcotics Anonymous, Alcoholics Anonymous and others; and referral for cultural/tribally specific, group therapy techniques such as Talking Circle, sweats, involvement of elders as story tellers, and group co-therapists or consultants.

g. Therapy with children may include: play therapy, individual, and group therapy; behavior modification; environmental modification (out of home placement) in order to reduce stress or provide respite; and culturally appropriate or tribal specific therapies.

h. Pharmacotherapy: The prescription of any drugs is the responsibility of a physician. Non-physician mental health staff should refer patients for evaluation of the need for medication, but may not prescribe, except as provided by the medical staff bylaws governing standing orders for non-physician professionals and in accordance with the laws of the state in which the program is located. Treatment of a child usually requires treatment of the family or significant care giver. Systematic peer review of drug utilization should include objectives of minimizing patient dependency, maintaining minimal effective doses, and other principles applicable to appropriate medication usage.

i. Environmental modification: All treatment settings should provide a therapeutic environment. Milieu therapy should be utilized whenever possible. Milieu therapy is the creation of an environment which is safe, secure, and helpful. The principles of a therapeutic milieu should be encouraged in other community setting such as jails, schools, group homes, and family homes.

j. Electroconvulsive Treatment (ECT): Referral for possible administration of ECT will be justified and approved by two psychiatrists, by the Service Unit/Tribal Health Director, the Area Chief Medical Officer, and the patient or guardian who will be given a clear statement of benefits and risks.[3]

Following the efforts of tribal groups to provide Native American substance-addiction counseling credentials at the state and regional levels, IHS developed its own certification for its programs. The IHS funds four hundred American Indian/Native Alaskan (AI/AN) substance abuse programs operating in 270 communities within Indian country, with over a thousand AI/AN counselors employed in these programs. According to the 1994 standards, the purposes of the IHS National Alcoholism and Substance Counselor Certification Program are:

To provide a certification program for substance abuse counselors and program administrators to enhance the skills of service providers to maximize the quality of care.

To provide national certification for counselors.

To promote uniform professional standards and quality for the alcoholism and substance abuse counseling profession and to give the profession greater visibility.

To provide reciprocity for alcoholism and substance abuse counselors when they relocate.

To provide support services, including consultation and training in the area of certification, i.e., establishment of standards, evaluation of competence, and the establishment and training of boards and committees.

To assure that service providers have a knowledge base of physiological, social, and psychological factors associated with substance abuse treatment and prevention services.

To provide a structured program of training to meet the needs of the certification process.

Principles: In developing the certification standards for Indian counselors, certain principles have been recognized.

A. Certification is based on competence and knowledge about alcoholism, drugs, and Indian people, rather than emphasis on academic achievement.

B. Authority for this certification come from the IHS Headquarters ASAPB, and is supported by those working in AI/AN alcoholism/substance abuse programs and who share the concern of the AI/AN programs for achieving a standard of excellence and competence.

C. Accreditation shall be required for all IHS-funded programs by FY 2000 (i.e., Joint Commission on Accreditation of hospitals, Commission on the Accreditation of Rehabilitation Facilities, State, IHS, etc.).

D. Certification is offered to counselors working within IHS-funded programs. A counselor may certify in a specialty area providing the applicant is currently certified at Level II.

E. Code of Ethics Statement.

F. National Advisory Certification Board.[4]

The training component for certification is similar to those prescribed by the National Certification Reciprocity Consortium (NCRC), in that the twelve core functions of counseling and professional ethics are stressed, along with other didactic, knowledge-based topics, such as chemical dependency, the physiology/pharmacology of substances, case management, individual and group counseling techniques, and nutrition and alcohol. The only difference is the IHS requirement for Native American Studies.

A Chemical Dependency Counselor I does not require a college degree per se, while an associate degree and two years (four thousand hours) of experience, or no college but three years (six thousand hours) of experience, are required for Counselor II certification (2,080 supervised hours are required for the Counselor I certification). Chemical Dependency Counselor III calls for three years of college work and five years (ten thousand hours) of experience, or no college and ten years of counseling experience. Certification and at least level II and two years of college are required to qualify for Program Administer I, while a four-year college degree or five years' managerial experience, two with an AI/AN substance abuse program, is required for certification as a Program Administer II. IHS also provides speciality certifications in the areas of Dual Diagnosis Counselor Specialist (substance-abuse counseling and medical/mental health), Adolescent Specific Counselor, Senior/Elder Specific Counselor, Female-Specific Counselor, and Prevention Specialist.

FEDERALLY FUNDED PROGRAMS

Nelson et al. looked at the effect of the 1987 national plan for Native American mental health services in their article on mental health services in Indian country in the 1990s. They argued that while IHS and tribal mental health programs are now available to identify and treat serious mental disorders, prevention needs to be rooted in tribal traditions:

Only Native American communities can create a climate for positive self-esteem, by recapturing, emphasizing, and enforcing positive tribal values and customs, by overcoming denial of embarrassing behavioral issues, by informing themselves and their people about the consequences of family violence and other dysfunctional behaviors, and by taking consistent concerted actions to reinforce and maintain efforts to create emotionally healthier communities. By taking these initiatives, Native American communities can significantly reduce the incidence of depression, family violence, alcoholism, and other psychosocial problems that impede the happiness and progress of individuals and families. These efforts can constitute important steps in restoring the well-being and traditional strengths of Native American peoples.[5]

In a similar vein, LeMaster and Connell reviewed programs funded under the IHS National Indian Fetal Alcohol Syndrome Prevention Program. Focusing on the IHS hospital-based FAS/FAE Prevention Project in Tuba City, the authors noted that this bilingual format had far-reaching effectiveness among the Navajo and Hopi Indians served by the IHS hospital. Over two thousand community members were involved in the program, and 147 tribal and school employees were trained in FAS/FAE recognition and awareness. A FAS/FAE diagnostic screening clinic was held five times during the course of the project, and case management was provided to high-risk women. The results showed that of thirty nine high-risk Navajo women, 56 percent abstained from alcohol or drank less as a result of the program. Nonetheless, LeMaster and Connell argue, these successes are far and few between. They note certain barriers to the implementation of these programs: mistrust among American Indians and Alaska Natives of interventions presented to them by outsiders, language barriers, the geographic isolation of Indian country.

Among their suggestions for greater participation is the incorporation of native cultural beliefs into the healing process and the use of tribal leaders and community members in the prevention programs.

The involvement of the community is particularly important when dealing with social problems, including substance abuse. Interventions and prevention programs that are community based, sanctioned by local gatekeepers (e.g., tribal authorities, health and education officials), and include tribal members and community resources (e.g., elders, schools, health care system, tribal government), may help to ensure cultural relevance. Specifically, the meaning of predisposing factors that contribute to substance abuse and other social problems among Native Americans must be understood prior to implementing a preventive or remedial intervention. An awareness of the cultural values that influence alcoholism and recovery is also essential.[6]

Indian Health Services published in 1995 a list of successes. One model that appears promising an interagency cooperation initiative in the Aberdeen area. The Aberdeen area (Iowa, Nebraska, and North and South Dakota) has the highest FAS/FAE rate in Indian country. This IHS-funded endeavor was in response to the needs in the rural western part of South Dakota, home to the Pine Ridge, Rosebud, and Cheyenne River reservations as well as the urban Indian population in Rapid City. Some of the problems in this vast rural area are recruitment and retention of health professionals, outdated medical facilities, travel required to the delivery health care services, lack of transportation for clients, and obstacles to health education for both the community and health care personnel.

In an effort to address some of these common issues, a Federal Hospital Consortium (FHC) was established in 1992. Partners in this consortium included the Department of Veterans Affairs (VA), Indian Health Service (IHS), and Air Force facilities west of the Missouri River in South Dakota. The original purpose of this collaboration among federal health care facilities was to improve patient access, expand buying power, share financial and human resources, and collaborate on projects that would be mutually beneficial. The Federal Consortium included four IHS service units (Pine Ridge, Rosebud, Cheyenne River, and Rapid City), two VA Medical Centers (Fort Meade and Hot Springs), and Ellsworth Air Force Base. Motivated by the interagency success of this larger FHC, the IHS service units have joined together to form an additional Lakota Consortium that has been the focal point for collaboration and coordination intramurally within the IHS as an agency. These service units continue to be involved with the FHC, as well.

... All of this collaboration has improved communication and coordination to the point that change is occurring within and among participants. The cooperation enables members to monitor changes in the local and national health care environment and provides impetus and additional resources for improvements in response to these needs. One example of this sharing from the Lakota Consortium is the telemedicine demonstration project with the Pine Ridge Service Unit and the Mayo Clinic (Rochester, Minnesota) that is discussed extensively in another article in this publication (*Telemedicine Successful on a Rural Reservation*). Based on the experience of this one service unit, the other three service units are exploring similar relationships with Mayo Clinic; St. Alexius Hospital, Bismark, ND; and Sioux Valley Hospital, Sioux Falls, SD. These other two private facilities have telemedicine programs, primarily for teleradiology, allowing access to faster

and improved telecommunication services at up to 50% reduction in costs compared to the current contractor for radiological services and interpretation.

Congress has for several years urged all agencies in the federal sector to work
cooperatively when this would be appropriate and mutually beneficial. These
efforts within the IHS and among federal health care providers in the Northern
Plains are in concert with this request. They have yielded increased access, cost
savings, improved efficiency, better federal inter- and intra-agency relations and,
in general, better managed patient care for all.[7]

Without question, Public Law 99–570, the Indian Alcohol and Substance Abuse Prevention and Treatment Act of 1986, has led to a number
of initiatives. It has also led to improved health-care delivery in general
within Indian country. However, a number of obstacles still exist, mainly
for IHS-funded programs, which need to comply with professional services standards. These policies and procedures, for the most part, are
rooted in the Euro-American clinical tradition and the protestant ethic
and are not sensitive to the Native American harmony ethos. Whether
or not this is a manifest or latent intent of the IHS, it unintentionally
contributes to the process of cultural genocide and psychocultural marginality.

It could be argued that the treatment of medical conditions other than
substance abuse, most notably physical disorders, transcends culture. To
a certain extent this is true. State-of-the-art medical and surgical procedures speak for themselves in cases of diabetes, heart disease, hyperten-
sive disorders, and corrective surgery. Nonetheless, preventive medicine,
the most significant health issue in Indian country, needs to be culturally
sensitive if we are to reduce the high incidence of accidents and pre-
mature death among American Indians and Alaska Natives. The sections
in the IHS manual that address culture-specific approaches appear as
afterthoughts and certainly do not fit the other Euro-American treatment
standards. "Culturally appropriate or tribal specific therapies" needs to
be the driving force relevant to mental disorder, including substance-
related disorders.[8] This author, in an ethnomethodological analysis of
the Unity IHS RYTC—the only IHS RYTC fulfilling its fiscal year 2000
goal of accreditation—found that while a culture specific component is
part of its program, it does not receive the support it should from administrators and clinical staff.

In 1987, after passage of Public Law 99–570 in 1986, IHS began to
provide funding for RYTCs. Six of the Area Agencies elected to develop
IHS Regional Youth Treatment Centers: the Portland area, with two facilities; the California area, with one facility; the Phoenix area, with one
facility; and Nashville area, with one facility.

Unity, located with the Eastern Band of Cherokee Indians in Cherokee,
North Carolina, is the Nashville area facility. Its primary responsibility

is to the Nashville area, which takes in all the recognized eastern tribes, all tribes from Maine to Florida and east of the Mississippi River. In 1987, renovations began on the old Cherokee Indian Hospital, a beautiful field-stone structure, to accommodate the Unity RYTC. In October 1988 key personnel were hired, and in 1989 the program became operational. It was originally designed to be a twenty-four-bed coed facility for youth between the ages of twelve and twenty-four, but due to the limited space at that time it was reduced to twenty, ten males and ten females. Unity's program philosophy is based on the belief that "Chemical Dependency is treated as a disease through a multidisciplinary approach, incorporating the cultural uniqueness of each individual, Adventure Based Counseling, and the twelve-step approach. Because the disease affects the entire family system, family education is a component of the program. Unity believes that continuing care is imperative for the patient to succeed outside of the impatient setting.[9] In 1993, Unity RYTC was accredited with commendation by the JCAHO. This is the highest level of accreditation awarded by JCAHO, and, as noted above, Unity is the only IHS RYTC to hold it. It has maintained this status to date. While designated to serve the twenty-four Nashville area federally recognized tribes and three Indian urban centers, IHS headquarters opened Unity in 1992 to all IHS-eligible youth (ages 12–19).

This author worked at Unity RYTC as a volunteer, federally certified clinical psychologist for a six-month period in 1996. He found that it had a well developed pan-Indian cultural program, run by Lloyd Carl Owle, an enrolled Cherokee and student of the Sioux native healer Fools Crow. Owle maintains two sweat lodges, one for boys and one for girls, on a hill facing east and overlooking the Cherokee Veterans Memorial Park. He also has constructed a ceremony/medicine wheel on the front lawn of the Unity facility across from the Cherokees' sacred waters, the Oconaluftee River. This is indeed a spiritual environment, one conducive to Native American healing. The program incorporates a horizontal program-progression model, by which newcomers are regulated to a status outside the medicine/healing circle; they are labeled "Coyotes." They can progress to "Deer" status and enter the medicine/healing circle. Next is "Wolf," followed by "Bear" status. The highest is that of "Eagle," the status needed to graduate from the Unity RYTC program.

The major problem observed was the failure of the clinical staff, even those who were Native Americans, to take Owle's cultural component seriously. The program failed to incorporate the cultural element in any of its other treatment components. The twelve-step program followed the Euro-American format, as did all other therapeutic components. Indeed, the protestant–ethic concepts of individual guilt and culpability, competition, and confrontation were all stressed, while harmony-ethos concepts were ignored or challenged. Another practice was a Christian conversion effort by both non-Indian and Native American lay preachers, who appeared to have special access to this captive population of marginal American Indian youth.

The message for Indian country is that if Native American cultures are to preserved, two things have to happen: attempts these therapeutic environments at cultural genocide must end, and culture specific treatment models must drive the healing process.[10]

IV

INDIAN GAMING—
THE NEW ADDICTION

9

INDIAN GAMING AND
U.S./INDIAN POLICY

—————————— ❖ ——————————

INTRODUCTION

Indian gaming has become a critical social issue in Indian country. On one side of the argument are those who posit the economic benefit gaming brings to otherwise impoverished tribes. The opponents, on the other hand, believe that tribal gaming contributes to the social ills already plaguing American Indians. Indian gaming appears to represent yet another federally directed public policy having a latent intent to undermine federal trust (monetary) responsibilities to the tribes. While some tribes claim a newfound financial base from gaming, an unintended consequence of Indian gaming per se is a renewed hostility toward American Indians on the part of many non-Indians. A more subtle negativism is the impact gaming has on traditional cultures and on the enculturation of young Native Americans under this influence. At one level, Indian gaming represents a form of tribal addiction to a new and needed source of revenues. Another level is the introduction of gaming to Indian youth and marginal adults as the way out of poverty and related personal and social problems. At the third level are the few gamblers, Indian and non-Indian alike, who fulfill the DSM-IV criteria for a clinical diagnosis of pathological gambling.

THE HISTORICAL CONTEXT OF GAMING CONTROL

Indian gaming was a common aboriginal practice, one that survived Euro-American contact and attempts at cultural genocide. Pre-Columbian Indians were ambivalent about this practice. "Chance" was portrayed by the aboriginal Cherokees as a shifty character, much as the Coyote is presented in southwestern Indian myths. Untsaiyi, the gambler, is listed among Monney's aboriginal Cherokee "wonder stories."

Thunder lives in the west, or a little to the south of west, near the place where the sun goes down behind the water. In the old times he sometimes made a journey to the east, and once after he had come back from one of these journeys a child was born in the east who, the people said, was his son. As the boy grew up it was found that he had scrofula sores all over his body, so one day his mother said to him, "Your father, Thunder, is a great doctor. He lives in the west, but if you can find him he can cure you."

So the boy set out to find his father to be cured. He traveled long toward the west, asking of every one he met where Thunder lived, until at last they began to tell him it was only a little way ahead. He went on and came to Untiguhi, on Tennessee, where lived Untsaiyi, "Brass." Now Untsaiyi was a great gambler, and made his living that way. It was he who invented the *gatayusti* game that we play with a stone wheel and a stick. He lived on the south side of the river, and everybody who came that way he challenged to play against him. The large flat rock, with the lines and grooves where they used to roll the wheel, is still there, with the wheels themselves and the stick turned to stone. He won almost every time, because he was so tricky, so that he had his house filled with all kinds of fine things. Sometimes he would lose, and then he would bet all that he had, even to his own life, but the winner got nothing for his trouble, for Untsaiyi knew how to take on different shapes, so that he always got away.

As soon as Untsaiyi saw him he asked him to stop and play a while, but the boy said he was looking for his father, Thunder, and has no time wait. . . . He went on, and soon the news came to Thunder that a boy was looking for him who claimed to be his son. . . . He asked the boy why he had come. "I have sores all over my body, and my mother told me you were my father and a great doctor, and if I came here you would cure me." "Yes," said his father, "I am a great doctor, and I'll soon fix you." . . . The boy told his father how Untsaiyi had dared him to play, and had even offered to play for the spots on his skin. "Yes," said Thunder, "he is a great gambler and makes his living that way, but I will see that you win." He brought a small cymling gourd with a hole bored through the neck, and tied it on the boy's wrist. . . . "Now," said his father, "go back the way you came, and as soon as he sees you he will want to play for the beads. He is very hard to beat, but this time he will lose every game. When he cries out for a drink, you will know he is getting discouraged, and then strike the rock with your war club and water will come, so that you can play on without stopping. At last he will bet his life, and lose. Then send at once for your brothers to kill him, or he will get away, he is so tricky."

The boy took the gourd and his war club and started east along the road by which he had come. As soon as Untsaiyi saw him he called to him, and when he saw the gourd with the bead string hanging out he wanted to play for it. . . . They began the game with the wheel and stick and the boy won. Untsaiyi did not know what to think of it, but he put up another stake and called for a second game. The boy won again, and so they played on until noon, when Untsaiyi had lost nearly everything he had and was about discouraged. . . . They played until Untsaiyi had lost all his buckskins and beaded work, his eagle feathers and ornaments, and at last offered to bet his wife. They played and the boy won her. Then Untsaiyi was desperate and offered to stake his life. "If I win I kill you, but if you win you may kill me." They played and the boy won.

"Let me go and tell my wife," said Untsaiyi, "so that she will receive her new husband, and then you may kill me." He went into the house, but it had two doors, and although the boy waited long Untsaiyi did not come back. When at last he went to look for him he found that the gambler had gone out the back way and was nearly out of sight.[1]

In aboriginal times, oral tales were the basis of education, with the grandparents serving as the teachers. In this tale, the moral of the story is that while games have their place within the culture, excessive gaming is unacceptable and reflects, at minimum, a serious character flaw. Untasaiyi, or "Brass—the gambler," illustrated the problems associated with compulsive gambling.

The proscription after Euro-American contact against these traditional games of chance fell under the larger category of outlawed heathen practices. The intensity of enforcement depended on a number of factors, including the tribe's ability to conceal these practices, the rigor of the white controlling agents, and to a lesser degree, the dominant society's attitudes toward gaming. Regarding the latter, gaming was generally accepted up until the 1840s, followed by mild laws during the Civil War, but it was prohibited in the late 1880s with the advent of the WASP (white Anglo-Saxon protestant) movement against Catholic and Jewish immigrants. The Great Depression provided another period of license and acceptability for gambling, resulting in the Nevada phenomenon, where casino gaming was legalized in 1931. The use of gaming as a revenue source for states began in 1964, when New Hampshire introduced a state-operated lottery for the manifest purpose of providing support to education without a state income or sales tax. In 1999, only two states outlaw gaming, Utah and Hawaii. Regardless of public attitudes toward gaming, however, overzealous military, religious, and civilian administrators in Indian country, armed with federal laws, punished traditional practices, gaming included, despite state laws to the contrary.[2]

In Indian country, a succession of laws and vehicles for their implementation emerged in order to curb Indian practices that offended the Christian-oriented federal regulators. The earliest efforts were made by the religious groups awarded federal contracts to run the Indian boarding schools, whose main function was the resocialization of Indian children. The motto of these harsh environments was: *kill the Indian (culture) to save the child.* Once a group of Indians were resocialized (civilized and Christianized), it was groomed to be put in charge of the other tribal members. In an early attempt to legislate for Indian county, Congress passed the Federal Enclaves Act (18 U.S.C.A.: 1152), also known as the General Crimes Act:

Except as otherwise expressly provided by law, the general laws of the United States as to the punishment of offenses committed in any place within the sole and exclusive jurisdiction of the United States, except the District of Columbia, shall extend to the Indian country.

This section shall not extend to offenses committed by one Indian against the person of property of another Indian, nor to any Indian committing any offense in the Indian country who has been punished by the local law of the tribe, or to any case where, by treaty stipulations, the exclusive jurisdiction over such offenses is or may be secured to the Indian tribes respectively.[3]

This law brought into Indian country the entire body of federal criminal law, opening the door for the Assimilative Crime Act (18 U.S.C.A.: 13), which was passed in 1825. A subsection added in 1948 addresses a significant contemporary problem in Indian country, that of driving while impaired.

13. Laws of States adopted for areas within federal jurisdiction:
(a) Whoever within or upon any of the places now existing or hereafter reserved or acquired as provided in section 7 of the title (18 U.S.C.: 7), is guilty of any act or ommission which, although not made punishable by any enactment of Congress, would be punishable if committed or omitted within the jurisdiction of the State, Territory, Possession, or District in which such place is situated, by the laws thereof in force at the time of such act or omission, shall be guilty of a like offense and subject to a like punishment.
(b) For purposes of subsection (a) of this section, that which may or shall be imposed through judicial or administrative action under the law of a State, Territory, Possession, or District, for a conviction for operating a motor vehicle under the influence of a drug or alcohol, shall be considered to be a punishment provided by that law.[4]

Clearly, the Assimilative Crimes Act (ACA) opened Indian country to the laws of the state, especially if a state prohibited gaming. The ACA's expansion of the Federal Enclaves Act provided the judicial foundation for the Courts of Indian Offenses, which were specially devised to use white-enculturated Native Americans to impose federal laws in Indian country and to prosecute outlawed aboriginal practices. These courts continue to be the major vehicle for Euro-American control within Indian country. Indeed, a Court of Indian Offenses was established by the Bureau of Indian Affairs among the Eastern Band of Cherokee Indians as late as 1981.[5] In 1924, the BIA added gaming prohibitions to the Code of Federal Courts, including the Court of Indian Offenses. Federal courts within Indian country had unusual powers, a point illustrated by the U.S. Court for the Western District of Arkansas at Fort Smith, which had jurisdiction through Indian Territory, later known as Oklahoma. Federal Judge Isaac Parker, from 1875 until 1896, had absolute power and authority regarding federal laws, including gaming restrictions, in Indian Territory.

On March 1, 1837, Congress approved an act giving the Court of the United States for the District of Arkansas "the same jurisdiction and power in all respects, whatever, that was given to the several district courts of the United States, by an act of Congress entitled, 'An Act to Regulate Trade and Intercourse With the Indian Tribes and Preserve Peace on the Frontiers,' " and provide that "the courts of the United States in and for the District of Arkansas be and hereby are vested with the same power and jurisdiction to hear, try, determine and punish all crimes committed within that Indian country designated in the twenty-fourth section of the act to which this is a supplement. . . ."

That Judge Parker's administration was stern to the extreme is attested by the fact that he sentenced 160 men to die and hanged 79 of them. His court was the most remarkable tribunal in the annals of jurisprudence, the greatest distinctive criminal court in the world; none ever existed with jurisdiction over so great an area, and it was the only trial court in history from the decisions of which there was, for more than fourteen years (of his tenure), no right of appeal. . . . In cases of homicide, his tribunal functioned as a circuit court, and federal statutes made no provision for having his findings reviewed by the Supreme Court of the United States. To that extent his court was greater than the Supreme Court, for it possessed both original and final jurisdiction. His decisions were absolute and irrevocable.[6]

Parker's view of his judicial wards was quoted in the local press at the time: "United States marshals and Winchester rifles will not solve the outlaw question in Indian Territory. Civilization will. And civilization can only come through a change in the conduct of the Indian governments which are crude and uncivilized, and will remain so as long as the influence of the white man is excluded. This farce of treating them as independent nations with whom it is necessary to have treaties is a great mistake."[7] Parker's anti-Indian biases and prejudices were considerable, given that he was speaking of all the tribes in Indian Territory, including the removed Civilized Tribes (Cherokee, Creek, Chickasaw, Choctaw, and Seminole), who patterned their governments after the federal U.S. system.

Following allotment and statehood for Oklahoma (the Dawes and Curtis Acts), the Assimilative Crimes Act continued to be enforced within Indian country, via Courts of Indian Offenses for tribes not allotted. These controls upon traditional practices continued even under reorganization in the 1930s. It was in the 1950s, with termination and relocation, that the current conflict over state versus federal control over Indian gaming emerged. Public Law 280, enacted on August 15, 1953, was an extension of the termination policy in that it extended state jurisdiction to offenses committed by or against Indians in Indian country. The ultimate failure of termination did not reverse this situation among the so-called mandatory states, California, Minnesota, Nebraska, Oregon, and Wisconsin. Even then there were exceptions regarding state control—in Minnesota (Red Lake Reservation is exempt), Oregon (Warm Spring Reservation), and Wisconsin (Menominee Reservation).[8]

The federal government, often through the BIA, enticed other states to assume complete or partial jurisdiction within Indian country. Ten optional states did this, prior to passage of the Civil Rights Act of 1968. Titles II–VII of the Civil Rights Act addressed Indian matters and became known as the Indian Civil Rights Act of 1968. A significant portion was the provision of a bill of rights for Native Americans, including a model code for Courts of Indian Offenses and a requirement that Indian consent be given before any additional states could enforce the dictates of Public Law 280. As noted above, since this rule ending the unilateral authorization of a state to assume jurisdiction within Indian country, no tribe has consented to it. The Indian Civil Rights Act, however, did not reverse the prior agreements made between the states and the federal government without tribal input. The Indian Bill of Rights included the following provisions.

SECTION 202. No Indian tribe in exercising powers of self-government shall:

(1) make or enforce any law prohibiting the free exercise of religion, or abridging the freedom of speech, or of the press, or the right of the people peaceably to assemble and to petition for a redress of grievances;

(2) violate the right of the people to be secure in their persons, houses, papers, and effects against unreasonable search and seizures, nor issue warrants, but upon probable cause, supported by oath or affirmation, and particularly describing the place to be searched and the person or thing to be seized;

(3) subject any person for the same offense to be twice put in jeopardy;

(4) compel any person in any criminal case to be a witness against himself;

(5) take any private property for a public use without just compensation;

(6) deny to any person in a criminal proceeding the right to a speedy and public trial, to be informed of the nature and cause of the accusation, to be confronted with the witnesses against him, to have compulsory process for obtaining witnesses in his favor, and at his own expense to have the assistance of counsel for his defense;

(7) require excessive bail, impose excessive fines, inflict cruel and unusual pun-

ishments, and in no event impose for conviction of any one offense any penalty or punishment greater than imprisonment for a term of six months or a fine of $500, or both;

(8) deny to any person within its jurisdiction the equal protection of its laws or deprive any person of liberty or property without due process of law;

(9) pass any bill of attainder or ex post facto law; or

(10) deny to any person accused of an offense punishable by imprisonment the right, upon request, to a trial by jury of not less than six persons.

SECTION 203. The privilege of the writ of habeas corpus shall be available to any person, in a court of the United States, to test the legality of his detention by order of an Indian tribe.[9]

These rights have been in effect for barely thirty years in Indian country, and they are necessary to protect tribal members from police and judicial excesses regardless of source, whether tribe, state, or federal governments. Where gaming is concerned, it must be realized that since passage of the Indian Gaming Regulatory Act (IGRA) in 1988, within most tribal jurisdictions only tribal gaming enterprises are authorized, and consequently considered legal. The gaming picture became more complicated with passage of the Organized Crime Control Act (OCCA) in 1970 (PL 91–452, 84 Stat. 941), augmenting the Gambling Devices Act (GDA) of 1951. A section of OCCA (18 U.S.C.A.: 1955) deals specifically with illegal gambling.[10] This has specific relevance to Indian gaming, where going to Indian country can be construed as interstate or foreign travel in violation of OCCA. Indeed, a number of appeals of convictions for gaming in Indian country, under either the Assimilative Crimes Act (ACA) or the OCCA, entered the case law system prior to passage of the Indian Gaming Regulatory Act (IGRA) in 1988. Nonetheless, the current controversy focuses mainly around these issues as they pertain to the IGRA.

THE INDIAN GAMING REGULATORY ACT CONTROVERSY

The need for on-reservation gaming in Indian country arose as a result of cutbacks due to the Reagan administration's interpretation of self-determination and U.S. treaty and trust responsibilities. While appropriations and expenditures for Indian affairs had been stipulated under the Snyder Act of 1921, no particular funding formula had ever been derived, allowing the federal government to determine the appropriate amount for "general and incidental expenses in connection with the administration of Indian affairs."[11]

The first federal Indian gaming court case involved a PL 280 state, Florida. In 1979, the Seminole Tribe began operating a high-stakes bingo operation on reservation land near a major metropolitan area in southern Florida. Threatened with criminal prosecution under PL 280 regulations by the county sheriff, the Seminole went to the federal court. In 1981, the 5th U.S. Circuit Court, in *Seminole Tribe of Florida v. Butterworth*, ruled in favor of the Seminole Tribe, since Florida allowed gambling under other circumstances. More significantly, the court stipulated that Indian gaming issues were civil/regulatory, not criminal/prohibitory, cases as stipulated under Public Law 280. Given that Florida allowed bingo gaming, the court argued, Indian gaming on a federal Indian reservation, PL 280 aside, did not constitute conduct prohibited as being against the public policy of the state of Florida. Other Public Law 280 cases (regarding Indian gaming among federally recognized tribes within Indian country) were heard in federal courts as well. These rulings led to a proliferation of high-stakes bingo operations on federally recognized reservations in Indian country.[12]

This author has noted that by 1984 tribal gaming was seen within Indian country as an avenue of economic stability:

At the 1984 National Congress of American Indians (NCAI) annual convention, many tribal leaders eagerly anticipated the report of the Indians' National Bingo Task Force, Joe De La Cruz, president of the NCAI that year, reported that up to one-third of the tribes offer bingo. He saw bingo as an economic godsend for tribes that have limited resources, minimal capital, and high unemployment—a description of most reservations. At this same meeting, the proposed $1.5 million Mohawk Bingo Palace, designed to seat 1,500 players with a grand prize of $100,000, was considered to be the Las Vegas of Indian bingo. About the same time, bingo was started at the Sandia Pueblo in New Mexico.[13]

It took a U.S. Supreme Court decision, *California v. Cabzon Band of Mission Indians* in 1987, to move Congress to establish a federal regulatory ruling regarding gaming within Indian country. *Cabzon* was yet another PL 280 case, where a state had attempted to enforce laws restricting the operation of bingo games in Indian country. The Supreme Court upheld the 5th Circuit Courts civil/regulatory precedent in the 1981 Seminole case, as against the California criminal/prohibitory PL 280 standards. The high court found that California public policy did not prohibit gaming, since it already permitted bingo, parimutuel horse-race betting, and even a state-run lottery. The Supreme Court held that federal and tribal interests outweighed the interests of the state in attempting to criminalize gaming selectively within federally recognized tribes within the state.[14]

With both the Supreme Court and the executive branch supporting Indian gaming, Congress set forth to authorize and regulate Indian gaming among federally recognized tribes. It attempted to write a law that would provide a statutory foundation for Indian gaming while at the same time promoting the self-determination economic considerations indicated by President Reagan. Congress also wanted to ensure that the tribes benefited from these activities, not outside interests, including organized crime. These federal standards were incorporated the Indian Gaming Regulatory Act of 1988 (Public Law 100–497).

The Congress finds that:

1. numerous Indian tribes have become engaged in or have licensed gaming activities on Indian lands as a means of generating tribal governmental revenue;

2. Federal courts have held that section 2103 of the Revised Statutes (25 U.S.C. 81) requires Secretarial review of management contracts dealing with Indian gaming, but does not provide standards for approval for such contracts;

3. existing Federal Law does not provide clear standards or regulations for the conduct of gaming on Indian lands;

4. a principal goal of Federal Indian policy is to promote tribal economic development, tribal self-sufficiency, and strong tribal government; and

5. Indian tribes have the exclusive right to regulate gaming activity in Indian lands if the gaming activity is not specifically prohibited by Federal law and is conducted within a State which does not, as a matter of criminal law and public policy, prohibit such gaming activity.

Declaration of Policy

The purpose of this Act is:

1. to provide a statutory basis for the operation of gaming by Indian tribes as a means of promoting tribal economic development, self-sufficiency, and strong tribal governments;

2. to provide a statutory basis for the regulation of gaming by an Indian tribe adequate to shield it from organized crime and other corrupting influences, to ensure that the Indian tribe is the primary beneficiary of the gaming operation, and to assure that gaming is conducted fairly and honestly by both the operator and players; and

3. to declare that the establishment of independent Federal regulatory authority for gaming on Indian lands, the establishment of Federal standards for gaming on Indian lands, and the establishment of a National Indian Gaming Commission are necessary to meet congressional concerns regarding gaming and to protect such gaming as a means of generating tribal revenue.

National Indian Gaming Commission

There is established within the Department of the Interior a Commission to be known as the National Indian Gaming Commission.

1. The Commission shall be composed of three full-time members who shall be appointed as follows:

(A) a Chairman, who shall be appointed by the President with the advice and consent of the Senate; and

(B) two associate members who shall be appointed by the Secretary of the Interior.

2. (A) The Attorney General shall conduct a background investigation on any person considered for appointment to the Commission.

(B) The Secretary shall publish in the Federal Register the name and other information the Secretary deems pertinent regarding a nominee for membership on the Commission and shall allow a period of not less than thirty days for receipt of public comment.

3. Not more than two members of the Commission shall be of the same political party. At least two members of the Commission shall be enrolled members of any Indian tribe. . . .

Tribal Gaming Ordinances

1. Class I gaming on Indian lands is within the exclusive jurisdiction of the Indian tribes and shall not be subject to the provisions of this Act.

2. Any Class II gaming on Indian lands shall continue to be within the jurisdiction of the Indian tribes, but shall be subject to the provisions of this Act.

(b) (1) An Indian tribe may engage in, or license and regulate, class II gaming on Indian lands within such tribe's jurisdiction, if:

(A) such Indian gaming is located within a State that permits such gaming for any purpose by any person, organization or entity (and such gaming is not otherwise specifically prohibited on Indian lands by Federal law), and

(B) the governing body of the Indian tribe adopts an ordinance or resolution which is approved by the Chairman.

A separate license issued by the Indian tribe shall be required for each place, facility, or location on Indian lands at which Class II gaming is conducted. . . .

Net revenues from any tribal gaming are not to be used for purposes other than: to fund tribal government operations or programs; to provide for the general welfare of the Indian tribe and its members; to promote tribal economic development; to donate to charitable organizations; or to help fund operations of local government agencies.

3. Class III gaming activities shall be lawful on Indian lands only if such activities are:

(A) authorized by an ordinance or resolution that: is adopted by the governing body of the Indian tribe having jurisdiction over such lands; and is approved by the Chairman,

(B) located in a State that permits such gaming for any purpose by any person, organization, or entity, and

(C) conducted in conformance with a Tribal-State compact entered into by the Indian tribe and the States . . . [and] that is approved by the Chairman.

Civil Penalties

Subject to such regulations may be prescribed by the Commission, the Chairman shall have authority to levy and collected appropriate civil fines, not to exceed $25,000 per violation, against the tribal operator of an Indian game or a management contractor engaged in gaming for any violation of any provision of this

Act, any regulation prescribed by the Commission pursuant to this Act, or tribal regulations, ordinances, or resolutions. . . . The Chairman shall have power to order temporary closure of an Indian game for substantial violation of the provisions of this Act. . . .

Criminal Penalties

The United States shall have exclusive jurisdiction over criminal prosecutions of violations of State gambling laws that are made applicable under this section to Indian country, unless an Indian tribe pursuant to a Tribal-State compact approved by the Secretary of the Interior under section 11(d)(8) of the Indian Gaming Regulatory Act, or under any other provision of Federal law, has consented to the transfer to the State of criminal jurisdiction with respect to gambling on the lands of the Indian tribe.[15]

The IGRA distinguishes between three types of gaming in Indian country, with Class I activities reserved for traditional Indian games of chance, those that have survived from aboriginal times. Under the IGRA, Public Law 280, or federal authority under the Assimilative Crimes Act (ACA), outsiders can no longer attempt to outlaw these traditional customs. Class II gaming pertains to bingo, pull-tabs, and similar games. This had been the initial form of Indian gaming, and the federal court rulings had protected these activities from PL 280 criminal interference by a state, providing the state had some policy permitting gaming. (Only Hawaii and Utah have no such policy.) This had led to high-stake bingo parlors in Indian country. The third stage of evolution of Indian gaming within Indian country was Class III gaming: slot machines, casino games, and sports and racing gambling.

However, the tribal-state compact for Class III, or casino-type, gaming bothered many tribal leaders. They saw the IGRA and the National Indian Gaming Commission as yet another layer of federal micromanagement, with little to do with the real intent of Indian self-determination. More bothersome was the extension of state influence in this process, under the tribe-state compact arrangements required for Class III gaming in Indian country.

This control was seen as the result of the influence of white-owned casinos and such religious groups as the Mormons. The twenty-five-million-square-mile Navajo Nation includes parts of Utah, Arizona, and New Mexico and the Mormon church has been a major source of opposition to gaming of any type in Diné land. Many tribal leaders saw the IGRA as Congress's way of reintroducing the PL 280 constraints previously overruled in federal court cases. Indeed, it could be argued that PL 280 authority was expanded to non-PL 280 states through the tribe-state compact. At any rate, in 1989 the Red Lake Band of Chippewa Indians and the Mescalero Apache in New Mexico filed suit against the constitutionality of the Indian Gaming Regulatory Act, on the grounds that the tribe-state compact undermined both tribal sovereignty and federal responsibility to Indian tribes. In 1992, seven more tribes joined the class-action suit, including the Eastern Band of Cherokee Indians of North Carolina and the Isleta Pueblo Indians in New Mexico. Litigation over the IGRA continues today, with the greatest obstacle coming from the western states—those that seem to harbor the greatest prejudice against Native Americans. One of the strongest anti-Indian voices, in addition to the Mormons, is the Western Governors' Association. Another region of white, right-wing hostility is the Southeast.

10

INDIAN GAMING: SOCIAL, POLITICAL, AND CLINICAL ISSUES

INTRODUCTION

A major social and political issue surrounds the question of what constitutes a legitimate Indian gaming enterprise. Once the Las Vegas and Atlantic City casino giants realized that Indian gaming was here to stay, they began to lobby tribes for contact with their casinos. The influence of big-name casinos in Indian country merely increased the resolve of anti-Nevada states, like California. Californian, a PL 280 state and the state with the highest number of Native Americans, California insisted on greatly restricting both the type and distribution of Indian gaming. Gov. Pete Wilson also wanted the state to determine the distribution of Indian gaming profits. This plan included profits for the state and local communities.

Under the Pala agreement between the state and some California tribes, Wilson wanted slot machines removed from tribal casinos and only lottery devices approved by the state allowed. Wilson's agreement was designed to eliminate all Class III gaming in Indian country within the state, an attempt to reverse a practice that had begun when the U.S. Supreme Court authorized Indian gaming in 1987, a year before Congress passed the Indian Gaming Regulatory Act. Wilson's definition of acceptable gaming devices envisioned a computerized high-speed lottery game where players bet against themselves and not the house. There would also be a statewide limit on the number of gaming devices allotted to tribes for use in gaming. Less than twenty thousand devices would be distributed among the one hundred federally recognized tribes in California, whether they had a casino or not. Each tribe would be allocated 199 approved gaming devices, with the option of forming a cooperative with smaller tribes to raise the level to a maximum of 975 devices. According to Wilson, this limit would prevent any gambling centers in California like Las Vegas, Reno, and Laughlin in Nevada. Wilson's plan also called for state interference in tribal matters with respect to how gaming profits would be spent by Native Americans. Moreover, under this plan employees at tribal gaming facilities, Indian and non-Indian alike, would be subject to the state's worker's compensation law; unemployment insurance and disability insurance laws and all service employees would be granted collective bargaining rights; and each gaming tribe would have to maintain public liability insurance, in the amount of five million dollars per occurrence. One of the most controversial elements of Governor Wilson's intrusive PL 280 Indian gaming plan was that local non-Indians would have a significant voice over tribe-state compacts, for instance regarding compensation for local police and other services.

In March 1998, Wilson gave gaming tribes in California sixty days either to accept the conditions of the Pala compact or cease games not approved by the state. However, the state's wealthiest tribes submitted for the November 1998 ballot an initiative (Proposition 5) to continue the lucrative video slot machines. Seventy million dollars were spent on this proposition, making this the costliest ballot initiative in the California's history. Proposition 5 passed, 63 percent to 37 percent, allowing video slot machines to continue at the forty-one tribal casinos that used these devices. In the end, 85 percent of California's tribes supported Proposition 5. The proposition also required the governor to approve within thirty days any tribe's request to run a casino. One element of Wilson's Pala agreement was included in Proposition 5, that a trust fund would be generated by the gaming tribes to benefit smaller and more rural California tribes that did not have gaming on their reservations.[1]

Another Native American group in the limelight is the small (318 members) Mashantucket Pequot tribe in Connecticut. Part of its problem is that half of the current tribal members are phenotypically African American and most of the others are phenotypically Caucasoid. The race factor certainly plays a role here, not only among non-Indians but among Native Americans as well. Many wondered how a 216-acre reservation containing only two elderly half-sisters in 1970 could emerge as a five-thousand-acre tribal holding and the state's largest taxpayer and the most profitable casino in the world in the mid-1990s. Donald Trump is quoted as angrily referring to the Mashantucket Pequot as "Michael Jordan Indians." They are the state's largest taxpayer, due to a tribe-state compact whereby they have agreed to pay 25 percent, or a minimum of a hundred million dollars, from their gaming profits to Connecticut each year. Tribal members, who have at least one-sixteenth Pequot Indian blood, are provided new houses, managerial jobs or training paying a minimum of fifty thousand dollars a year, free education through graduate school (with a thirty-thousand-dollar stipend while in college), and free health care and day care.

While the Pequots' success is phenomenal, it is not representative of other tribal situations. By the same token, the "black Indian" stigma has relevance historically, especially among eastern tribes during the colonial era. The Pequot were almost annihilated 350 years ago by white physical genocide and disease. Those not massacred were enslaved and mixed with black slaves, hence the mixed race genopool of the tribe today.[2] Regarding the issue of Indian slaves, this author has noted

all the horrors long associated with the worst image of slavery—beatings, killings, and family breakups. Indeed, it was routine policy to separate members of Indian families, sending the females and children to one location and the males to another. These actions were deemed necessary due to the rebellious nature of Indian males once subjected to servitude. Indian and black slaves were further exploited by being forced to quell the other's slave uprising. . . . Interbreeding among Indian and black slaves also occurred, which is most evident among the 40,000 Lumbee Indians of Lumberton County, North Carolina. The combination of lost tribal traditionalism and the mix with black slaves led to a loss of their aboriginal roots and a long struggle for recognition as an Indian tribe.[3]

The success of the Pequot has led to competition from other long-lost tribes in the region, including the Mohegan Tribe, just across the county line from the Pequot's lucrative Foxwoods Resort and Casino, and from the Narragansett Indian Tribe of Rhode Island. Regarding the Narragansett Indians, the Bureau of Indian Affairs provided the following evidence supporting their federal recognition:

The Narragansett Indian Tribe is the modern successor of the Narragansett and Niantic tribes which, in aboriginal times, inhabited the area which is today the state of Rhode Island. . . . The tribe has a documented history dating from 1614. . . . After the Narragansett nation was essential destroyed in 1675 in King Philip's War, the Niantics combined with the remnants of the Narragansetts. The tribe was placed under a form of guardianship by the colony of Rhode Island in 1709, a relationship which continued until 1880, when the state legislature of Rhode Island enacted a so-called "detribalization" act. This ended the state's relationship with the tribe except for retention of two acres surrounding the Narragansett

Indian church which continued to be held in special status. . . . The state again effectively recognized the group beginning in 1934. . . . Essentially all of the current membership are believed to be able to trace to at least one ancestor on the membership lists of the Narragansett community prepared after the 1880 Rhode Island "detribalization" act. . . . Federal law imposes no general blood degree requirements for tribal membership.[4]

The Mohegans received federal recognition as a tribe in 1994. Like the Pequot, the Mohegans and Narragansett tribes are within hours of New York City and Boston. The Mohegan are also a small, highly diluted tribe of about a thousand members; until federal recognition, they owned only half an acre of land. Some in Indian country have questioned why these long-ignored Indian groups in the populated northeast are being federally recognized since passage of the Indian Gaming Regulatory Act, while other "real" tribes have been ignored for decades. Two factors seem to emerge here—better acceptance of non-Indian-looking Native Americans among the dominant society, and the riches that can be made via tribe-state compacts. The exploitation of Indian gaming by the federal, state, and local governments, along with private interests, and the resurrection of small, long-lost, culturally dead, and blood-weak groups of Native American descendants, for profit, seems to some obscene.[5]

Indeed, Indian gaming has become such big business that management consortiums have emerged, as have Indian-gaming legal specialists. Capital Gaming International is the largest manager of Indian gaming contracts in the United States, representing eight tribes in five states. There is no end in sight for the growth of Indian gaming. The Coeur d' Alene Tribe of Idaho has plans to establish a national Indian lottery, with an expected annual profit of two hundred million dollars. This has led to state-tribe competition for these resources and legal challenges in both Congress and state legislatures. Part of the problem is that some states have allowed tribes to acquire off-reservation casino land near major population centers if the tribes agree to share revenues with the state. On the other hand, the National Indian Gaming Association, which represents 133 of the 550 recognized tribes, is against any amendment to the Indian Gaming Regulatory Act. As it stands now, the Senate has agreed to review and revise Indian gaming policy, with a view to providing increased federal oversight over this burgeoning industry.[6]

A COMPARISON OF TWO SYSTEMS: THE CHEROKEE OF NORTH CAROLINA AND THE INDIANS OF NEW MEXICO

The Eastern Band of Cherokee Indians was well suited for Indian gaming, given its tourist-based industry, part of the federal development of the Great Smoky National Park. Four-lane highways link the Qualla Boundary, deep in the Appalachian Mountains, with large urban centers within a two-hundred-mile radius. Millions of tourists still come in during the tourist season, from April to October, but now, with Indian gaming, the tribe has a steady clientele year-round. The twelve-thousand-member band is the only recognized tribe in North Carolina, having successfully kept the forty-thousand–strong Lumbee Indians from receiving federal recognition, despite their Indian–black slave heritage, like that of the tiny Pequot Tribe of Connecticut. The Eastern Band began with high-stakes bingo, soon after the successful Seminole court case. In the early 1990s, the band made arrangements for Class III gaming and established two small casinos near its major tourist center. In November 1997, a new mega-casino replaced these smaller facilities. Managed by Harrah's, the new Cherokee casino, with 1,800 video machines, is the largest such facility between Atlantic City, New Jersey, and the Indian casino on the Choctaw Reservation in Philadelphia, Mississippi. The tribe continues to run its big bingo hall as well as the new casino.

The Eastern Band of Cherokee Indians had little trouble obtaining a tribe-state compact, given their role as a tourist magnet for the western part of the state. Moreover, the tribe's unique state and federal status also served to facilitate this process. In the tribe's current code (1993), gaming regulations are stated as follows:

16–1. *Policy.*

(a) The Tribal Council finds that the Eastern Band of Cherokee Indians has conducted Bingo gaming operations continuously since December 1982 as a means of generating tribal government revenue.

(b) The federal courts and Congress have declared that Indian tribal gaming operations are a lawful and valid means of promoting economic development, self-sufficiency, and for strengthening tribal governments.

(c) Congress has established federal regulatory authority and standards for gaming on Indian lands in order to protect such gaming from organized crime and other corrupting influences and to preserve such gaming as a means of generating tribal revenue.

(d) The Eastern Band of Cherokee Indians does enact this Gaming Ordnance in compliance with the Indian Gaming Regulatory Act, 15 U.S.C. 2701 et seq., to replace its prior Bingo Ordinance and to provide appropriate regulation of these essential governmental activities.

16–2. *Interpretation.*

The provisions in this Ordinance, being necessary for the welfare of the Tribe and its members, shall be liberally construed to effect the purpose and objects hereof.

16–3. *Penalties.*

(a) It shall constitute a violation of the laws of the Eastern Band of Cherokee

Indians to violate the provisions of this Ordinance, any regulations promulgated by the Tribe under this Ordinance, or any proper order issued by the Cherokee Gaming Commission issued under the authority of this Ordinance. Any persons so violating these laws or regulations may be charged with criminal or civil violation in the Cherokee Court.

(b) Any member of the Eastern Band of Cherokee or of any other federally recognized Indian tribe residing on Eastern Cherokee trust lands may be charged with a criminal violation and upon conviction shall be punished by a fine of not more than one thousand dollars ($1,000), by imprisonment not to exceed twelve (12) months, for each separate offense, or by both fine and imprisonment or other sentencing alternatives under tribal law.

(c) Any person who is not an enrolled member of any federally recognized Indian tribe may be charged with a civil violation of Tribal law and shall, upon judgment, be required to pay a civil fee of not more than one thousand dollars ($1,000) per offense or violation plus such civil damages as may be awarded by the Court.

16–5. *Definitions.*

(a) "Bingo" shall mean a game wherein participants pay a sum of money for the use of one or more cards or sheets. Numbers are drawn by chance, one by one, and announced until a participant announces that he has matched his card with enough randomly drawn numbers to complete the desired winning pattern of numbers. The player calls out "Bingo" and is declared the winner of a pre-determined prize.

(b) "Instant Bingo/Instant Lotto" shall mean a game wherein participants pay a sum of money for the use of one or more cards. Winning patterns are amounted upon the card. When a card is played, paper tabs are pulled off the cardboard backing or a covering is scratched off to reveal the patterns printed on the card. If a player receives patterns which are printed as winning patterns, the player turns in the card for a predetermined prize.

(c) "Lotto" shall mean a game wherein participants pay a sum of money for the use of one or more cards. Numbers are preprinted on the card. At a specified date and time each day, numbers are drawn by chance, one by one, and announced. A participant whose card contains enough of the randomly drawn numbers turns in the card for a predetermined prize.

(d) "You-Pick-Em Bingo" shall mean a game wherein participants pay a sum of money for the use of one or more cards. The participant select numbers and enters them on the card. Numbers are drawn by chance, one by one, until a specified total of numbers are drawn. A participant whose card contains enough of the randomly drawn numbers turns in the card for a predetermined prize.

(e) "Electronic Bingo/Lotto" shall mean coin operated electronic devices that offer games based upon the principles of bingo or lotto.

(f) "Other Electronic Games" shall mean coin operated games that are based on the players ability to master judgment, reaction, hand/eye coordination, skill or adroitness. These elements must be a dominant factor in affecting the success or outcome of the game.

(g) "Amusement Games" shall mean coin operated games that are played for amusement only, in which the player receives nothing of value as a result of the play, or in which the player can receive something of value but the value of which is less than the cost of playing the game.

16–6. *Gaming Authorized.*

All forms of gaming defined and listed in 16–5 shall be lawful if operated by the Tribe as a tribal enterprise or by any other person, firm or entity under license duly issued by the Tribe.

16–19. *Revenue from Gaming.*

The net revenues received by the Eastern Band of Cherokee Indians from any gaming activity shall be used only for the following purposes:

(a) to fund tribal government operations or programs,

(b) to provide for the general welfare of the Tribe and its members,

(c) to promote tribal economic development,

(d) to donate to charitable organizations, or

(e) to help fund operations of local government agencies.

16–26. *Establishment.*

(a) There is established by the Eastern Band of Cherokee Indians a Commission to be known as the Cherokee Gaming Commission.

(b) The Commission shall be composed of three members, who shall be the persons who are occupying the following positions:

(1) The Principal Chief,

(2) The chairman of the Tribal Council.

(3) A person appointed by the Tribal Council.

(c) Upon election of a new Principal Chief or Tribal Council Chairman, the newly elected person shall assume a position on the Commission on the date they assume such position. The third Commission member shall be appointed by the Tribal Council to serve a term of three years.[7]

The tribe-state compact agreement between the tribes in New Mexico represents an entirely different situation. Fiercely independent and with high blood degrees, the nineteen Pueblo tribes, the two Apache tribes, and the Navajo Nation have combatted for over five hundred years colonial exploitation and brutality from the Spanish, Mexican, and U.S. governments. In 1680, the Pueblo tribes drove the Spanish from what is now New Mexico and Arizona, and they have maintained a special status that preceded U.S. intrusion in this area under the colonial justification of Manifest Destiny. The Mescalero and Jicarilla Apache are descendants of the Apache driven from New Mexico and Arizona as a result of the fifty-one-year Apache/American War, which ended with Geronimo's surrender in 1886. When Geronimo surrendered, his entire band was transported from the New Mexico Territory to a federal military prison at Fort Pickens, Florida. The 720-square-mile Mescalero reservation, located in the middle-eastern portion of the state, was created by treaty in 1852, while the 1,360-square-mile Jicarilla reservation, located in the four-corners section of the state, was established in 1887 by executive order. The Navajo experienced similar hostility, from the Spanish, Mexicans, and U.S. governments. During Col. Kit Carson's punitive expeditions in 1863, Navajo crops, herds, and villages were destroyed, and all those who refused to be removed were systematically executed regardless of age or gender. The first of these three-hundred-mile forced marches began in March 1864. Eventually eight thousand Navajo were forcefully removed to Fort Sumner, New Mexico. Those who could not endure these "Long Walks" were killed by the soldiers. Many more died at Fort Sumner, until this experience was reversed in 1868 and the Navajo were allowed to return to their traditional homeland.[8]

Today, the Native Americans in New Mexico continue to suffer under the Hispanics and Anglos, who have maintained a constant neo-colonial battle for the resources of the state. Indeed, Native Americans were not allowed to hold public office or vote in the state until 1982, despite their right to vote in federal elections since 1924 (when Congress passed the Indian Citizenship Act). In 1995, Gov. Gary Johnson signed a tribe-state compact for Class III gaming in Indian country that required the gaming tribes to give 16 percent of their profits to the state—in violation of the IGRA. This exploitation of the tribes is even more blatant when it is realized that the state has paid little attention to Indian issues, regardless of the political affiliation (Republican or Democrat) or ethnicity (Anglo or Hispanic) of the leaders of the executive or legislative branches.

The history of Indian gaming in New Mexico is described in the report of the "Twenty-first New Mexico First Town Hall."

By 1989, a few tribes had introduced electronic machine gambling into their bingo halls. By 1991, both the Mescalero Apache and the Pueblo of Sandia presented compacts to then Democratic Governor Bruce King to negotiate. He refused, whereupon the tribes took him to federal court. The suit was dismissed after the court determined that the state's own limited immunity prevented the tribes from suing. In the meantime, several other tribes introduced newer electronic machines and in spite of threats by federal agents to seize the equipment, no action was taken against them.

In 1989, the first attempt to introduce state tribal gaming legislation failed. Republican Garry Curruthers directed the NM Office of Indian Affairs to negotiate the gaming compacts. A reinstated Governor Bruce King vetoed it. The veto ultimately backfired. In 1994, the gaming tribes initiated an election campaign and provided over $270,000 for the political war chests of pro-gaming candidates. With the clear backing of the gaming tribes, Republican Gary Johnson defeated incumbent Bruce King for the Office of Governor. During the same ballot, New Mexico voters approved a constitutional amendment to allow video gaming in New Mexico and a statewide lottery to provide additional revenues for funding state programs.

In July, 1995, the US Attorney General signed non-prosecution deals with 8 tribes. In exchange, the 8 tribes agreed to limit the number of devices pending a good-faith negotiation of a gaming compact. Early in 1995, Gov. Johnson signed a compact that permitted 14 tribes to offer unlimited casino-style, Class III gaming. In November, the NM Supreme Court determined that the compact was invalid. The ruling indicated that the state legislative process and that authorization first required the passage of a state gaming statute.

Anti-gaming foes used various measures to thwart the compact. One such attempt was a law suit initiated by gamblers against the 13 financial institutions who provided ATM withdrawal machines in the Indian casinos. There was even an attempt to resurrect an 1857 Territorial Law allowing for the recovery of lost wagers. The anti-gaming sentiment reached a pinnacle in 1997 after US District Court Judge James A. Parker ruled, on balance, in favor of a 61 year-old grandmother, Loretta Martinez. Although she had robbed the Tesuque Pueblo Camel Rock Casino of $7,100 at gunpoint, she was only sentenced to six months house arrest with five years probation. The determination stated that she did not need to pay back the money as the casino had been operating "illegally" at the time of the incident.

Other actions included the seizure of all electronic games from charitable organizations. In August 1996, the Mescalero Apache tribe, which refused to negotiate on state terms, had their tribal gaming operations forcibly shut down for a period of several months. In 1996, there was a staged traffic slowdown and a threatened road block by the Pueblos of Pojoaque and Isleta. And, in a show of support, Indian and non-Indian casino employees organized rallies throughout the state in support of the industry and the thousands of jobs they provided.

After embittered negotiations, the NM legislature finally approved the NM Indian Gaming Compact in 1997. The Mescalero Apache Tribe, however, has refused to make any payment to the state under the terms of that compact. They continue to hold out by putting funds in an escrow account, with the hope that renegotiations will force the state to make "individualized" compacts rather than one single compact.

Overall, in the early stages, it was the inability of the US District Attorney and the NM Attorney General to act decisively that fueled the gaming controversy. Moreover, the issue is far from resolved. In the face of all this controversy, a fervid disquiet has engaged the public. Beginning in 1995, Indian gaming has been voted 3 consecutive years by the Associated Press as the number one story in New Mexico. In addition to hundreds of newspaper articles and op-eds, the visual and print media has tracked every nuance of this controversy.

The federal Indian Gaming Regulatory Act requires that tribes and states negotiate compacts prior to Indian tribes engaging in Class III gaming within any state. The Act provides little other procedural or substantive guidance to tribes or to states.

From the State of New Mexico's point of view, there is currently a single version of a gaming compact that representatives of the State drew up and presented to New Mexico tribes to sign in 1997. There appears to be no room for negotiated changes to accommodate any particular tribe, as consistency is seen as an administrative convenience to the State of New Mexico. This is the main point of contention as protested by the Mescalero tribe. From the tribes' points of view, the State's lack of flexibility and unwillingness to engage in meaningful negotiations with each individual New Mexico tribe could be construed as a lack of good faith. Furthermore, the regulatory, revenue sharing, monitoring and other fees charged by the State of New Mexico in the gaming compact are supposed to be paid by the tribes in exchange for exclusive access to Class III gaming within the State of New Mexico. This is not what the tribes are currently receiving. The State and other organizations continue to engage in many forms of Class III gaming.

Many New Mexico tribes believe the various fees charged by the State of New Mexico in the gaming compact amount to no more than a series of taxes. The regulatory fees changed could be construed as an *ad valorem* property tax levied on the value of tribal gaming equipment. Although the New Mexico Constitution gives the State the power to impose such a tax on New Mexico residents, the 1995 US Supreme Court cases of *Potawatomi* and *Chickasaw* indicate otherwise.

The 10th Circuit case of *Indian Country USA* is additional binding authority for New Mexico. Even if New Mexico could tax the equipment of Indian tribes located on Indian land, the tax is still limited under the New Mexico Constitution to 33 1/3% of the value of the equipment. The current rate being paid by tribes is about 32% of the value of their gaming equipment, and the compact provides for the regulatory fees to escalate 5% per year. Again, these monetary payments to be made by each of the tribes on each of their slot machines, gaming tables, poker machines, etc. are not called taxes, but are effectively the same thing.

New Mexico state lottery continues to operate unrestricted, and is classified as a Class III gaming operation. Moreover, the lottery is available to anyone 18 years old or over, while Indian gaming is restrict to those 21 years old and over. Horse racing, such as that at Sante Fe Downs also constitutes Class III gaming, as the horse races are simulcast, thus allowing customers in New Mexico to bet on horse races happening in other states. Horse tracks and fraternal orders are exempted from the exclusivity provision of gaming compact, and so are still able to have and operate slot machines on their premises, thus constituting Class III gaming as well.

Under the case of *State vs Schwartz*, New Mexico citizens cannot be criminally prosecuted for illegal gambling. All that is required is for a citizen, before being arrested, to file a civil action declaring her/his gambling losses. By filling the civil suit, the citizen stops the criminal action, and therefore cannot be prosecuted for illegal gambling. This is yet another "hole" in the exclusive contract for Class III gaming which New Mexico tribes are supposed to have with the State. The effect is that virtually anyone can engage in Class III gambling in New Mexico and there are no sanctions. No other state has a similar law.[9]

New Mexico presented their Twenty-First "New Mexico First Town Hall" on June 4–7, 1998, in Albuquerque. On the basis of these town meetings, New Mexico First recommended that, on a government-to-government basis, New Mexico and the twenty-one tribes find acceptable solutions to the following issues: the dual taxation of American Indians in Indian country; the sharing of revenue derived from activities, including but not limited to gross receipts taxes, tourism, severance taxes, and law enforcement revenues; support for funding for American Indian education; state funding of preschools for all prekindergarten students living below the poverty level; the problem of American Indian student school attendance; and representation of American Indians on rural and urban school boards.

Indian gaming has strong support among tribal leaders throughout the country, due mainly to the recognized economic gains. Cozzetto, in his research on Minnesota tribes, argued that the positive effects of gaming are impressive, and fuel economic development, including employment opportunities for tribal members. Indeed, for the Milles Lacs Band, one of the eleven Minnesota tribes operating seventeen casinos, not only has unemployment been resolved (it had been nearly 70 percent before gaming), but the amount of money made has greatly improved life for tribal members. The Sault Ste. Marie, Minnesota, tribe of Chippewa Indians, like many other tribes, relies heavily on gaming funds for education—which is seen by many tribes as a vehicle for preserving their traditional culture and languages. Even the Southern Ute tribe, overcoming the influence of the Mormon church, has established the Sky Ute Lodge and Casino, on tribal land in southeastern Colorado.[10]

Another significant problem with tribal gaming is exploitation by non-Indians and corrupt tribal leaders—a problem clearly illustrated by the violence that erupted in 1990 over gaming among the Mohawk Indians in New York State. The problem arose because the Akwesasne (St. Regis Mohawk) Reservation lies partly in the United States (New York State) and partly in Canada (Quebec), with the St. Lawrence River dividing its twenty-five thousand tribal members. Following passage of the IGRA in 1988, the U.S. portion of the tribe established gaming houses. The Canadian faction, along with the more traditional Iroquois Indians, known as the "Followers of the Longhouse Tradition," were against gaming. Radical Indians in the American Indian Movement (AIM) supported gaming. These tensions erupted into violence, resulting in the death of two Indians. The Mohawk Gambling War, the Federal Bureau of Investigation (FBI), the New York State Police, and the Royal Canadian Mounted Police raided the reservation in an attempt to restore order. Leaders of the progambling, AIM-sponsored Warrior Society were arrested and convicted in both the United States and Canada. An upshot of this highly publicized intratribal conflict was the disclosure that the Gotti Mafia family of New York City had most likely been involved in the Akwesasne gambling controversy.[11]

This is a problem with other tribes as well: the scenario where white management companies run Indian gaming enterprises for high margins of profit. Lueders has used the St. Croix Chippewa Tribe of Wisconsin to illustrate this problem. Two white businessmen, Roy C. Palmer and Ronald G. Brown, formed a management firm with the Indian-sounding name of Buffalo Brothers Management, Inc. Not only have these two non-Indians skimmed tens of millions of dollars from the St. Croix casinos, but they are linked to corruption, bribery, and inciting violence.

Corruption and violence continues to surface in reference to Indian gaming. On March 25, 1995 there was a shootout on the Cattaraugus Indian Reservation, and three were killed on the Seneca Nation. These are but a few of the reasons that better oversight and protection needs to be provided by an impartial federal agency.[12]

PREVENTION AND TREATMENT ISSUES

Benefits to the tribe aside, there is a downside to gaming in general. Conzzetto, in his research, found a dramatic increase in compulsive gambling among both Indians and non-Indians in the Minnesota tribal casinos.[13] Ben Nighthorse Campbell, the only American Indian in the U.S. Senate, has warned about the ills of Indian gaming in a *New York Times* article. He argued that the Foxwood success is not representative of conditions and circumstances existing in *real* Indian country.[14] A similar sentiment was expressed in the U.S. Congress by Senator Paul M. Simon, Republican from Illinois.

The Explosive Growth of Gambling in the United States

Mr. President, in November of last year, when I announced I would retire from the Senate after 1996, President Clinton suggested that with the freedom from political restraint I now have, and with slightly more credibility because political opportunism would not be the immediate cry of critics, I should, from time to time, make observations about our Nation, where we are going, and where we should go.

One of the marks of our civilization, virtually unnoticed as we discuss the Nation's problems, is our fastest-growing industry: gambling.

Local governments, Indian tribes, and States—all desperate for revenue—increasingly are turning to what appears to be a quick and easy solution: legalized gambling. And, temporarily, it often works. Poverty-stricken Indian tribes suddenly have revenue. Cities like East St. Louis, IL, with every possible urban malady, find themselves with enough revenue to at least take care of minimal services.

There are four basic questions:

First, how rapidly is this phenomenon growing?

Second, what are its advantages?

Third, what are it disadvantages,

Fourth, is there a role for the Federal Government to play, and should it play a role?

Gambling is not a new phenomenon. The Bible and early historical records tell of its existence. Gambling surfaced early in U.S. history, then largely disappeared as a legal form of revenue for State and local governments. It remained very much alive, however, even though illegal, in the back rooms of taverns and in not-so-hidden halls, often with payoffs to public officials to "look the other way" while it continued.

. . . Early in our Nation's history, almost all States had some form of lottery, my State of Illinois being no exception. When Abraham Lincoln served in our State legislature from 1834 to 1842, lotteries were authorized, and there apparently was no moral question raised about having them. . . . In Illinois and other States the loose money quickly led to corruption, and the States banned all forms of gambling. Illinois leaders felt so strongly about it, they put the ban into the State constitution. For many years, Louisiana had the only lottery, and then in 1893—after a major scandal there—the Federal Government prohibited all lottery sales. Even the results of tolerated but illegal lotteries could not be sent through the mail. But the lottery crept back in, first in New Hampshire in 1963, and then in 36 other States. Last year States sold $34 billion in lottery tickets. Forty-two States now have some form of legalized gambling.

. . . What we know as casino gambling was legal only in Nevada, then in New Jersey and now in 23 States. From a small enterprise in a few States, gambling has matured. In 1974, $17 billion was legally wagered in the Nation. By 1992, it reached $329 billion, and it is now over $500 billion. Three-fourths of the Nation's citizens now live within 300 miles of a casino. One article reports, "Airlines are exploring the installation of back-of-seat slot machines on some flights." Other nations—particularly poorer ones—are expanding gambling operations. Within our country, the magazine *Gaming and Wagering Business* reports, "Old attitudes have been shattered. Barriers are crumbling, and doors have been flung open." (Dec. 15, 1991–Jan. 15, 1992.)

. . . Indian reservations have misery as their constant companion. Unemployment rates, and poverty indexes all combine to paint a grim picture that should be a matter of shame for our Nation. Not only has the Federal Government been weak in its response to these needs, but State governments, sometimes dominated by prejudice against Native Americans, often have been even worse. Listen to this Department of Health and Human Services report, given to a Senate committee this year: "In 15 of the 24 states with the largest Native American populations, eligible Tribes receiving nothing in 1993 from the more than $3 billion in Federal funds (Title XX and Title IV-E child welfare services and protection programs) the States received. In the other nine States, Indians received less than three percent (George Crob, Deputy Inspector General, HHS, April 5, 1995, Senate Committee on Indian Affairs.) It should not surprise anyone that tribal leaders who want to produce for their people seize what some view as a legal loophole that our courts and laws have created to get revenue for their citizens; 115 tribes now have some form of casino gambling. The gross revenue for the 17 tribes in Wisconsin is $655 million. And about one-fifth of that revenue comes from people who live outside of Wisconsin, higher than in most States, much lower than Nevada or Atlantic City. Connecticut is the prime example of a small tribe gaining big money. A casino operated by the Mashantucket Pequot Tribe in Ledyard, CT, brings in approximately $800 million in gross revenue annually. Native American leaders who see long-term harm to their tribes from the gambling enterprises are hard-pressed by those who see immediate benefits, and not too much hope for sizable revenue outside of gambling.

. . . Gambling addiction is a serious problem. We know that men are more likely to become addicted than women, that the appeal of gambling is greater for low-income people than those of above average income, that there are approximately 9 million adults and 1.3 million teenagers with some form of gambling behavior problem and that the availability of gambling enterprises—their closeness to where a person lives—causes a significant increase in the addiction problem. Nationally, less than 1 percent, 0.77 percent, of the population are compulsive gamblers, but when enterprises are located near a population, that number increases two to seven times. The greatest growth is among teenagers.

. . . The suicide rates for problem gamblers is significantly higher than it is for the general population. One out of five attempt suicide, a higher rate than for alcoholism or drug addiction. Pathological gamblers are much more likely to be violent with their spouses and abuse their children. Children of these gamblers generally do worse in school and have a suicide rate twice that of their classmates.

A survey of compulsive gamblers found 22 percent divorced because of gambling, 40 percent had lost or quit a job due to gambling, 49 percent stole from work to pay gambling debts, 23 percent alcoholic, 26 percent compulsive overeaters, 63 percent had contemplated suicide and 79 percent said they wanted to die. (Henry Lesieur and Christopher Anderson.)

Treatment for gambling compulsion is rarely covered by health insurance policies, though physicians often will simply list depression as the cause for needed therapy, and that may be covered.

Let a commission look at where we are and where we should go. My instinct is that sensible limits can be established. For example, what if any new gambling enterprise established after a specific date had to pay a tax of 5 percent on its gross revenue? Those who are already in the field who are not too greedy should support it because it prevents the saturation of the market. . . . Or suppose we were to move to some form of supplement to local and State revenue again? States, Indian tribes, and local governments that do not have any form of legalized gambling would be eligible for per capita revenue-sharing assistance. It would require creating a source of revenue for such funding, but would bring some relief to non-Federal governments who do not want gambling but are desperate for additional revenue. There is no way—let me underscore this—of reducing the gambling problem without facing the local revenue problem.[15]

Elia and Jacobs examined the prevalence rate of potential and pathological gambling in a 1991 survey of American Indians and whites being treated in a veterans' hospital in South Dakota. The eighty-five patients in their sample were being treated primarily for alcohol problems. American Indians had nearly twice the proportion (41% to 2%) of substance abusers who were also addicted to gambling.[16] The Seminole Tribe of Florida, one of the first to incorporate gaming as a means of tribal economic development, bans compulsive gamblers from its gaming establishments. Other tribes might want to adopt this model in an attempt to prevent gambling addiction at their casinos.[17] The editor of *The Cherokee One Feather* wrote an editorial about compulsive gambling eighteen months prior to the opening of Harrah's mega-casino on the reservation. Martin noted that Harrah's has a staff training program, "Operation Bet

Smart," where employees learn to provide information and assistance to their guests who they think might be getting in over their heads: "They refer the guests to various programs or help lines. The National Council on Problem Gambling is one of the sources they will refer them to. They also place brochures on the subject near the cashier cages, visitor centers and anywhere else brochures may be found." Martin noted that there are no such groups or activities in the Cherokee area for problem gamblers.[18]

What is confusing here is the loose definition of *pathological gambling*. "Problem gambling" is a better term for the seemingly irresponsibility of Indians and non-Indians who spend more than they should on gambling. According to DSM-IV, pathological gambling is an "Impulse-Control Disorder Not Elsewhere Classified," along with intermittent explosive disorder, kleptomania, pyromania, and trichotillomania. The essential feature of these disorders is the failure to resist an internal impulse, drive, or temptation to engage in the particular of behavior. It has little to do with a plan to get rich quick.

The individual may be preoccupied with gambling (e.g., reliving past gambling experiences, planning the next gambling venture, or thinking of ways to get money with which to gamble). Most individuals with Pathological Gambling say that they are seeking "action" (an arousal, euphoric state) even more than money. Increasingly larger bets, or greater risks, may be needed to continue to produce the desired level of excitement. Individuals with Pathological Gambling often continue to gamble despite repeated efforts to control, cut back, or stop the behavior. There may be restlessness or irritability when attempting to cut down or stop gambling.[19]

DSM-IV notes that there are cultural variations in types of gambling activities, including Chinese pai go, cockfights, horse racing, and the stock market. About one-third of individuals diagnosed as pathological gamblers are females. Moreover, females with the pathological gambling disorder are more likely also to be depressed. Females with this disorder are also grossly underrepresented in treatment programs, including Gamblers Anonymous. Current clinical research indicates that the prevalence of pathological gambling may be as high as 1 to 3 percent of the adult population. This disorder usually begins in early adolescence in males, later in life in females. Stress and depression can exacerbate the condition. However, the most common comorbid clinical picture is that of pathological gambling and alcohol dependence. Pathological gambling needs to be distinguished from characterologic flaws, social gambling, professional gambling, and a loss of judgment during a manic episode secondary to Type I or II bipolar disorders.

Marginal Indians are likely to be better represented among Native

Americans with a substance abuse problem, with alcohol being the most abused substance. Substance abuse, coupled with a stressful life and bouts of depression, provides a clinical picture where irresponsible gambling is likely. Among non-Indian patrons of Indian gaming facilities, the largest group of gamblers in Indian country, problem gambling is more likely to occur than of pathological gambling. Someone who gets caught up in the casino environment and unwisely spends his or her money due either to excitement or the chance of getting rich quick is not diagnosable as a pathological gambler. Unfortunately, many confuse poor socialization skills and behavioral control with pathological gambling.

Pathological gambling is not synonymous with poor frontal-lobe executive functioning, per se. Impulse-control disorders involve subcortical urges with dysregulation in both the greater limbic and endocrine systems. The thinking and reasoning part of the central nervous system, the cortex—notably the frontal lobe—plays only a secondary role in this CNS dysregulation. This is a critical distinction with respect to prevention and treatment issues. In this sense, pathological gambling involves the same mechanism of action that is involved in impulsive behaviors associated with PTSD. Intervention is critical to any reduction in this cycle of abuse within Indian country, and it needs to begin prior to the fetus's being compromised by the stress associated with psychocultural marginality and the popular form of self-medication—alcohol abuse. Prevention of substance addiction, PTSD, bouts of depression and chain smoking, excessive caffeine use, and problematic gambling become difficult if the Native American's neurophysiology has been already compromised by FAS.

Clearly, the single most significant treatment focus in Indian country should be promoting a healthy sense of tribal traditionalism, coupled with tribe-centered efforts at reducing paternal drinking and the incidence of fetal alcoholism. This will not be an easy task as long as public policy continues to support cultural genocide. The dominant society needs to lose its Christian-based (protestant ethic) ethnocentrism and missionary zeal in dealing with Native Americans and become more tolerant of other cultural orientations. Only then can American Indians and Alaska Natives break the stigma associated with their traditional heritage and get back to a physically and mentally healthier lifestyle. Until then, treatment will be reactive. Tribe-specific twelve-step programs, traditional rituals (purifications sweats, corn pollen blessings, medicine wheels, vision quests, peyote sacraments, round dances, singings, sun dances, etc.), and the participation of respected elders within the schools illustrate a few programs that are helpful in retroactive preventive and treatment strategies.

These Native-run programs have recently shown promise in reducing inhalant use and alcohol abuse, but the need to be more widely used, not relegated to adjunct status, as it stands now in IHS-funded programs. Native-run prevention and treatment programs need to become the primary focus in Indian country and not merely discarded as a hindrance to the Christian conversion treatment model so prevalent in so-called treatment programs like the Unity IHS RYTC in Cherokee, North Carolina.

The science-practitioner and Native traditional models can operate effectively together, especially when the division of labor is such that the science-practitioner aspects pertain to assessment, evaluation, and diagnoses while the Native, traditional approach is utilized in intervention, prevention, and treatment. Some medical interventions, including psychopharmacology, can be used to augment the Native treatment approach. Clinical psychopharmacology is not necessarily contrary to Native cures, in that more is being learned about the psychoactive and medical uses of traditional plants and herbs including their mechanisms of action. At any rate, impulsive behaviors, notably those secondary to fetal alcoholism and pervasive psychocultural stress—such as PTSD, substance-abuse disorders, and pathological gambling—respond best to an agent that diminishes the excessive impulses stemming from the subcortical emotional portions of the CNS (greater limbic and endocrine systems) while at the same time augmenting the serotonergic activity in the dense neuronet within the frontal lobe.

Western-type medicines for subcortical urges include mood stabilizers such as lithium, Depakote (divalproex or valporic acid), and Tegretol (carbamazapine). In some cases, beta blockers are used in an attempt to keep the sympathic mode of the autonomic nervous system from activating. Select serotonin reuptake inhibitors (SSRIs), such as Prozac (fluoxetine), Zoloft (sertraline), Paxil (paroxetine), and Luvox (fluvoxamine), are indicated for frontal-lobe augmentation and regulation of other relevant neurotransmitter, such as norepinephrine and dopamine. Buspar (buspirone) is often used for long-term anxiety as well as depression. Other new medications may also be indicated if a client is not responsive to any of these combinations. However, it is important to distinguish between PRN (as needed) medication and that needed for steady-state blood levels. All the medications mentioned above are steady-state agents; even this, however, does not mean that they have to be used forever. Research has indicated that neurocompensation occurs when medications are coupled with relevant therapies.

Hence, medications coupled with a viable Native traditional treatment plan can result in eventual discontinuation of the medications once the CNS compensates for the initial dysregulation. It is important that the client not discontinue his or her prescribed medicines, including herbal remedies, without the consent and knowledge of the primary therapist. Abrupt discontinuation can result in a rebound effect, whereby the initial condition being treated reappears, (refractory rebound) but in a more extreme state—one that may be difficult to treat again.

NOTES

INTRODUCTION

1. P. C. Rivers, *Alcohol and Human Behavior, Theory, Research, and Practice* (Englewood Cliffs, NJ: Prentice-Hall, 1994); and Laurence A. French, *The Winds of Injustice: American Indians and the U.S. Government* (New York: Garland, 1994).

2. T. L. Taylor, *Improving the Health of Native Americans* (Princeton, NJ: Robert Wood Johnson Foundation, 1991); and E. Gordis, "Alcohol and Minorities," *Alcohol Alert 23 (PH 347)* (Rockville, MD: NIH, January, 1994).

3. D. Schultz and S. E. Schultz, *Theories of Personality*, 6th Ed. (Pacific Grove, CA: Brooks/Cole, 1998).

4. M. Weber, *The Protestant Ethic and the Spirit of Capitalism* (T. Parsons, trans.) (New York: Charles Scribner's Sons, 1930); and Laurence A. French and Jim Hornbuckle, *The Cherokee Perspective* (Boone, NC: Appalachian Consortium Press, 1981).

5. Laurence A. French, *Counseling American Indians* (Lanham, MD: University Press of America, 1997).

CHAPTER 1: THE ABORIGINAL WORLDVIEW AND LIFESTYLE

1. Laurence A. French and Jim Hornbuckle, *The Cherokee Perspective* (Boone, NC: Appalachian Consortium Press, 1981), 12–13.

2. Max Weber, *The Protestant Ethic and the Spirit of Capitalism* (T. Parsons, trans.) (New York: Charles Scribner's Sons, 1930).

3. Laurence A. French, *The Winds of Injustice: American Indians and the U.S. Government* (New York: Garland, 1994).

4. P. Holder, *The Hoe and the Horse on the Plains: A Study of Cultural Development among North American Indians* (Lincoln: Univ. of Nebraska Press, 1970).

5. J. Mooney, *Myths of the Cherokee and Sacred Formulas of the Cherokees.* (Nashville, TN: Charles Elder, 1972).

6. J. Adair, *History of the American Indians* (S. Williams, ed.) (Johnson City: East Tennessee Univ. Press, 1930).

7. Laurence A. French, "The Early Cherokee," *The Qualla Cherokee Surviving in Two Worlds* (Lewiston, NY: Edwin Mellen Press, 1998), 23–61.

8. Ibid., 23–32.

9. French and Hornbuckle, (Chapter 1) "The Cherokees—Then and Now," in *The Cherokee Perspective* 3–14.

10. Ibid., 5–8.

CHAPTER 2: ABORIGINAL USES OF PSYCHOACTIVE AGENTS

1. Laurence A. French, "Indian Marginality," *The Winds of Injustice: American Indians and the U.S. Government* (New York: Garland, 1994), 143–178.

2. James Mooney, "The Sacred Formulas of the Cherokees," *Seventh Annual Report of the Bureau of Ethnology to the Secretary of the Smithsonian Institute 1885–86* (J. W. Powell, dir.) (Washington, DC: Government Printing Office, 1891), 424.

3. Ibid., 423.

4. J. E. Brown, *The Sacred Pipe: Black Elk's Account of the Seven Rites of the Oglala Sioux* (Norman: Univ. of Oklahoma Press, 1953).

5. J. Wilbert, "Tobacco and Shamanistic Ecstasy among the Warao Indians of Venezuela," *Flesh of the Gods: The Ritual Use of Hallucinogens* (P. T. Furst, ed.) (New York: Praeger, 1972), 57.

6. Ibid., 60.

7. Public Law 103–344, *American Indian Religious Freedom Act Amendments of 1994* (103d Congress of USA, Second Session, January 25, 1994), H.R. 4230–3.

8. R. E. Schultes, "An Overview of Hallucinogens in the Western Hemisphere," *Flesh of the Gods: The Ritual Use of Hallucinogens* (P. T. Furst, ed.) (New York: Praeger, 1972), 13.

9. Peter T. Furst, "To Find Our Life: Peyote among the Huichol Indians of Mexico," *Flesh of the Gods: The Ritual Use of Hallucinogens* (New York: Praeger, 1972), 151.

10. Ibid., 420–427.

11. Schultes, 31–32.

CHAPTER 3: FEDERAL POLICIES AND MARGINALITY

1. R. Snake, "Snyder Act of 1921," *Report on Alcohol and Drug Abuse (Task Force Eleven: Alcohol and Drug Abuse). First Report to the American Indian Policy Review Commission* (Washington, DC: Government Printing Office, 1976), 31–32.

2. Ibid.

3. Ibid., 32–33.

4. Snake, Issues, Problems, and Recommendations in the Indian Alcoholism and Drug Abuse Field, 13.

5. E. R. Rhoades, "Historical and Legal Review (Cpt. 4)," *Report on Indian Health (Task Force Six: Indian Health) Final Report to the American Indian Review Commission* (Washington, DC: Government Printing Office, 1976), 27.

6. A. Jackson, *First Annual Message to Congress* (Washington, DC: *Congressional Record*, December 8, 1829), 1.

7. *Indian Removal Act* (*U.S. Statutes at Large*, 4: 411–12, May 28, 1830), 411.

8. W. Medill, *Annual Report to the Commissioner of Indian Affairs* (Washington, DC: House Executive Document No. 1, 30th Congress, Second Session, Serial 537, November 30, 1848: 385–389), 385.

9. Stephanson Anders, *Manifest Destiny* (New York: Hill and Wang, 1995); and Laurence A. French, "A Review of U.S./Indian Policy: A Unique Chapter in U.S. History," *Free Inquiry in Creative Sociology* 25, no. 2 (1997): 169–177.

10. J.D.C. Atkins, *Annual Report of the Commissioner of Indian Affairs* (Washington, DC: House Executive Document No. 1, 49th Congress, Second Session, Serial 2467, September 28, 1886: 81–82, 86–88), 81–82.

11. G. Shirley, *Law West of Fort Smith: A History of Frontier Justice in the Indian Territory, 1834–1896* (Lincoln; Univ. of Nebraska Press, 1968).

12. *Indian Citizenship Act* (*U.S. Statutes at Large*, 43: 253, June 24, 1924).

13. Lewis Meriam, *The Problem of Indian Administration* (Baltimore: Johns Hopkins Univ. Press, 1928).

14. *Johnson-O'Malley Act* (*U.S. Statutes at Large*, 48: 596, April 16, 1934).

15. *Wheeler-Howard Act (Indian Reorganization Act)* (*U.S. Statutes at Large*, 48: 984–988, June 18, 1934).

16. J. S. Sando, *The Pueblo Indians* (San Francisco: Indian Historian Press, 1976).

17. *House Concurrent Resolution 108* (*U.S. Statutes at Large*, 67: B132, August 1, 1953).

18. D. L. Fixico, *Termination and Relocation: Federal Indian Policy, 1945–1960* (Albuquerque: Univ. of New Mexico Press, 1992).

19. R. Costo and J. Henry, *Indian Treaties: Two Centuries of Dishonor* (San Francisco: Indian Historian Press, 1977), 41.

20. Public Law 93–638, *Indian Self-Determination and Education Assistance Act* (*U.S. Statutes at Large*, 88: 2203–2214, January 4, 1975), 2203.

21. Public Law 94–437, *Indian Health Care Improvement Act* (*U.S. Statutes at Large*, 90: 1400–1407, 1410–1412, September 30, 1976), 1402.

22. Public Law 99–570, *The Indian Alcohol and Substance Abuse Prevention Act of 1986* (H.R. 5484, 99th Congress, Second Session, Section 4201, 100 STAT: 3207-1-133, October 27, 1986), 1.

23. Ibid., 137.

24. U.S. Senate, "Part One: The Executive Summary: A New Federalism for American Indians," *Final Report and Legislative Recommendations: A Report of the Special Committee on Investigations of the Select Committee on Indian Affairs, United States Senate* (101st Congress, First Session, S.Prt 101–60, November 1989), 3–4.

CHAPTER 4: PSYCHOCULTURAL FACTORS

1. W. LeBeau, "Juvenile Justice Detention Issues in Indian Country," paper presented at the Strategic Planning Meeting on Crime and Justice Research in Indian Country, Portland, Oregon, on October 14, 1998. (Program sponsored by U.S. Department of Justice, Office of Justice Programs, National Institute of Justice, Office of Juvenile Justice and Delinquency Prevention, and American Indian and Alaska Native Affairs Office), 1–15.

2. Laurence A. French, "Politics of Tribal Survival," *The Winds of Injustice: American Indians and the U.S. Government* (New York: Garland, 1994), 169–178.

3. Laurence A. French, "The History of the Qualla Cherokee," in *The Qualla Cherokee: Surviving in Two Worlds* (Lewiston, NY: Edwin Mellen Press, 1998), 63–94.

4. Ibid., 23–31.

5. Laurence A. French, "The Sioux," *Psychocultural Change and the American Indian: An Ethnohistorical Analysis* (New York: Garland, 1987), 93–97.

6. Everett R. Rhoades, "The History of Federal Involvement in Health Care to the Indians," *Report on Indian Health (Task Force Six: Indian Health)* (Washington, DC: American Indian Policy Review Commission, Government Printing Office, 1976), 27–32.

7. Reuben Snake, "Snyder Act of 1921," *Report on Alcohol and Drug Abuse (Task Force Eleven: Alcohol and Drug Abuse)* (Washington, DC: American Indian Policy Review Commission, Government Printing Office, 1976), 31–33.

8. Public Law 94–437, *Indian Health Care Improvement Act* (94th Congress S. 522, 25 USC 1601, September 30, 1976, 90 STAT: 1400–1414).

9. P. C. Rivers, "Sociocultural Factors in Alcohol Use and Abuse," in *Alcohol and Human Behavior: Theory, Research, and Practice* (Englewood Cliffs, NJ: Prentice-Hall, 1994), 156–180; and E. H. Mizruchi and R. Perrucci, "Norm Qualities and Differential Effects of Deviant Behavior: An Exploratory Analysis," *American Sociological Review* 27 (1962): 391–399.

10. *Indian Intercourse Act (U.S. Statutes at Large, 4: 564, July 9, 1832).*

11. Laurence A. French, "Indian Marginality," in *The Winds of Injustice*, 143–151.

12. *Indian Intercourse Act,* 564

13. Snake, "Snyder Act of 1921," 32–33.

14. E. M. Jellinek, "The World and Its Battle," *World Health* 10, no. 4 (1957): 4–6.

15. M. B. First, *Diagnostic and Statistical Manual of Mental Disorders*, Fourth Edition (DSM-IV) (Washington, DC: American Psychiatric Association Press, 1994).

16. Laurence A. French, "The Aboriginal Harmony Ethos," *The Winds of Injustice*, 5–14.

17. Laurence A. French, *The Qualla Cherokee Surviving in Two Worlds*, 79, 125.

18. Erik Erikson, *Identity: Youth and Crisis* (New York: Norton, 1968).

19. French, Laurence A. "Native American Alcoholism: A Transcultural Counseling Perspective," *Counselling Psychology Quarterly* 2, no. 2 (1989): 153–166.

20. N. Finkelstein, "The Changing Needs of Today's Addicted Woman," *The Counselor* 8 (1990): 21–23.

21. First, *Diagnostic and Statistical Manual of Mental Disorders*, Fourth Edition, 317–444, 477–492, 629–674.

22. Finkelstein, "Changing Needs," 21–23.

23. L. Weiner, B. Morse, and P. Garrdio. "FAS/FAE: Focusing Prevention on Women at Risk," *International Journal of Addictions* 24 (1989): 385–395.

24. Laurence A. French, "Breaking the FAS Cycle of Abuse," *The Winds of Injustice*, 214–221.

25. First, "Posttraumatic Stress Disorder," *Diagnostic and Statistical Manual of Mental Disorders*, Fourth Edition, 424–429.

26. "Addictions '98: Comorbidity across the Addictions." Symposium, September 25–27, 1998, Newcastel-upon-Tyne, United Kingdom; and P. M. Miller and Michael Hersen, "Annual Review of Addictions Research and Treatment," *Addictive Behaviors: An International Journal* 23, no. 6 (1998): 715–946.

27. Laurence A. French, "Neuropsychology of Violence," *Corrective and Social Psychiatry* 37, no. 1 (1991): 12–17.

28. T. J. Guilmette, "Autobiographical Memory," *Pocket Guide to Brain Injury, Cognitive, and Neurobehavioral Rehabilitation* (San Diego, CA: Singular, 1997), 64.

29. M. Dorris, *The Broken Cord* (New York: Harper & Row, 1989).

30. B. S. Nelson and D. W. Wright, "Understanding and Treating Post-Traumatic Stress Disorder Symptoms in Female Partners of Veterans with PTSD," *Journal of Marital and Family Therapy* 22, no. 4 (1996): 455–467; and E. Duran and B. Duran, *Native American Postcolonial Psychology* (Albany: State Univ. of New York Press, 1995).

CHAPTER 5: STUDIES ON SUBSTANCE ABUSE IN INDIAN COUNTRY

1. Joan Weibel-Orlando, "American Indians and Prohibition: Effect Or Affect? Views from the Reservation and the City," *Contemporary Drug Problems* (New York: Federal Legal, 1990), 293–322.

2. Ibid., 302.

3. S. F. Black et al., "Alcohol Abuse and Alcoholism," *The Farmington Report: A Conflict of Cultures* (Sante Fe: New Mexico Advisory Committee to the U.S. Commission on Civil Rights, July 1975), 139–143.

4. Ibid., 143–146.

5. R. Barker, *The Broken Circle: A True Story of Murder and Magic in Indian Country* (New York: Ballantine Books, 1992).

6. Black et al., 143.

7. Ibid., 144.

8. M. Haederle, "Quiet Nights of Despair," *Arizona Republic* 101 (1990): C1–C3.

9. B. H. Ellis, Jr., *Taking the Long View: A Review of Substance Abuse–Related Social Indicators in McKinley County, New Mexico* (Albuquerque, NM: Fighting Back National Program, 1994), 1, 2.

10. Ibid., 35.

11. "Senator: Indians' Lives Not Improving," *Albuquerque Journal* 118, no. 298 (1998): B9.

12. T. J. Cole, "Against the Iron Horse," *Albuquerque Journal* 118, no. 291 (1998): A1, A10.

13. Laurence A. French, "A Review of U.S./Indian Policy: A Unique Chapter in U.S. History," *Free Inquiry in Creative Sociology* 25, no. 2 (1997): 169–177.

14. Joan Weibel-Orlando, 293–321.

15. Enoch Gordis, "Alcohol and the Liver," *Alcohol Alert 19 (PH 329)* (January 1993): 1–4; "Alcohol and Nutrition," *Alcohol Alert 22 (PH 346)* (October 1993): 1–4; "Alcohol and Hormones," *Alcohol Alert 26 (PH 352)* (October 1994): 1–4; "Alcohol and Tolerance," *Alcohol Alert 28, (PH 356)* (April 1995): 1–4.

16. T. M. Pinkert, *Consequences of Maternal Drug Abuse (Research Monograph 59)* (Rockville, MD: DHHS Publication no. ADM 87-1400, 1987); M. M. Kilbey and A. Khursheed, *Methodological Issues in Epidemiological, Prevention, and Treatment Research on Drug-Exposed Women and Their Children (Research Monograph 117)* (Rockville, MD: DHHS Publication no. ADM 92–1881, 1992); and W. A. Hunt and S. Zakhari, *Stress, Gender, and Alcohol-Seeking Behavior, (Research Monograph 29)* (Rockville, MD: NIH Publication no. 95–3893, 1995).

17. F. E. Lancaster, *Alcohol and Glial Cells (Research Monograph 27)* (Rockville, MD: NIH Publication no. 94–3742, 1994); W. A. Hunt and S. J. Nixon, *Alcohol-Induced Brain Damage (Research Monograph 22)* (Rockville, MD: NIH Publication no. 93–3549, 1993); C. W. Sharp, F. Beauvais, and R. Spence, *Inhalant Abuse (Research Monograph 129)* (Rockville, MD: NIH Publication no. 93–3480, 1992); S. E. Martin, *Alcohol and Interpersonal Violence (Research Monograph 24)* (Rockville, MD: NIH Publication no. 93–3496, 1993); R. Zucker, B. Gayle, and J. Howard, *The Development of Alcohol Problems (Research Monograph 26)* (Rockville, MD: NIH Publication no. 94–3495, 1994); and M. R. De la Rosa, and J. L. Recio Adrados (editors), *Drug Abuse among Minority Youth (Research Monograph 130)* (Rockville, MD: NIH Publication no. 93–3479, 1993).

18. J. King and J. F. Thayer, "Examining Conceptual Models for Understanding Drug Use Behavior among American Indian Youth," *Drug Abuse among Minority Youth (Research Monograph 130)* (De La Rosa and Recio Adrados, eds.). (Rockville, MD: NIH Publication no. 93–3479, 1993), 129–143.

19. Enoch Gordis, "Alcohol and Minorities," *Alcohol Alert*, 1.

20. Ibid., 3, 4.

21. R. W. Blum et al., "American Indian—Alaska Native Youth Health," *JAMA* 267, no. 12 (1992): 1637–1644.

22. L. Burd and M.E.K. Moffatt, "Epidemiology of Fetal Alcohol Syndrome in American Indians, Alaskan Natives, and Canadian Aboriginal Peoples: A Review of the Literature," *Public Health Reports* 109, no. 5 (1994): 688–693.

23. F. Beauvais, "Trends in Drug Use among American Indian Students and Dropouts, 1975 to 1994," *American Journal of Public Health* 86, no. 11 (1996): 1594–1598.

24. P. A. May, "The Epidemiology of Alcohol Abuse among American Indians: The Mythical and Real Properties," *American Indian Culture and Research Journal* 18, no. 2 (1994): 121–143.

25. M. H. Kaufman, "The Teratogenic Effects of Alcohol following Exposure during Pregnancy, and Its Influence on the Chromosome Constitution of the Pre-ovulatory Egg," *Alcohol and Alcoholism* 32, no. 2 (1997): 113–128.

26. K.S.D. Kopera-Frye and A. P. Streissguth, "Impairments of Number Pro-

cessing Induced by Prenatal Alcohol Exposure," *Neuropsychologia* 34, no. 12 (1996): 1187–1196.

27. S. N. Mattson et al., "A Decrease in the Size of the Basal Ganglia in Children with Fetal Alcohol Syndrome," *Alcoholism: Clinical and Experimental Research* 20, no. 6 (1996): 1088–1093.

28. M. W. Church and J. A. Kaltenbach, "Hearing, Speech, Language, and Vestibular Disorders in the Fetal Alcohol Syndrome: A Literature Review," *Clinical and Experimental Research* 21, no. 3 (1997): 495–512.

29. W. M. Kaneko et al., "Auditory Event-Related Potentials in Fetal Alcohol Syndrome and Down's Syndrome Children," *Alcoholism: Clinical and Experimental Research* 20, no. 1 (1996): 35–42.

30. C. M. Fleming, "Cultural Formulation of Psychiatric Diagnosis," *Culture, Medicine and Psychiatry* 20, no. 2 (1996): 145–154.

31. M. H. Irwin and S. Roll, "The Psychological Impact of Sexual Abuse of Native American Boarding-School Children," *American Academy of Psychoanalysis* 23, no. 3 (1995): 461–473.

32. Laurence A. French, *Counseling American Indians* (Lanham, MD: University Press of America, 1997).

33. J. King et al., "A Structural Equation Model of Factors Related to Substance Use among American Indian Adolescents," *Drugs & Society* 6, (1992): 253–268.

34. B. M. Gfellner, "A Matched-Group Comparison of Drug Use and Problem Behavior among Canadian Indian and White Adolescents," *Journal of Early Adolescence* 14, no. 1 (1994): 24–48.

35. J. Roski et al., "Psychosocial Factors Associated with Alcohol Use among Young Adolescent American Indians and Whites," *Journal of Child & Adolescent Substance Abuse* 7, no. 2 (1997): 1–18.

36. B. Finley, "Social Network Differences in Alcohol Use and Related Behaviors among Indian and Non-Indian Students, Grades 6–12," *American Indian Culture and Research Journal* 13, nos. 3 and 4 (1989): 33–48.

37. Laurence A. French and N. Picthall-French, "The Role of Substance Abuse among Rural Youth by Race, Culture and Gender," *Alcohol Treatment Quarterly* 16, no. 3 (1998): 101–108.

38. F. Beauvais, E. R. Oetting, and R. W. Edwards, "Trends in the Use of Inhalants among American Indian Adolescents," *White Cloud Journal* 3, no. 4 (1985): 3–11.

39. P. Jumper-Thurman and F. Beauvais, "Treatment of Volatile Solvent Abusers," *Inhalant Abuse: A Volatile Research Agenda* (C. W. Sharp, F. Beauvais, and R. Spence, eds.) (Rockville, MD: NIDA Research Monograph 129, 1992), 203–213.

40. P. Jumper-Thurman, "What Works' in Crime Prevention and Control: Promising Models in Indian Country," paper presented at the Strategic Planning Meeting on Crime and Justice Research in Indian Country (Portland, OR: sponsored by the U.S. Department of Justice, National Institute of Justice, Office of Juvenile Justice and Delinquency Prevention and American Indian and Alaska Native Affairs Office, October 14, 1998), 1–24.

41. M. Adrian, N. Layne, and R. T. Williams, "Estimating the Effect of Native Indian Population on County Alcohol Consumption: The Example of Ontario," *The International Journal of the Addictions* 25 (1991): 731–765; and C. Linklater,

"Comprehensive Community Approach to an Alcohol/Drug Program" (Edmonton, Alberta: 1986).

42. Adrian et al., 746, 754.

43. C. W. Duclos et al., "Prevalence of Common Psychiatric Disorder among American Indian Adolescent Detainees," *Journal of the Academy of Child Adolescent Psychiatry* 37, no. 8 (1998): 866–873.

44. E. S. Grobsmith, "The Relationship between Substance Abuse and Crime among Native American Inmates in the Nebraska Department of Corrections," *Human Organization* 48, no. 4 (1989): 285–298.

45. M. O. Howard et al., "Substance-Use and Psychiatric Disorders among American Indian Veterans," *Substance Use & Misuse* 31, no. 5 (1996): 581–598.

46. I. Chang, S. C. Lapham, and K. J. Barton, "Drinking Environment and Sociodemographic Factors among DWI Offenders," *Journal of Studies on Alcohol* 58 (1996): 659–669.

47. Laurence A. French, "MMPI Cultural Profiles of Anglos, Mexican Americans, and American-Indians in the U.S. Southwest," paper presented at the XXVI International Congress of Psychology (Montreal: August 16–21, 1996).

48. R. Bynum, "Indians, Native Alaskans Have Higher Diabetes Risk," *Albuquerque Journal* 118, October 30, 1998, A8.

49. M. P. Nowak, E. M. Sellers, and R. F. Tyndale, "Canadian Native Indians Exhibit Unique CYP2A6 and CYP2C19 Mutant Allele Frequencies," *Clinical Pharmacology & Therapeutics* 64, no. 4 (1998): 378–383.

50. Enoch Gordis, "Alcohol and the Liver Research Update," *Alcohol Alert* 42 (Rockville, MD: NIAAA Publication Distribution Center, 1998), 1–4.

CHAPTER 6: UNDERSTANDING CULTURE-SPECIFIC PRIMARY AND SECONDARY CLINICAL DIAGNOSES

1. Frances First, "Ethnic and Cultural Considerations," *Diagnostic and Statistical Manual on Mental Disorders*, Fourth Edition (DSM-IV) (Washington, DC: American Psychiatric Association Press, 1994), xxiv–xxv.

2. Ibid., Appendix C (Glossary of Technical Terms), Appendix I (Outline for Cultural Formulation), and Glossary of Culture-Bound Syndromes, 763–771, 843–849.

3. H. M. Teller, "Courts of Indian Offenses," *Annual Report of the Secretary of the Interior* (Washington, DC: House Executive Document no. 1, 48th Congress, 1st Session, serial 2190, 1883), x–xiii.

4. *Major Crimes Act* (18 U.S. U.S.C.A. 1153, *U.S. Statutes at Large*, 23: 385, March 3, 1885); and C. Gentry, *J. Edgar Hoover: The Man and His Secrets* (New York: W. W. Norton, 1991).

5. Z. Snyder-Joy, "Self-Determination and American Indian Justice" *Native Americans, Crime, and Justice* (M. O. Nielsen and R. A. Silverman, eds.) (Boulder, CO: Westview Press, 1996), 38–45.

6. D. Schultz and S. E. Schultz, "Sigmund Freud (Chapter 2) Erik Erikson (Chapter 8)," *Theories of Personality* 6th Edition (Pacific Grove, CA: Brooks/Cole, 1998), 38–80, 201–226.

7. American Psychiatric Association, *Diagnostic and Statistical Manual on Men-

tal Disorders, Third Edition; Third Edition Revised; Fourth Edition (Washington, DC: American Psychiatric Association Press, 1980; 1987; 1994); and M. K. Jones et al., *St. Anthony's Compact ICD-9-CM*, Fifth Edition (Volumes 1 and 2) (Reston, VA: St. Anthony, 1997).

8. P. T. Trzepacz and R. W. Baker, *The Psychiatric Mental Status Examination* (New York: Oxford Univ. Press, 1993).

9. K. S. Pope, J. N. Butcher, and J. Seelen, *The MMPI, MMPI-2 & MMPI-A in Court* (Washington, DC: American Psychological Association, 1993); and J. R. Graham, *MMPI-2: Assessing Personality and Psychopathology* (New York: Oxford Univ. Press, 1993).

10. Frances First, Substance-Related Disorders; Differential Diagnosis of Substance-Induced Disorders (Not including Dependence and Abuse), 175–272, 692–693. *Diagnostic and Statistical Manual on Mental Disorders—Fourth Edition* (DSM-IV). Washington, DC. American Psychiatric Association, 1994.

11. J. Lewis, R. Q. Dana, and G. A. Blevins, "Assessment and Diagnosis of Substance Use Disorders," *Substance Abuse Counseling* (Pacific Grove, CA: Brooks/Cole, 1988), 74–117; W. R. Miller and A. G. Marlatt, *Manual CDP: Comprehensive Drinker Profile* (Odessa, FL: Psychological Assessment Resources, 1984); and G. Miller, *The Substance Abuse Subtle Screening Inventory Manual* (Spencer, IN: Spencer Evening World, 1994).

12. Richard Ries, *Assessment and Treatment of Patients with Coexisting Mental Illness and Alcohol and Other Drug Abuse (TIP-9)* (Rockville, MD: U.S. Department of Health and Human Services, Publication no. SMA 95–3061, 1995); Peter O. Rostenberg, *Alcohol and Other Drug Screening of Hospitalized Trauma Patients (TIP-16)* (Rockville, MD: U.S. Department of Health and Human Services DHHS Publication no. SMA 95–3041, 1995); J. P. Allen, and M. Columbus (eds). *Assessing Alcohol Problems: A Guide for Clinicians and Researchers (NIAAA Treatment Handbook Series 4)* (Bethesda, MD: NIH Publication no. 95–3745, 1995).

13. American Psychiatric Association, *Structured Clinical Interview for DSM-IV, Patient Edition (SCID-P)* (Washington, DC: American Psychiatric Association Press, 1996).

14. J.R.T. Davidson et al., "Assessment of a New Self-Rating Scale for Post-Traumatic Stress Disorder," *Psychological Medicine* 27 (1997): 153–160.

15. R. F. Mollica et al., "The Harvard Traumatic Questionnaire," *The Journal of Nervous and Mental Disease* 180, no. 2 (1992): 111–116.

16. L. Peters et al., "The Composite International Diagnostic Interview Post-Traumatic Stress Disorder Module: Preliminary Data," *International Journal of Methods in Psychiatric Research* 6 (1996): 167–174.

17. E. R. Kandel, J. H. Schwartz, and T. M. Jessell, *Essentials of Neural Science and Behavior* (Norwalk, CT: Appleton & Lange, 1995); and B. Kolb and I. Q. Whishaw, *Fundamentals of Human Neuropsychology* (New York: W. H. Freeman, 1990).

18. M. B. First (ed.). Posttraumatic Stress Disorder. *Diagnostic and Statistical Manual on Mental Disorders—Fourth Edition (DSM-IV)* (Washington, DC: American Psychiatric Association, 1994). Hans Selye, *The Stress of Life* (New York: McGraw-Hill, 1956); and R. Plotnik, "Physiological Responses," *Introduction to Psychology*, 4th Edition. (Pacific Grove, CA: Brooks/Cole, 1996): 446–449.

19. M. S. Gazzaniga, R. B. Ivry, and G. R. Mangun, *Cognitive Neuroscience: The Biology of the Mind* (New York: W. W. Norton, 1998).

20. Kandel, Schwartz, and Jessell, 625.

21. Ibid., 626.

22. Laurence A. French, "Suicide: A Biopsychosocial Review," *The Forensic Examiner* 6, nos. 9 and 10 (1997): 11–15.

23. G. W. Lawson and C. Cooperrider (eds.), "Psychoses and Schizophrenia," *Clinical Psychopharmachology* (Rockville, MD: Aspen, 1998), 33–40.

24. R. Plotnik, "Brain's Building Blocks," *Introduction to Psychology 4th Edition* (Pacific Grove, CA: Brooks/Cole, 1996). 42–59.

25. M. J. Gitlin, *The Psychotherapists Guide to Psychopharmacology* (New York: Free Press, 1990); J. Preston, J. H. O'Neal, and M. C. Talaga, *Handbook of Clinical Psychopharmacology for Therapists* (Oakland, CA: New Harbinger, 1994); Jonathan Piel (ed.), *Mind and Brain* (New York: W. H. Freeman, 1993); and W. Stone Trevor, *Neuropharmacology* (New York: W. H. Freeman, 1995).

26. Laurence A. French, "Eagle Dancer, Apache Male: A Case Study in Ethnopsychopharmacology," *The American Journal of Pharmacopsychology* 1, no. 2 (1997): 13–15.

CHAPTER 7: CULTURAL TREATMENT CONSIDERATIONS

1. Lisa Rabasca, "Indians Need More Access to Behavioral Medicine" *APA Monitor* 29, no. 8 (1998), 38.

2. L. S. Onken et al., *Treatment of Drug-Dependent Individuals with Comorbid Mental Disorders* (Rockville, MD: NIDA Research Monograph 172, NIH Publication no. 97–4172, 1997); L. Henderson et al., *National Admissions to Substance Abuse Treatment Services: The Treatment Episode Data Set (TEDS) 1992–1996* (Rockville, MD: SAMHSA, Office of Applied Studies: Drug and Alcohol information System Series S-5, DHHS Publication no. SMA 98–3244, 1998); and J. P. Allen and Megan Columbus (eds.), *Assessing Alcohol Problems: A Guide for Clinicians and Researchers*. NIAAA Treatment Handbook Series 4, (Bethesda, MD: NIH Publication no. 95-3745, 1995).

3. Joan Weibel-Orlando, "Hooked on Healing: Anthropologists, Alcohol and intervention," *Human Organization* 48, no. 2 (1989): 148–155.

4. Public Law 99–570, *Anti-Drug Abuse Prevention Act of 1986* (H.R. 5484, 99th Congress, Second Session, Section 4,2100 100 STAT. 3207, 1–153, October 27, 1986), 133–145.

5. S. K. Clarren, D. M. Bowden, and S. Astley, "The Brain in the Fetal Alcohol Syndrome," *Alcohol Health & Research World* 10, no. 1 (1985): 20–23.

6. P. D. Connor and A. P. Steissguth. "Effects of Prenatal Exposure to Alcohol across the Life Span," *Alcohol Health & Research World* 20, no. 3 (1996): 170–174.

7. D. H. Barrett et al., "Cognitive Functioning and Posttraumatic Stress Disorder," *American Journal of Psychiatry* 153, no. 11 (1996): 1492–1494.

8. A. Bleich et al., "Post-Traumatic Stress Disorder and Depression," *British Journal of Psychiatry* 170 (1997): 479–482; and E. Y. Deykin and S. L. Buka, "Prevalence and Risk Factors for Posttraumatic Stress Disorders among Chemically

Dependent Adolescents," *American Journal of Psychiatry* 154, no. 6 (1997): 752–757.

9. Enoch Gordis, "Alcohol and Women," *Alcohol Alert 10 (PH 290)* (Rockville, MD: U.S. Department of Health and Human Services, National Institute on Alcohol Abuse and Alcoholism, 1990), 1–4.

10. Enoch Gordis, "Fetal Alcohol Syndrome," *Alcohol Alert 13 (PH 297)* (Rockville, MD: U.S. Department of Health and Human Services, NIAAA, July, 1991), 1–4.

11. Enoch Gordis, "Alcohol and Minorities," *Alcohol Alert 23 (PH 347)* (Rockville, MD: Health and Human Services, NIAAA, 1994), 1–4.

12. Philip A. May, "Fetal Alcohol Syndrome and American Indians: A Positive Challenge in Public Health and Prevention," *Mashkirki: Old Medicine Nourishing the New* (E. W. Haller and L. P. Aitken, eds.) (Lanham, MD: University Press of America, 1992): 62–68.

13. T. Prugh, "FAS among Native Americans," *Alcohol Health & Research World* 10, no. 1 (1985): 36–37.

14. R. A. LaDue and B. A. O'Hara, "Documentation of Critical Issues Related to the Comprehensive Indian Fetal Alcohol Syndrome (FAS) Prevention and Treatment Act," *Focus* 6, no. 2 (1992): 8–10.

15. Gordis, "Alcohol and Women," 1–4.

16. L. Weiner, B. A. Morse, and P. Garrido, "FAS/FAE: Focusing Prevention on Women at Risk," *The International Journal of the Addictions* 24, no. 5 (1989): 385–395.

17. Laurence A. French, "Little Hawk: The Case Study of a FAS Adoptee," *Alcoholism Treatment Quarterly* 13, no. 4 (1995): 75–82; Louise Erdrich, *The Antelope Wife* (New York: HarperCollins, 1998); and M. Dorris, *The Broken Cord* (New York: Harper & Row, 1989).

18. D. K. Novins et al., "Substance Abuse Treatment of American Indian Adolescents: Comorbid Symptomatology, Gender Differences, and Treatment Patterns," *Journal of the American Academy of Child Adolescence Psychiatry* 35, no. 12 (1996): 1593–1601.

19. R. W. Robin et al., "Factors Influencing Utilization of Mental Health and Substance Abuse Services by American Indian Men and Women," *Psychiatric Services* 48, no. 6 (1997): 826–832.

20. C. C. Brant, "Native Ethics and Rules of Behavior," *Canadian Journal of Psychiatry* 35 (1990): 534–539.

21. J. T. Garrett and M. W. Garrett, "The Path of Good Medicine: Understanding and Counseling Native American Indians," *Journal of Multicultural Counseling and Development* 22 (1994): 134–144.

22. E. N. Anderson, "A Healing Place: Ethnographic Notes on a Treatment Center," *Alcoholism Treatment Quarterly* 9, nos. 3 and 4 (1992): 1–21.

23. R. D. Walker et al., "Treatment Implications of Comorbid Psychopathology in American Indians and Alaska Natives," *Culture, Medicine, and Psychiatry* 16 (1993): 555–572.

24. M. P. Nofz, "Alcohol Abuse in Culturally Marginal American Indians," *Social Casework* 69 (1988): 67–73.

25. M. D. Terrell, "Ethnocultural Factors and Substance Abuse: Toward Cul-

turally Sensitive Treatment Models," *Psychology of Addictive Behaviors* 7, no. 3 (1993): 162–167.

26. C. A. Dolan, "A Study of the Mismatch between Native Students' Counseling Needs and Available Services," *Canadian Journal of Counseling* 29, no. 3 (1995): 234–243.

27. J. Wiebe and K. M. Huebert, "Community Mobile Treatment," *Journal of Substance Abuse Treatment* 13, no. 1 (1996): 23–31.

28. N. Dorpat, "PRIDE: Substance Abuse Education/Intervention Program," *American Indian and Alaska Native Mental Health Research* 4 (1994): 122–133.

29. K. R. VanStelle, G. A. Allen, and R. D. Moberg, "Alcohol and Drug Prevention among American Indian Families: The Family Circles Program," *Drugs & Society* 12, nos. 1 and 2 (1988): 53–60.

30. J. Navarro et al., "Substance Abuse and Spiritually: A program for Native American Students," *American Journal on Health Behavior* 21, no. 1 (1997): 3–11.

31. T. D. LaFromboise, "American Indian Mental Health Policy," *American Psychologist* 43, no. 5 (1988): 388–397.

32. P. Jumper-Thurman, " 'What Works' in Crime Prevention and Control: Promising Models in Indian Country," paper presented at the Strategic Planning Meeting on Crime and Justice (Portland, OR, U.S. Department of Juvenile Justice and Delinquency Prevention, American Indian and Alaska Native Affairs Office, October 14–15, 1998), 1–14.

33. R. Vicks, Sr., L. M. Smith, and C.I.R. Herrera, "The Healing Circle: An Alternative Path to Alcoholism Recovery, *Counseling and Values* 42, no. 2 (1998): 133–141; and Laurence A. French" The 'Talking Circle' Technique: The Navajo Adaptation," *The Winds of Injustice* (New York: Garland, 1994), 208–214.

34. Weibel-Orlando, "Hooked on Healing," 148–155.

35. P. Zah, *President Peterson Zah Report to the Navajo People on the American Indian Religious Freedom Legislation* (Window Rock, AZ: Navajo Nation, October 29, 1994), 1–8.

36. J. Zion and E. B. Zion, "Hazho's Sokee'—Stay Together Nicely," *Native Americans, Crime, and Justice* (M. O. Nielsen and R. A. Silverman, eds.) (Boulder, CO: Westview Press, 1996), 96–112.

37. *Indian Inmates of the Nebraska Penitentiary v. Joseph Vitek* (U.S. District Court for the District of Nebraska, Civil No. 72-L-156, October 31, 1974); and Elizabeth S. Grobsmith, *Indians in Prison* (Lincoln: Univ. of Nebraska Press, 1994).

38. Laurence A. French, "Sioux Healing," *Counseling American Indians* (Lanham, MD: University Press of America, 1997), 111–144.

39. J. E. Brown, *The Sacred Pipe* (Norman: Univ. of Oklahoma Press, 1953).

CHAPTER 8: THE FEDERAL RESPONSE: STANDARDS AND PRACTICE GUIDELINES

1. Everett R. Rhoades, "Alcoholism/Substance Abuse Program," *Indian Health Manual (Part 3)* (Washington, DC: IHS, TN 91–3, 1993), 1–70.

2. Public Law 99–570. *Anti-Drug Abuse Prevention Act of 1986* (21 USC 801 note HR 5484, 100 SAT. 3207).

3. M. E. Lincoln, "Mental Health Programs," *Indian Health Manual (Part 3– Professional Services)* (Washington, DC: IHS, TN 93–14), 1–70.

4. Indian Health Service Alcoholism and Substance Abuse Program Branch, *Manual for Alcohol and Substance Abuse Counselors* (Washington, DC: 1994), 1–33.

5. S. H. Nelson et al., "An Overview of Mental Health Services for American Indians and Alaska Natives in the 1990s," *Hospital and Community Psychiatry* 43, no. 3 (1992): 257–261.

6. Pamela L. LeMaster and Cathleen M. Connell, "Health Education Interventions among Native Americans: A Review and Analysis," *Health Education Quarterly* 21, no. 4 (1994): 521–538.

7. A. J. Albert, et al., "Success through Interagency Cooperation in the Aberdeen Area," *Successful Strategies for Increasing Direct Health Care Quality, Accessibility, and Economy for American Indians and Alaska Natives* (Washington, DC: IHS Publication no. 95-85016, 1995), 61–62.

8. Lincoln, "Mental Health Programs," 44.

9. *History of Unity 1987–1997* (Cherokee, NC: Unity, 1998), 1–5.

10. Laurence A. French, "The Cherokee Cultural Therapy Model," *Counseling American Indians* (Lanham, MD: University Press of America, 1997), 77–110.

CHAPTER 9: INDIAN GAMING AND U.S./INDIAN POLICY

1. James Mooney, "Untsaiyi, the Gambler," *Nineteenth Annual Report of the Bureau of American Ethnology to the Secretary of the Smithsonian Institution- 1897–98 (Part 1)* (J. W. Powell, ed.) (Washington, DC: Government Printing Office, 1900), 311–314.

2. G. R. Blakey and H. Kurland, "The Development of the Federal Law of Gambling," *Cornell Law Review* 63, no. 6 (1978): 923–1021; I. Nelson Rose, *Gambling and the Law* (Los Angeles: Gambling Times, 1986); and Ronald Rychlak, "The Introduction of Casino Gambling: Public Policy and the Law," *Mississippi Law Journal* 64, no. 2 (1995): 291–362.

3. W. C. Canby, Jr., "Present Division of Criminal Jurisdiction in Indian Country," *American Indian Law* (St. Paul, MN: West, 1988), 119–142.

4. N. Abrams and S. S. Beale, "The Assimilative Crimes Act and the Special Maritime and Territorial Jurisdiction," *Federal Criminal Law*, (second edition) (St. Paul, MN: West, 1993), 671–692.

5. B. O. Bridgers, *The Cherokee Code* (Cherokee, NC: Eastern Band of Cherokee Indians 1993).

6. Glenn Shirley, "Appeals and Reversals," *Law West of Fort Smith* (Lincoln: Univ. of Nebraska Press, 1968), 139–158.

7. Issac Parker, quoted in *Oklahoma Star* (Caddo, OK) (November 2, 1876): 1.

8. Public Law 280 (*U.S. Statutes at Large*, August 15, 1953, 67: 588–90).

9. Indian Bill of Rights, *Civil Rights Act of 1968* (*U.S. Statutes at Large*, 82:77–81, April 11, 1968).

10. Abrams and Beale, "The Racketeer Influenced and Corrupt Organizations Statute," *Federal Criminal Law, Second Edition* (St. Paul, MN: West, 1993), 451–567.

11. *Snyder Act*, (*U.S. Statutes at Large*, 42: 208–209, November 2, 1921).

12. *Seminole Tribe of Florida v. Butterworth*, 658 F.2d 310 (5th Cir. 1981); *Lac du Flambeau Band v. Williquette*, 629 F. Wupp. 689 (W.D. Wis. 1986); *Lac du Flambeau*

Band of Lake Superior Chippewa Indians v. Wisconsin, 743 F. Supp. 645 (W.D. Wis. 1990); and *Oneida Tribe of Indians of Wisconsin v. State of Wisconsin*, 518 F. Supp. 719 (W.D. Wis. 1981).

13. Laurence A. French, "Reservation Ills: Gambling, Mineral Exploration, Toxic Dumps, and Water Issues," *The Winds of Injustice* (New York: Garland, 1994), 179–205.

14. *California v. Cabzon Band of Mission Indians*, 480 U.S. 202 (1987); and Public Law 280 (*U.S. Statutes at Large, 67: 588–90, August 15, 1953*).

15. *Indian Gaming Regulatory Act* (*U.S. Statutes at Large*, 102: 2467–69, 2472, 2476, October 17, 1988).

CHAPTER 10: INDIAN GAMING: SOCIAL, POLITICAL, AND CLINICAL ISSUES

1. A. Nakao, "With $70 Million, Proponents Won Right to Keep Slots," *San Francisco Examiner*, November 4, 1998: A28.

2. K. Chappell, "Black Indians Hit Jackpot in Casino Bonanza," *Ebony* 50, no. 8 (1995): 46, 48, 56; and Steve Kemper, "This Land Is Whose Land," *Yankee*, September 1998: 46–54, 120–123.

3. Laurence A. French, "Government Policy and Practices during the 'Indian War' Era," *The Winds of Injustice* (New York: Garland, 1994), 23–43.

4. "Federal Acknowledgement of Narragansett Indian Tribe of Rhode Island (February 2, 1983)," *Federal Register* 48 (February 10, 1983): 6177–6178.

5. T. A. Reeves and D. Hess, "Wall Street Signs On for Casino," *Albuquerque Journal* 115, October 1, 1995: A12.

6. C. Del Valle, "Odds Are against This Lottery," *Business Week* 3442 September 18, 1995: 6; P. N. Filzer, "Gaming Law," *National Law Journal* 18 no. 2 (1995): B5–B6; J. McTague, D.C. Current: Roll Over Sitting Bull," *Barron's*, December 26, 1994: 17; W. J. Moore, "When It Comes to Congress, Why Gamble?" *National Journal* 27, June 24, 1995. 1656–1657; F. Shafroth, "Senate Agrees to Overhaul Nation's Indian Gaming Policy," *Nation's Cities Weekly* 18 August 14, 1995: 12; and R. M. Wells, "Bill Would Widen Federal Role in Regulating Gambling," *Congressional Quarterly Weekly Report* 53, August 12, 1995: 2445.

7. B. O. Bridgers, "Gaming," *The Cherokee Code* (Cherokee, NC: Eastern Band of Cherokee Indians, 1993), 65–74.

8. French, *Winds of Injustice* (Chapter Three), 23–43; Laurence A. French, "The Navajo Beauty Way Perspective," *Counseling American Indians* (Lanham, MD: University Press of America, 1997), 145–177; and C. Kluckholn and D. Leighton, *The Navajo* (Cambridge, MA: Harvard Univ. Press, 1946).

9. T. P. Tinnin, *American Indians in New Mexico and Their Neighbors: Building Bridges of Understanding* (Albuquerque: New Mexico First, 1998), 60–62, 85–86.

10. Dan A. Cozzetto, "The Economic and Social Implications of Indian Gaming," *American Indian Culture & Research Journal* 19, no. 1 (1995): 119–131.

11. French, *Winds of Injustice* (Chapter Eight), 179–189.

12. Bill Lueders, "Buffaloed," *Progressive* 58 (August 1994): 30–33.

13. Cozzetto, 119–131.

14. B. N. Campbell, "The Foxwood Myth," *New York Times* March 29, 1995: A23.

15. P. M. Simon, "The Explosive Growth of Gambling in the United States," *Congressional Record*—Senate, July 31, 1995: 10912–10916.

16. C. Ellia and D. F. Jacobs, "The Incidence of Pathological Gambling among Native Americans Treated for Alcohol Dependence," *International Journal of Addictions* 28, no. 7 (1993): 659–666.

17. J. Testerman, "Seminole Indian Reservation," *St. Petersburg Times* (February 27, 1995): 1B.

18. J. Martin, "Compulsive Gambling Like Drug Addiction," *Cherokee One Feather* 30, no. 20, May 15, 1996. 1.

19. Michael B. First, "Pathological Gambling" *Diagnostic and Statistical Manual of Mental Disorders*, Fourth Edition (Washington, DC: American Psychiatric Association Press, 1994), 615–618.

BIBLIOGRAPHY

———————— ❖ ————————

Abrams, N., and S. S. Beale. "The Assimilative Crimes Act and the Special Maritime and Territorial Jurisdiction." *Federal Criminal Law*, Second Edition. St. Paul, MN: West, 1993, 671–692.

Adair, J. *History of the American Indians*. (Williams, S., ed.). Johnson City: East Tennessee Univ. Press, 1930.

Adams, E. *American Indian Education*. New York: Kings Crown Press, 1946.

Addictions '98: Comorbidity across the Addictions. Symposium held September 25–27, 1998, Newcastel-Upon-Tyne, United Kingdom.

Adrian, M., N. Layne, and R. T. Williams. "Estimating the Effect of Native Indian Population on Country Alcohol Consumption: The Example of Ontario." *The International Journal of the Addictions* 25 (1991): 731–765.

Albert, A. J., et al. "Success through Interagency Cooperation in the Aberdeen Area." *Successful Strategies for Increasing Direct Health Care Quality, Accessibility, and Economy for American Indians and Alaska Natives*. Washington, DC: IHS Publication no. 95–85016, 61–62.

Allen, J. P., and M. Columbus (eds.) *Assessing Alcohol Problems: A Guide for Clinicians and Researchers* (NIAAA Treatment Handbook Series 4) Bethesda, MD: NIH Publication no. 95–3745, 1995.

American Psychiatric Association. *Diagnostic and Statistical Manual on Mental Disorders*, Third Ed. (DSM-III) (Williams, J. B. W., ed); Third Ed. Revised (DSM-III-R); (Williams, J. B. W., ed), Fourth Edition (DSM-IV). (First F., ed.) Washington, DC: American Psychiatric Association Press, 1980; 1987; 1994.

———. *Structured Clinical Interview for DSM-IV—Patient Edition (SCID-P)*. Washington, DC: American Psychiatric Association Press, 1996.

Anderson, E. N. "A Healing Place: Ethnographic Notes on a Treatment Center." *Alcoholism Treatment Quarterly* 9, nos. 3 and 4 (1992): 1–21.

Atkins, J.D.C. *Annual Report of the Commissioner of Indian Affairs*. Washington, DC: House Executive Document no. 1, 49th Cong. 2d sess. serial 2467, September 28, 1886: 81–82, 86–88.

Barker, R. *The Broken Circle: A True Story of Murder and Magic in Indian Country*. New York: Ballantine Books, 1992.

Barrett, D. H., et al. "Cognitive Functioning and Posttraumatic Stress Disorder." *American Journal of Psychiatry* 153, no. 11 (1996): 1492–1494.

Bauer, F. B. *Land of the North Carolina Cherokee*. Brevard, NC: Buchanan Press, 1970.

Beauvais, F. Trends in Drug Use among American Indian Students and Dropouts, 1975 to 1994." *American Journal of Public Health* 86, no. 11 (1996): 1594–1598.

Beauvais, F., E. R. Oetting, and R. W. Edwards. "Trends in the Use of Inhalants among American Indian Adolescents." *White Cloud Journal* 3, no. 4 (1985): 3–11.

Black, S. F., et al. *The Farmington Report: A Conflict of Cultures*. Sante Fe: New Mexico Advisory Committee to the U.S. Commission on Civil Rights, July 1975.

Blakey, G. R., and H. Kurland. "The Development of the Federal Law of Gambling." *Cornell Law Review* 63, no. 6 (1978): 923–1021.

Bleich, A., et al. "Post-Traumatic Stress Disorder and Depression." *British Journal of Psychiatry* 170 (1997): 479–482.

Blum, R. W., et al. "American Indian—Alaska Native Youth Health." Journal of the American Medical Association (*JAMA*) 267, no. 12 (1992): 1637–1644.

Brant, C. C. "Native Ethics and Rules of Behaviour." *Canadian Journal of Psychiatry* 35 (1990): 534–539.

Bridgers, B. O. *The Cherokee Code*. Cherokee, NC: Eastern Band of Cherokee Indians, 1993.

Browder, N. C. *The Cherokee Indians and Those Who Came After*. Hayesville, NC: Land of the Big Sky Press, 1974.

Brown, D. *Bury My Heart at Wounded Knee*. New York: Bantam Books, 1970.

Brown, J. E. *The Sacred Pipe: Black Elk's Account of the Seven Rites of the Oglala Sioux*. Norman: Univ. Oklahoma Press, 1953.

Brown, J. P. *Old Frontiers*. Kingsport, TN: Southern, 1938.

Burd, L., and M.E.K. Moffatt. "Epidemiology of Fetal Alcohol Syndrome in American Indians, Alaskan Natives, and Canadian Aboriginal Peoples: A Review of the Literature." *Public Health Reports*. 109, no. 5 (1994) 688–693.

Bynum, R. Indians, "Native Alaskans Have Higher Diabetes Risk." *Albuquerque Journal*. October 30, 1998, A8.

California v. Cabzon Band of Mission Indians, 480 U.S. 202, 1987.

Campbell, B. N. "The Foxwood Myth." *New York Times*. March 29, 1995, 23.

Canby, Jr., W. C. *American Indian Law* (2d ed.). St. Paul, MN: West, 1988.

Chang, I., S. C. Lapham, and K. J. Barton. "Drinking Environment and Sociodemographic Factors among DWI Offenders." *Journal of Studies on Alcohol* 58 (1996): 659–669.

Chappell, K. "Black Indians Hit Jackpot in Casino Bonanza." *Ebony* 50, no. 8 (1995): 46, 48, 56.

Church, M. W., and J. A. Kaltenbach. "Hearing, Speech, Language and Vestibular Disorders in Fetal Alcohol Syndrome: A Literature Review." *Clinical and Experimental Research* 21, no. 3 (1997): 495–512.

Clarren, S. K., D. M. Bowden, S. Astley. "The Brain in the Fetal Alcohol Syndrome." *Alcohol Health & Research World* 10, no. 1 (1985): 20–23.

Coblentz, C. C. *Sequoyah.* New York: David McKay, 1946.

Cole, T. J. "Against the Iron Horse." *Albuquerque Journal* 118, no. 291 (1998): A1, A10.

Collier, J. *Indians of the Americas.* New York: Norton, 1947.

———. *American Indian Ceremonial Dances.* New York: Bounty Books, 1977.

Collier, P. *When Shall They Rest.* New York: Holt, Rinehart and Winston, 1973.

Connor, P. D., and A. P. Steissguth. "Effects of Prenatal Exposure to Alcohol across the Life Span." *Alcohol Health & Research World* 20, no. 3 (1996): 170–174.

Cordran, D. H. *The Cherokee Frontier: Conflict and Survival.* Norman: Univ. of Oklahoma Press, 1966.

Costo, R., and J. Henry. *Indian Treaties: Two Centuries of Dishonor.* San Francisco: Indian Historian Press, 1977.

———. *Texts and the American Indian.* San Francisco: Indian Historian Press, 1970.

Cotterill, R. S. *The Southern Indians: The Story of the Civilized Tribes before Removal.* Norman: Univ. of Oklahoma Press, 1954.

Cozzetto, D. A. "The Economic and Social Implications of Indian Gaming." *American Indian Culture & Research Journal* 19, no. 1 (1995): 119–131

Dale, F. M., and G. Little. *Cherokee Cavaliers.* Norman: Univ. of Oklahoma Press, 1939.

Daves, F. M. *Cherokee Woman.* Boston: Branden Press, 1973.

David, J., ed. *The American Indian—The First Victim.* New York: Morrow, 1972.

Davidson, J.R.T., et al. "Assessment of a New Self-Rating Scale for Post-Traumatic Stress Disorder." *Psychological Medicine* 27 (1997): 153–160.

De La Rosa, M. R., and J-L. Recio Adrados (Editors). *Drug Abuse among Minority Youth (Research Monograph 130).* Rockville, MD: NIH Publication no. 93-3479, 1993.

Del Valle, C. "Odds Are Against This Lottery." *Business Week* 3442, September 18, 1995, 6.

Deloria, Jr., V. *Behind the Trail of Broken Treaties.* New York: Dell, 1974.

Dent, F. B. 1974. *Federal and State Indian Reservations.* Washington, DC: Government Printing Office, 1974.

Deykin, E. Y., and S. L. Buka. "Prevalence and Risk Factors for Posttraumatic Stress Disorders among Chemically Dependent Adolescents." *American Journal of Psychiatry* 154, no. 6 (1997): 752–757.

Dial, A., and D. Eliades. *The Only Land I Know.* San Francisco: Indian Historian Press, 1975.

Dolan, C. A. "A Study of the Mismatch between Native Student's Counseling

Needs and Available Services." *Canadian Journal of Counseling* 29, no. 3 (1995): 234–243.

Dorpat, N. "PRIDE: Substance Abuse Education/Intervention Program." *American Indian and Alaska Native Mental Health Research* 4 (1994): 122–133.

Dorris, M. *The Broken Cord*. New York: Harper & Row, 1989.

Driver, H. *Comparative Studies of the North American Indians*. Philadelphia: American Philosophical Society, 1957.

Duclos, C. W., et al. "Prevalence of Common Psychiatric Disorders among American Indian Adolescent Detainees." *Journal of the Academy of Child Adolescent Psychiatry* 37, no. 8 (1998): 866–873.

Duran, E., and B. Duran. *Native American Postcolonial Psychology*. Albany: State Univ. of New York Press, 1995.

Eaton, R. C. *John Ross and the Cherokee Indians*. Menasha, WI: George Banta, 1914.

Eggan, F. *The American Indian: Perspectives for New Study of Social Change*. Chicago: Aldine, 1964.

Elia, C., and D. F. Jacobs. "The Incidence of Pathological Gambling among Native Americans Treated for Alcohol Dependence." *The International Journal of Addictions* 28, no. 7 (1993): 659–666.

Ellis, Jr., B. H. *Taking the Long View: A Review of Substance Abuse–Related Social Indicators in McKinley County, New Mexico*. Albuquerque, NM: Fighting Back National Program, 1994.

Erdrich, L: *The Antelope Wife*. New York: HarperCollins, 1998.

Erikson, E. *Identity: Youth and Crisis*. New York: Norton, 1968.

"Federal Acknowledgment of Narragansett Indian Tribe of Rhode Island (February 2, 1983)." *Federal Register*, February 10, 1983, 6177–6178.

Fenton, W., and J. Gulick. *Symposium on Cherokee and Iroquois Cultures*. Washington, DC: Government Printing Office, 1966.

Filler, L., ed. *The Removal of the Cherokee Nation*. Boston: Health, 1962.

Filzer, P. N. "Gaming Law." *National Law Journal* 18, no. 2 (1995): B5–B6.

Finger, J. R. *Cherokee Americans*. Lincoln: Univ. of Nebraska Press, 1991.

Finkelstein, N. "The Changing Needs of Today's Addicted Woman." *The Counselor* 8 (1990): 21–23.

Finley, B. "Social Network Differences in Alcohol Use and Related Behaviors among Indian and Non-Indian Students, Grades 6–12." *American Indian Culture and Research Journal* 13, nos. 3 and 4 (1989): 33–48.

First, M. B. *Diagnostic and Statistical Manual of Mental Disorders*, Fourth Ed. (DSM-IV). Washington, DC: American Psychiatric Association Press, 1994.

Fixico, D. L. *Termination and Relocation: Federal Indian Policy, 1945–1960*. Albuquerque: Univ. of New Mexico Press, 1992.

Fleming, C. M. "Cultural Formulation of Psychiatric Diagnosis." *Culture, Medicine and Psychiatry* 20, no. 2 (1996): 145–154.

Foreman, G. *Advancing the Frontier, 1830–1860*. Norman: Univ. of Oklahoma Press, 1933.

———. *Sequoyah*. Norman: Univ. of Oklahoma Press, 1937.

———. *Last Trek of the Indians*. Chicago: Univ. of Chicago Press, 1946.

———. *The Five Civilized Tribes*. Norman: Univ. of Oklahoma Press, 1966.

Forrest, W. *Trail of Tears*. New York: Crown Publishers, 1959.

French, Laurence A. "Missionaries among the Eastern Cherokee." *Interethnic*

Communication (E. Ross, ed.). Athens: Univ. of Georgia Press, 1978: 100–112.

———. "Native American Correctional Treatment." *Contemporary Issues in Corrections* (S. Letman et al., eds.). Cincinnati, OH: Pilgrimage, 1981: 63–78.

———. *Indians and Criminal Justice.* Totowa, NJ: Littlefield, Adams, 1982.

———. *Psychocultural Change and the American Indian* (Vol. 12, Garland Library of Sociology/Vol. 381, Garland Reference Library of Social Sciences). New York: Garland. 1987.

———. "Native American Alcoholism." *Counselling Psychology Quarterly* (Special Counselling Women and Ethnic Minority Issue) 2, no. 2 (1989): 153–166.

———. "Substance Abuse Treatment among American Indian Children." *Alcohol Treatment Quarterly* 7, no. 3 (1990): 63–76.

———. "Neuropsychology of Violence." *Corrective and Social Psychiatry* 37, no. 1 (1991): 12–17.

———. *The Winds of Injustice: American Indians and the U.S. Government.* New York: Garland, 1994.

———. "Adaptations of Aboriginal Justice in the United States." *Journal of Human Justice* 6, no. 2 (1995): 72–78.

———. "Little Hawk: The Case Study of a FAS Adoptee." *Alcoholism Treatment Quarterly* 13, no. 4 (1995): 75–82.

———. "MMPI Cultural Profiles of Anglos, Mexican-Americans, and American Indians in the U.S. Southwest." Paper presented at the XXVI International Congress of Psychology: Montreal: August 16–21, 1996.

———. "Eagle Dancer, Apache Male: A Case Study in Ethnopsychopharmacology." *The American Journal of Pharmacopsychology* 1, no. 2 (1997): 13–15.

———. *Counseling American Indians.* Lanham, MD: University Press of America, 1997.

———. "A Review of U.S./Indian Policy: A Unique Chapter in U.S. History." *Free Inquiry in Creative Sociology* 25, no. 2 (1997): 169–178.

———. "Suicide: A Biopsychosocial Review." *The Forensic Examiner* 6, nos. 9 and 10 (1997): 11–15.

———. *The Qualia Cherokee: Surviving in Two Worlds* (Vol. 5, Native American Studies). Lewiston, NY: Edwin Mellen Press, 1998.

French, Laurence A., and R. Crowe (eds.). *Wee Wish Tree: Qualla Cherokee* Issue 5, no. 1 (1976).

French, Laurence A., and Jim Hornbuckle. "Suicides Questioned by Carolina Cherokee." *Wassaja* 4, no. 5 (1976) 3.

———. "Cultural Clash in Our Educational System." *Indian Historian* 10, no. 4 (1977): 33–39.

———. "Historical Influences of Eastern Indians on Contemporary Pan-Indianism." *Indian Historian* 10, no. 2 (1977): 23–27.

———. "Analysis of Indian Violence." *American Indian Quarterly* 3, no. 4 (1977–78) 335–356.

———. "Indian Stress and Violence." *Journal of Alcohol and Drug Education* 25, no. 1 (1979): 36–43.

———. "Analysis of Indian Alcoholism." *Social Work* 25, no. 4 (1980): 275–280.

———. *The Cherokee Perspective.* Boone, NC: Appalachian Consortium Press, 1981.

French, Laurence A., and N. Picthall-French. "The role of Substance Abuse among Rural Youth by Race, Culture and Gender." *Alcohol Treatment Quarterly* 16, no. 3 (1998): 101–108.

Furst, Peter T. (ed). *Flesh of the Gods: The Ritual Use of Hallucinogens.* New York, NY: Praeger, 1972.

Garrett, J. T., and M. W. Garrett. "The Path of Good Medicine: Understanding and Counseling Native American Indians." *Journal of Multicultural Counseling and Development* 22 (1994) 134–144.

Gazzaniga, M. S., R. B. Ivry, and G. R. Mangun. *The Biology of the Mind.* New York: W. W. Norton, 1998.

Gearing, F. *Priests and Warriors.* Masasha, WI: American Anthropological Association, 1962.

Gentry, C. J. *Edgar Hoover: The Man and His Secrets.* New York: W. W. Norton, 1991.

Gfellner, B. A. "A Matched-Group Comparison of Drug Use and Problem Behavior among Canadian Indian and White Adolescents." *Journal of Early Adolescence* 14, no. 1 (1994): 24–48.

Gilbert, W. H. *The Eastern Cherokee.* Washington, DC: Government Printing Office, 1943.

Gitlin, M. J. *The Psychotherapists Guide to Psychopharmacology.* New York: Free Press, 1990.

Gordis, E. "Alcohol and Women." *Alcohol Alert 10 (PH 290).* Rockville, MD: NIH, October 1990, 1–4.

———. "Fetal Alcohol Syndrome." *Alcohol Alert 13 (PH 297).* Rockville, MD: NIH, July 1991, 1–4.

———. "Alcohol and the Liver." *Alcohol Alert 19 (PH 329).* January 1993: 1–4.

———. "Alcohol and Nutrition." *Alcohol Alert 22 (PH 346).* Rockville, MD: NIH, October 1993: 1–4.

———. "Alcohol and Minorities." *Alcohol Alert 23 (PH 347).* Rockville, MD: NIH, January 1994, 1–4.

———. "Alcohol and Hormones." *Alcohol Alert 26 (PH 352).* Rockville, MD: NIH, October 1994: NIH, 1–4.

———. "Alcohol and Tolerance." *Alcohol Alert 28 (PH 356).* Rockville, MD: NIH, April 1995: 1–4.

———. "Alcohol and the Liver: Research Update." *Alcohol Alert 42.* October 1998.

Graham, J. R. *MMPI-2: Assessing Personality and Psychopathology.* New York: Oxford Univ. Press, 1993.

Grobsmith, E. S. "The Relationship between Substance Abuse and Crime among Native American Inmates in the Nebraska Department of Corrections." *Human Organization* 48, no. 4 (1989): 285–298.

———. *Indians in Prison.* Lincoln: Univ. of Nebraska Press, 1994.

Guilmette, T. J. *Pocket Guide to Brain Injury, Cognitive, and Neurobehavioral Rehabilitation.* San Diego; Singular, 1997.

Gulick, J. *Cherokees at the Crossroads.* Chapel Hill: Univ. of North Carolina Press, 1960.

Haederle, M. "Quiet Nights of Despair." *Arizona Republic* 101 (1990) C1–C3.

Haywood, J. *Natural and Aboriginal History of Tennessee.* Nashville, TN: George Wilson, 1823.

Henderson, L., et al. *National Admissions to Substance Abuse Treatment Services: The Treatment Episode Data Set (TEDS) 1992–1996.* Rockville, MD: SAMHSA,

Office of Applied Studies: Drug and Alcohol Information System Series S-5, DHHS Publication no. SMA 98–3244, 1998.

Holder, P. *The Hoe and the Horse on the Plains: A Study of Cultural Development among North American Indians.* Lincoln: Univ. of Nebraska Press, 1970.

House Concurrent Resolution 108. U. S. Statutes at Large, 67: B132, August 1, 1953.

Howard, M. O., et al., "Substance-Use and Psychiatric Disorders among American Indian Veterans." *Substance Use & Misuse* 31, no. 5 (1996): 581–598.

Hudson, C. M., ed. *Red, White and Black.* Athens: Univ. of Georgia Press, 1973.

Hunt, W. A., and S. J. Nixon. *Alcohol-Induced Brain Damage (Research Monograph 22).* Rockville, MD: NIH Publication no. 93–3549, 1993.

Hunt, W. A., and S. Zakhari. *Stress, Gender, and Alcohol-Seeking Behavior (Research Monograph 29).* Rockville, MD: NIH Publication no. 95–3893, 1995.

Indian Bill of Rights. Civil Rights Act of 1968: U.S. Statutes at Large, 82: 77–81, April 11, 1968.

Indian Citizenship Act. U.S. Statutes at Large, 43: 253, June 24, 1924.

Indian Gaming Regulatory Act, U.S. Statutes at Large, 102: 2467–69, 2472, 2476. October 17, 1988.

Indian Health Service Alcoholism and Substance Abuse Program Branch. *Manual for Alcohol and Substance Abuse Counselors.* Washington DC: IHS, 1994, 1–33.

Indian Inmates of the Nebraska Penitentiary v. Joseph Vitek. U.S. District Court for the District of Nebraska, Civil No. 72-L-156, October 31, 1974.

Indian Intercourse Act. U.S. Statutes at Large, 4: 564, July 9, 1832.

Indian Removal Act. U.S. Statutes at Large, 4: 411–12, May 28, 1830.

Irwin, M. H., and S. Roll. "The Psychological Impact of Sexual Abuse of Native American Boarding-School Children. *American Academy of Psychoanalysis* 23, no. 3 (1995): 461–473.

Jackson, A. *First Annual Message to Congress.* Washington, DC: *Congressional Record,* December 8, 1829.

Jellinek, E. M. "The World and Its Battle." *World Health* 10, no. 4 (1957): 4–6.

Johnson, H. W. *American Indians in Transition.* Washington, DC: Department of Agriculture, 1975.

Johnson-O'Malley Act. U.S. Statutes at Large, 48: 596, April 16, 1934.

Jones, C. C. *Antiquities of Southern Indians.* New York: Appleton, 1873.

Jones, M. K., et al. *St. Anthony's Compact ICD-9-CM,* Fifth Ed. (Volumes 1 and 2). Reston, VA: St. Anthony, 1997.

Jumper-Thurman, P. " 'What Works' in Crime Prevention and Control: Promising Models in Indian Country." Paper presented at the Strategic Planning Meeting on Crime and Justice Research in Indian Country, Portland, OR: U.S. Department of Justice, National Institute of Justice, Office of Juvenile Justice and Delinquency Prevention, American Indian and Alaska Native Affairs Office, October 14, 1998: 1–24.

Jumper-Thurman, P., and F. Beauvais. "Treatment of Volatile Solvent Abusers." Inhalant Abuse: A Volatile Research Agenda." (C. W. Sharp, F. Beauvais, and R. Spence, eds.). Rockville, MD: NIDA Research Monograph 129, 1992: 302–213.

Kandel, E. R., J. H. Schwartz, and T. M. Jessell. *Essentials of Neural Science and Behavior.* Norwalk, CT: Appleton & Lange, 1995.

Kaneko, W. M., et al. "Auditory Event-Related Potentials in Fetal Alcohol Syndrome and Down's Syndrome Children." *Alcoholism: Clinical and Experimental Research* 20, no. 1 (1996): 35–42.

Kaufman, M. H. "The Teratogenic Effects of Alcohol following Exposure during Pregnancy, and Its Influence on the Chromosome Constitution of the Pre-Ovulatory Egg." *Alcohol and Alcoholism* 32, no. 2 (1997): 113–128.

Kemper, S. "This Land is Whose Land." *Yankee*, September 1998, 46–54, 120–123.

Kephart, H. *The Cherokees of the Smoky Mountains*. Ithaca, NY: Atkinson Press, 1936.

Kilbey, M. M., and A. Khursheed. *Methodological Issues in Epidemiological Prevention, and Treatment Research on Drug-Exposed Women and Their Children (Research Monograph 117)*. Rockville, MD: DHHS Publication no. ADM 92–1881, 1992.

King, J., et al. "A Structural Equation Model of Factors Related to Substance Use among American Indian Adolescents." *Drugs & Society* 6 (1992): 253–268.

King, J., and J. F. Thayer. "Examining Conceptual Models for Understanding Drug Use Behavior among American Indian Youth." *Drug Abuse among Minority Youth (Research Monograph 130)* (De la Rosa and Recio Adrados, eds.). Rockville, MD: NIH Publication no. 93–3479, 1993: 129–143.

Kluckholn, C., and D. Leighton. *The Navajo*. Cambridge, MA: Harvard Univ. Press, 1946.

Kolb, B., and I. Q. Whishaw. *Fundamentals of Human Neuropsychology*. New York: W. H. Freeman, 1990.

Kopera-Frye, K. S. D., and A. P. Streissguth. "Impairments of Number Processing Induced by Prenatal Alcohol Exposure." *Neuropsychologia* 34, no. 12 (1996): 1187–1196.

Kupferer, H. *The Principal People*. Washington, DC: U.S. Bureau of Ethnology, 1966.

Lac du Flambeau Band v. Williquette, 629 F. Wupp. 689, W.D. Wis. 1986.

Lac du Flambeau Band of Lake Superior Chippewa Indians v. Wisconsin, 743 F. Supp. 645, W.D. Wis. 1990.

LaDue, R. A., and B. A. O'Hara. "Documentation of Critical Issues Related to the Comprehensive Indian Fetal Alcohol Syndrome (FAS) Prevention and Treatment Act." *Focus* 6, no. 2 (1992): 8–10.

La Farge, O. *The Changing Indian*. Norman, OK: Symposium on the American Association on Indian Affairs, 1942.

LaFromboise, T. D. "American Indian Mental Health Policy." *American Psychologist* 43, no. 5 (1988): 388–397.

Lancaster, F. E. *Alcohol and Glial Cells (Research Monograph 22)*. Rockville, MD: NIH Publication no. 94–3742, 1994.

Lauber, A. W. *Indian Slavery in Colonial Times*. Williamstown, MA: Corner House, 1970.

Lawson, G. W., and C. A. Cooperrider (eds.). "Psychoses and Schizophrenia." *Clinical Psychopharmacology*. Rockville, MD: Aspen, 1998, 33–40.

LeBeau, W. "Juvenile Justice Detention Issues in Indian Country." Paper presented at the Strategic Planning Meeting on Crime and Justice Research in Indian Country. Portland, OR: U.S. Department of Justice, Office of Justice Programs, National Institute of Justice, Office of Juvenile Justice and Delinquency Prevention, American Indian and Alaska Native Affairs Office, October 14, 1998.

"Native Americans: A Review and Analysis." *Health Education Quarterly* 21, no. 4 (1994): 521–538.

Le Master, P. L., and C. M. Connell. "Health Education Interventions among Nature Americans: A Review and Analysis." *Health Education Quarterly*, 21, no. 4 (1994):521–538.

Levine, S., ed. *The American Indian Today*. Baltimore: Penguin Books, 1972.

Lewis, J., R. Q. Dana, and G. A. Blevins. "Assessment and Diagnosis of Substance Use Disorders." *Substance Abuse Counseling*. Pacific Grove, CA: Brooks/ Cole, 1988, 74–117.

Lincoln, M. E. "Mental Health Programs." *Indian Health Manual (Part 3 — Professional Services)*. Washington, DC: IHS, TN 93–14 (1993): 1–70.

Linklater, C. "Comprehensive Community Approach to an Alcohol/Drug Program." Edmonton, Alberta: Hobbema Four Bands, 1986.

Linton, R. *Acculturation in Seven American Indian Tribes*. New York: Columbia Univ. Press, 1940.

Lisa, R. "Indians Need More Access to Behavioral Medicine." *APA Monitor* 29, no. 8 (1998):38.

Lueders, B. "Buffaloed." *Progressive* 58, August 1994, 30–33.

Major Crimes Act. 18 U.S. U.S.C.A. 1153, *U.S. Statutes at Large*, 23:385, March 3, 1885.

Martin, J. "Compulsive Gambling Like Drug Addiction." *Cherokee One Feather* 30, no. 20, May 15, 1996, 1.

Martin, S. E. *Alcohol and Interpersonal Violence (Research Monograph 24)*. Rockville, MD: NIH Publication no. 93–3496, 1993.

Mattson, S. N., et al. "A Decrease in the Size of the Basal Ganglia in Children with Fetal Alcohol Syndrome." *Alcoholism: Clinical and Experimental Research* 20, no. 6 (1996): 1088–1093.

May, P. A. "Fetal Alcohol Syndrome and American Indians: A Positive Challenge in Public Health and Prevention." *Mashkirki: Old Medicine Nourishing the New* (E. W. Haller and L. P. Aiken, eds.). Lanham, MD: University Press of America, 1992, 62–68.

———. "The Epidemiology of Alcohol Abuse among American Indians: The Mythical and Renal Properties." *American Indian Culture and Research Journal* 18, no. 2 (1994) 121–143.

McKenny, T. L. *Memories, Official and Personal with Sketches of Travels among the Northern and Southern Indians*. Volumes 1 and 2. New York: Paine and Burgess, 1846.

McTague, J. "D.C. current: Roll Over Sitting Bull." *Barron's*, December 26, 1994, 17.

Medill, W. *Annual Report to the Commissioner of Indian Affairs*. Washington, DC: House Executive Document No. 1, 30th Cong., Second session serial 537, November 30, 1848: 385–389.

Meriam, L. *The Problem of Indian Administration*. Baltimore: Johns Hopkins Univ. Press, 1928.

Miller, G. *The Substance Abuse Subtle Screening Inventory Manual*. Spencer, IN: Spencer Evening World, 1994.

Miller, P. M., and M. Hersen. "Annual Review of Addictions Research and Treatment." *Addictive Behaviors: An International Journal* 23, no. 6 (1998): 715–946.

Miller, W. R., and A. G. Marlatt. *Manual CDP: Comprehensive Drinker Profile.* Odessa, FL: Psychological Assessment Resources, 1984.

Mizruchi, E. H., and R. Perrucci. "Norm Qualities and Differential Effects of Deviant Behavior: An Exploratory Analysis." *American Sociological Review* 27 (1962): 391–399.

Mollica, R. F., et al. "The Harvard Traumatic Questionnaire." *The Journal of Nervous and Mental Disease* 180, no. 2 (1992): 111–116.

Mooney, J. *Myths of the Cherokee and Sacred Formulas of the Cherokee.* Nashville, TN: Charles Elder, 1972.

———. "The Sacred Formulas of the Cherokees." *Seventh Annual Report of the Bureau of Ethnology to the Secretary of the Smithsonian Institute 1885–86* (J. W. Powell, dir.). Washington, DC: Government Printing Office, 1891.

———. "Untasaiyi, the Gambler." *Nineteenth Annual Report of the Bureau of American Ethnology to the Secretary of the Smithsonian Institution — 1897–98 (Part 1)* (J. W. Powell, ed.). Washington, DC: Government Printing Office, 1900, 311–314.

Moore, W. J. "When It Comes to Congress, Why Gamble?" *National Journal* 27, June 24, 1995, 1656–1657.

Murdock, G. P. *Ethnographic Bibliography of North America, Third Edition.* New Haven, CT: Human Relations area files, Yale Univ. Press, 1960.

Nakao, A. "With $70 Million, Proponents Won Right to Keep Slots." *San Francisco Examiner*, November 4, 1998, A28.

Nash, G. *Red, White and Black.* Englewood Cliffs, NJ: Prentice-Hall, 1974.

Navarro, J., et al. "Substance Abuse and Spirituality: A Program for Native American Students." *American Journal on Health Behavior* 21, no. 1 (1997): 3–11.

Neihardt, J. *Black Elk Speaks.* New York: Pocket Books, 1972.

Nelson, B. S., and D. W. Wright. "Understanding and Treating Post-Traumatic Stress Disorder Symptoms in Female Partners of Veterans with PTSD." *Journal of Marital and Family Therapy* 22, no. 4 (1996): 455–467.

Nelson, S. H., et al. "An Overview of Mental Health Services for American Indians and Alaska Natives in the 1990s." *Hospital and Community Psychiatry* 43, no. 3 (1992): 257–261.

Nofz, M. P. "Alcohol Abuse in Culturally Marginal American Indians." *Social Casework* 69 (1988): 67–73.

Novins, D. K., et al. Substance Abuse Treatment of American Indian Adolescents: Comorbid Symptomatology, Gender Differences, and Treatment Patterns." *Journal of the American Academy of Child Adolescence Psychiatry* 35, no. 12 (1996): 1593–1601.

Nowak, M. P., E. M. Sellers, and R. F. Tyndale. "Canadian Native Indians Exhibit Unique CYP2A6 and CYP2C19 Mutant Allele Frequencies." *Clinical Pharmacology & Therapeutics* 64, no. 4 (1998): 378–383.

Oneida Tribe of Indians of Wisconsin v. State of Wisconsin, 518 F. Supp. 719, W. D. Wis. 1981.

Onken, L. S., et al. *Treatment of Drug-Dependent Individuals with Comorbid Mental*

Disorders. Rockville, MD: NIDA Research Monograph 172, NIH Publication no. 97–4172, 1997.

Park, R. E. *Race and Culture*. New York: Free Press, 1964.

Parker, I. *Oklahoma Star*, November 2, 1876, 1.

Perdue, T. *Slavery and the Evolution of Cherokee Society, 1540–1866*. Knoxville: Univ. of Tennessee Press, 1979.

Peters, L., et al. "The Composite International Diagnostic Interview Post-Traumatic Stress Disorder Module: Preliminary Data." *International Journal of Methods in Psychiatric Research* 6 (1996): 167–174.

Philip, K. *John Collier's Crusade for Indian Reform, 1920–1954*. Tucson: Univ. of Arizona Press, 1977.

Piel, J. (ed.). *Mind and Brain*. New York: W. H. Freeman, 1993.

Pinkert, T. M. *Consequences of Maternal Drug Abuse (Research Monograph 59)*. Rockville, MD: DHHS Publication no. ADM 87–1400, 1987.

Plotnik, R. *Introduction to Psychology*, 4th Edition. Pacific Grove, CA: Brooks/Cole, 1996.

Pope, K. S., J. N. Butcher, and J. Seelen. *The MMPI, MMPI-2 & MMPI-A in Court*. Washington, DC: American Psychological Association, 1993.

Pratt, R. *Battlefield and Classroom* (R. Utley, ed.). New Haven, CT: Yale Univ. Press, 1964.

Preston, J., J. H. O'Neal, and M. C. Talaga. *Handbook of Clinical Psychopharmacology for Therapists*. Oakland, CA: New Harbinger, 1994.

Prucha, F. *Documents of United States Indian Policy (Second Edition, Expanded)*. Lincoln: Univ. of Nebraska Press, 1990.

Prugh, T. "FAS among Native Americans." *Alcohol Health & Research World* 10, no. 1 (1985): 36–37.

Public Law 93–638. *Indian Self-Determination and Education Assistance Act*, U.S. Statutes at Large, 88: 2203–1114, January 4, 1975: 2203.

Public Law 94–437. *Indian Health Care Improvement Act. U.S. Statutes at Large*, 90: 1400–1407, 1410–1412, September 30, 1976.

Public Law 99–570. *The Indian Alcohol and Substance Abuse Prevention Act of 1986*. H. R. 5484, 99th Congress, Second session, section 4210, 100 STAT: 3207–1-133, October 27, 1986.

Public Law 103–344. *American Indian Religious Freedom Act Amendments of 1994*. 103d Congress, Second session, January 25, 1994: H.R. 4230–3.

Public Law 280. *U.S. Statutes at Large*, August 15, 1953, 67: 588–590.

Rabasca, L. "Indians Need More Access to Behavioral Medicine." *APA Monitor*, 29, no. 8 (1998): 38.

Reeves, T. A., and D. Hess. "Wall Street Signs On for casino." *Albuquerque Journal* 115, October 1, 1995, A12.

Reid, J. *A Better Kind of Hatchet*. University Park: Pennsylvania State Univ. Press, 1967.

———. *A Law of Blood*. New York: New York Univ. Press, 1970.

Rhoades, E. R. Report on *Indian Health (Task Force Six: Indian Health)*. Final Report to the American Indian Review Commission. Washington, DC: Government Printing Office, 1976.

———. *Indian Health Manual (Part 3)*. Chapter 18. Washington, DC: IHS, TN 91–3, 1991, 1–116.

Ries, R. *Assessment and Treatment of Patients with Coexisting Mental Illness and Alcohol and Other Drug Abuse (TIP-9)*. Rockville, MD: U.S. Department of of Health and Human Services, Publication no. SMA 95–3061, 1995.

Rivers, P. C. *Alcohol and Human Behavior, Theory, Research, and Practice*. Englewood Cliffs, NJ: Prentice-Hall, 1994.

Robin, R. W., et al. "Factors Influencing Utilization of Mental Health and Substance Abuse Services by American Indian Men and Women." *Psychiatric Services* 48, no. 6 (1997): 826–832.

Rose, I. N. *Gambling and the Law*. Los Angeles, Gambling Times, 1986.

Roski, J., et al. "Psychosocial Factors Associated with Alcohol Use among Young Adolescent American Indians and Whites." *Journal of Child & Adolescent Substance Abuse* 7, no. 2 (1997): 1–18.

Rostenberg, P. O. *Alcohol and other Drug Screening of Hospitalized Trauma Patients (TIP-16)*. Rockville, MD: U.S. Department of Health and Human Services DHHS Publication no. SMA 95–3041, 1995.

Royce, C. C. *The Cherokee Nation of Indians (Fifth Annual Report)*. Washington, DC: U.S. Bureau of American Ethnology, 1883–1884.

Rychlak, R. "The Introduction of Casino Gambling: Public Policy and the Law." *Mississippi Law Journal* 64, no. 2 (1995): 291–362.

Sando, J. S. *The Pueblo Indians*. San Francisco: Indian Historian Press, 1976.

Scheirbeck, H., et al. *Report on Indian Education, Task Force Five*. Final Report to the American Indian Policy Review Commission. Washington, DC: Government Printing Office, 1976.

Schermerhorn, R. *Comparative Ethnic Relations*. New York: Random House, 1970.

Schultes, R. E. "An Overview of Hallucinogens in the Western Hemisphere." *Flesh of the Gods: The Ritual Use of Hallucinogens* (P. T. Furst, ed.). New York: Praeger, 1972.

Schultz, D., and S. E. Schultz. *Theories of Personality*, 6th edition. Pacific Grove, CA: Brooks / Cole, 1998.

Selye, H. *The Stress of Life*. New York: McGraw-Hill, 1956.

Seminole Tribe of Florida v. Butterworth, 658 F.2d 310 (5th Cir. 1981).

"Senator: Indian's Lives Not Improving." *Albuquerque Journal* 118, no. 298 (1998): B9.

Sharfroth, F. "Senate Agrees to Overhaul Nation's Indian Gaming Policy." *Nation's Cities Weekly* 18, August 14, 1995, 12.

Sharp, C. W., F. Beauvais, and R. Spence. *Inhalant Abuse (Research Monograph 129)*. Rockville, MD: NIH Publication no. 93–3480, 1992.

Sheehan, B. *Seeds of Extinction*. New York: W. W. Norton, 1974.

Shirley, G. *Law West of Fort Smith: A History of Frontier Justice in the Indian Territory, 1834–1896*. Lincoln: Univ. of Nebraska Press, 1968.

Simmel, G. *Conflict: The Web of Group Affiliation* (K. H. Wolff and R. Bendix trans.). Glencoe, IL: Free Press, 1955.

Simon, P. M. "The Explosive Growth of Gambling in the United States." *Congressional Record — Senate*, July 31, 1995, 10912–10916.

Snake, R. *Report on Alcohol and Drug Abuse (Task Force Eleven: Alcohol and Drug Abuse)*. First Report to the American Indian Policy Review Commission. Washington, DC: Government Printing Office, 1976.

Snyder Act. U.S. Statutes at Large, 42: 208–209, November 2, 1921.

Snyder, C. *Alcohol and the Jews*. Glencoe, IL: Free Press, 1958.

Snyder-Joy, Z. "Self-Determination and American Indian Justice." *Native Americans, Crime, and Justice* (M. O. Nielsen) and R. A. Silverman, eds. Boulder, CO: Westview Press, 1996: 38–45.

Sorokin, P. A. *Society, Culture, and Personality*. New York: Harper, 1947.

Standing Bear, L. *My People, the Sioux*. Lincoln: Univ. of Nebraska Press, 1975.

Stephanson, A. *Manifest Destiny*. New York: Hill and Wang, 1995.

Stone, T. W. *Neuropharmacology*. New York: W. H. Freeman, 1995.

Stonequist, E. *The Marginal Man*. New York: Russell and Russell, 1937.

Strickland, R. *Fire and Spirit*. Norman. Univ. of Oklahoma Press, 1975.

Sumner, W. G. *Folkways*. Boston: Ginn, 1906.

Swanton, J. R. *Indians of Southeastern United States (Bulletin 137)*. Washington, DC: Bureau of American Ethnology, 1946.

———. *The Indian Tribes of North America (Bulletin 145)*. Washington, DC: Bureau of American Ethnology, 1952.

Taylor, T. L. *Improving the Health of Native Americans*. Princeton, NJ: Robert Wood Johnson Foundation, 1991.

Teller, H. M. "Courts of Indian Offenses." *Annual Report of the Secretary of the Interior*. Washington, DC: House Executive Document no. 1, 48th Congress, 1st Session, Serial 2190, 1881: x–xiii.

Terrell, M. D. "Ethnocultural Factors and Substance Abuse: Toward Culturally Sensitive Treatment Models." *Psychology of Addictive Behaviors* 7, no. 3 (1993): 162–167.

Testerman, J. "Seminole Indian Reservation." *St. Petersburg Times*, February 27, 1995, 1B.

Tinnin, T. P. *American Indians in New Mexico and Their Neighbors: Building Bridges of Understanding*. Albuquerque: New Mexico First, 1998, 60–62, 85–86.

Thurman, P. J. " 'What Works' in Crime Prevention and Control: Promising Models in Indian Country." Paper presented at the Strategic Planning Meeting on Crime and Justice. Portland, OR: U.S. Department of Justice; National Institute of Justice; Office of Juvenile Justice and Delinquency Prevention; American Indian and Alaska Native Affairs Office, October 14–15, 1998, 1–14.

Toennies, F. *Fundamental Concepts of Sociology* (C. P. Loomis, ed.). New York: American Book, 1940.

Trzepacz, P. T., and R. W. Baker. *The Psychiatric Mental Status Examination*. New York: Oxford Univ. Press, 1993.

U.S. Senate. Part One: "Executive Summary: A New Federalism for American Indians." *Final Report and Legislative Recommendations: A Report of the Special Committee on Investigations of the Select Committee on Indian Affairs, United States Senate*. 101st Congress, First Session, S. Prt 101–60, November 1989.

VanStelle, K. R., G. A. Allen, and P. D. Moberg. "Alcohol and Drug Prevention among American Indian Families: The Family Circles Program." *Drugs & Society* 12, nos. 1 and 2 (1988): 53–60.

Vicks, R., Sr., L. M. Smith, and C.I.R. Herrera. "The Healing Circle: An Alternative Path to Alcoholism Recovery." *Counseling and Values* 42, no. 2 (1998): 133–141.

Walker, R. D., et al. "Treatment Implications of Comorbid Psychopathology in

American Indians and Alaska Natives." *Culture, Medicine, and Psychiatry* 16 (1993): 555–572.

Washburn, W. *The Assault on Indian Tribalism*. Philadelphia: J. B. Lippincott, 1975.

Weber, M. *The Protestant Ethic and the Spirit of Capitalism* (T. Parsons, trans.). New York: Charles Scribner's Sons, 1930.

Weibel-Orlando, J. "Hooked on Healing: Anthropologists, Alcohol and Intervention." *Human Organization* 48, no. 2 (1989): 148–155.

———. "American Indians and Prohibition: Effect of Affect? Views from the Reservation and the City." *Contemporary Drug Problems*. New York: Federal Legal, 1990, 293–322.

Weiner, L., B. Morse, and P. Garrdio. "FAS/FAE: Focusing Prevention on Women at Risk." *International Journal of Addictions* 24 no. 5 (1989): 385–395.

Wells, R. M. "Bill Would Widen Federal Role in Regulating Gambling." *Congressional Quarterly Weekly Report* 53, August 12, 1995, 2445.

Wheeler-Howard Act (Indian Reorganization Act). U.S. Statutes at Large, 48: 984–88, June 18, 1934.

Wiebe, J., and K. M. Huebert. Community Mobile Treatment. *Journal of Substance Abuse Treatment* 13, no. 1 (1996): 23–31.

Wilbert, J. "Tobacco and Shamanistic Ecstasy among the Warao Indians of Venezuela." *Flesh of the Gods: The Ritual Use of Hallucinogens* (P. T. Furst, ed.). New York: Praeger, 1972.

Winston, S. "Indian Slavery in the Carolina Region." *Journal of Negro History* 19 (1934): 43–42.

Young, T., and L. A. French. "Suicide and Social Status among Native Americans." *Psychological Reports* 73 (1993): 461–462.

———. "Status Integration and Suicide among Native American Women." *Social Behavior and Personality*. 23, no. 2 (1995): 155–158.

———. "Homicide Rates among Native American Children." *Adolescence* 32, no. 124 (1997): 57–59.

Zah, P. *President Peterson Zah Report to the Navajo People on the American Indian Religious Freedom Legislation*. Window Rock, AZ: Navajo Nation, October 29, 1994, 1–8.

Zion, J., and E. B. Zion. "Hazho's Sokee—Stay Together Nicely." *Native Americans, Crime, and Justice* (M. O. Nielsen and R. A. Silverman, eds.). Boulder, CO: Westview Press, 1996, 96–112.

Zucker, R., B. Gayle, and J. Howard. *The Development of Alcohol Problems (Research Monograph 26)*. Rockville, MD: NIH Publication no. 94–3495, 1994.

INDEX

About the Author

LAURENCE ARMAND FRENCH is Professor of Psychology and Chair of the Department of Social Sciences at Western New Mexico University. He is also a licensed clinical psychologist. His publications include *Psychocultural Change and the American Indian* (1987) and *The Winds of Injustice* (1994).

ISBN 0-275-96349-7

9 780275 963491

90000>

EAN

HARDCOVER BAR CODE